MOMENTS FOR NOTHING

MOMENTS FOR NOTHING

SAMUEL BECKETT AND THE END TIMES

GABRIELE SCHWAB

Columbia University Press   *New York*

Columbia University Press
Publishers Since 1893
New York   Chichester, West Sussex
cup.columbia.edu

Copyright © 2023 Columbia University Press
All rights reserved

Library of Congress Cataloging-in-Publication Data
Names: Schwab, Gabriele, author.
Title: Moments for Nothing : Samuel Beckett and
the End Times / Gabriele Schwab.
Description: New York : Columbia University Press, [2023] |
Includes bibliographical references and index.
Identifiers: LCCN 2023008232 (print) | LCCN 2023008233 (ebook) |
ISBN 9780231211604 (hardback) | ISBN 9780231211611 (trade paperback) |
ISBN 9780231558990 (ebook)
Subjects: LCSH: Beckett, Samuel, 1906–1989—Criticism and interpretation. |
End of the world in literature. | LCGFT: Literary criticism.
Classification: LCC PR6003.E282 Z8284 2023 (print) |
LCC PR6003.E282 (ebook) | DDC 848/.91409—dc23/eng/20230627
LC record available at https://lccn.loc.gov/2023008232
LC ebook record available at https://lccn.loc.gov/2023008233

Cover image: Samuel Beckett, *Quad I and II*, directed by
Michael Hackett (2020); costume design by Ruoxuan Li; performed by
Elliyah Banks, Gia Blakey, Kevin Hinton, and Gil Weissman.
Hammer Museum, UCLA School of Theater, Film and Television.
Photo by Josh Concepcion.

CONTENTS

Acknowledgments vii

Introduction 1

1 Moments for Nothing: *Endgame* and Its Discontents 41

2 The Transitional Space Between Life and Death: "The Calmative," *Molloy*, and *Malone Dies* 71

3 End Times of Subjectivity: *The Unnamable* 95

4 "Laughing wildly inmidst severest woe": *Happy Days* and the Last Humans 149

5 Cosmographical Meditations on the In/Human: *The Lost Ones* 173

Coda: *Breath* and the Vicissitudes of Animation 207

Notes 225
Bibliography 249
Index 259

ACKNOWLEDGMENTS

The gratitude I owe people for accompanying me on this decades-long journey with Beckett reaches back to the early 1970s. Since I have traced this journey in my introduction and acknowledged the people involved, I will focus here on those who, in one way or another, were supporting my writing of *Moments for Nothing*. Robert Barrett, my assistant, has been deeply involved in doing the final editing and formatting of the manuscript, and he also assembled the bibliography. He was a meticulous reader, engaging the text with notes on the margins and getting me through rough spots of the never-ending endgame of submitting a manuscript to the press. Christine Guiyangco helped me at an early stage with scanning texts and was ingenious in finding the accurate version of quotes I had cited from memory. Thank you, Robert and Christine. I can't imagine going through this process without you. Anirban Gupta also helped me through the purgatory of completion by finding additional missing quotes.

Ackbar Abbas, who read the entire manuscript, has unfailingly grasped its spirit. A Beckett scholar himself, he has been one of my most faithful readers for many years. Rare friends and colleagues like him inspire the pleasure of working with literature and make intellectual life exciting. Gregg Lambert visited me during a sabbatical in Berlin where we did veritable writing binges and sometimes talked about Beckett until late into the night. I also thank the students from my graduate seminar on Beckett who made me feel every minute that putting a Beckett monograph together in today's turbulent times was well worthwhile. Their excitement was contagious.

Since I worked on *Moments for Nothing* during the COVID-19 pandemic, I also want to thank the family members and friends who supported me in various ways during these trying times. My sons, Manuel and Leon Schwab, both ardent Beckett aficionados, were there for me during my extended periods of time in Berlin. I also thank my friends and colleagues in Berlin, Reinhold Görling, Ulla Haselstein, Bettine Menke, Klaus Milich, Ulrike Ottinger, Katharina Sykora, and Florian Sedlmeier, for their invitations to lecture and the inspired discussions afterward. In Constance, I thank Kirsten Mahlke and Renate Lachmann, who both engaged my work on Beckett and hosted me when I presented the annual Wolfgang Iser Lecture in 2022. I also owe an immense debt of gratitude to Tessa Theodorakopoulos for envisioning the trilingual version of *Happy Days*, in which I played the role of Winnie, that inspired my chapter on the play.

In California, I already acknowledged Ackbar Abbas, my most faithful reader. I also thank Ketu Katrak and Beheroze Shroff, with whom I am in a writing group and who nourished me with delicious food, literature, art, and film. Ketu and I discussed my emergent project during long walks at the beach or in the San Joaquin Wildlife Sanctuary. Tamara Beauchamp and Ben Garceau listened to my Beckett stories and got me through the pandemic lockdown with our weekly dinner-movie nights. I also am grateful for the support of Alicia Carroll,

David Goldberg, Adriana Johnson, Daphne Lei, Liron Mor, Jane Newman, and John Smith. Special thanks go to Molly Schneider and Kevin O'Brien for watching and discussing the entire DVD series *Beckett on Film* with me. Finally, I thank Chi Zhang for keeping my spirits high during the final stages of completing my manuscript and for long talks about Beckett and Buddhist philosophy, at times with the help of a translation app.

I'm grateful to Catherine Malabou, the last person at my house before the lockdown, for being one of my consistent interlocutors. While I dearly miss the regular exchanges with Gayatri Spivak in Irvine, we continue our discussions and collaborations remotely. I cannot thank Michael Levine enough for his support over the years, and our long discussions on Beckett, Kafka, and Derrida have certainly animated my work on this book. Steven Connor has republished my original essay on *Endgame* and invited me to present a keynote at his wonderful Beckett conference in London. His own work on Beckett, and particularly his essay on Beckett and Bion, were a true inspiration for me. Reinhold Görling invited me as a speaker at his conference on the Fold, and my lecture eventually turned into the chapter on *The Lost Ones*. Michael Fox recruited me to present at his Centennial Production of *Endgame* at the Rude Guerrilla Theater in Santa Ana and was the first to imagine me in the role of Winnie when he thought of staging *Happy Days*. Achille Mbembe, Sarah Nutall, and David Goldberg included me in their International Wiser/HRI Summer Seminar, Johannesburg, where I presented for the first time on *Happy Days*. Susan Winnett invited me to speak at the First European MLA, where I presented another lecture on *Happy Days*. These two lectures as well as my acting as Winnie at the University Theater in Constance became the basis of my chapter on *Happy*

Days. Finally, I'm grateful to Kathleen Woodward for still being out there somewhere in the Beckettian noosphere. Chapter 4, "'Laughing wildly inmidst severest woe': *Happy Days* and the Last Humans," was previously published as "Postnuclear Ecologies—Language, Body, and Affect in Beckett's *Happy Days*" in Gabrielle Schwab, *Radioactive Ghosts* (University of Minnesota Press, 2020). Copyright 2020 by the Regents of the University of Minnesota. Used by permission.

It is time to acknowledge the support of Columbia University Press. My heartfelt thanks also go to Philip Leventhal, whose excitement about *Moments for Nothing* carried me from the very beginning. I am happy to have had an editor who grasped the nature and spirit of the book so well. Philip made the process as smooth as possible, and it was a pleasure to work with him, as well as with Greg McNamee, my meticulous copyeditor, Susan Pensak, production editor, and Monique Laban, associate editor. Finally, I am deeply grateful to Michael Hackett for his invaluable help with getting the copyright for the book cover and to Josh Concepcion for his generosity in letting me use his photograph. I also thank the anonymous readers for the press as well as the board members who so enthusiastically supported the publication of the book.

Lastly, I want to acknowledge a few friends and colleagues who passed away during the time I worked on *Moments for Nothing*. Mihai Spariosu and John-Paul Riquelme belonged to a group of scholars deeply impacted by the work of my former mentor and adviser, Wolfgang Iser. We have collaborated in various capacities over the years, including Mihai's summer school for Critical Theory in Santiago de Compostela, where he invited me as one of the seminar leaders. More recently, they included me in two events for Iser's commemoration at which I presented on *Wolfgang Iser's Beckett*.

I was still able to tell Ruth Kluger about the project, but she died in October 2020 before I could share any drafts with her. One of the last things she said to me had a Beckettian ring in its paradoxical embrace and negation of the end. On the last evening before she passed away, and knowing full well that she was dying, she said to me, almost like a conjuration: "Man sieht sich sicher noch sehr oft!" ("Certainly, we'll see each other again very often").

Aijaz Ahmad was another friend and colleague with whom I had animated exchanges about Beckett. The conversations in his backyard during the lockdown are unforgettable, almost as if the pandemic presented us with a gift of rare intellectual intimacy. Also irreplaceable are my discussions with Dieter Henrich about Beckett, first in person and then on Zoom. He was finishing his book on Beckett and Hölderlin as I was beginning the work on *Moments for Nothing*. Beckett played a crucial role in helping to form the tie between us that lasted over decades. Sadly, both Aijaz Ahmad and Dieter Henrich passed away in 2022 and will never see the book in print.

MOMENTS
FOR NOTHING

INTRODUCTION

The buzzing, the buzzing in the skull

Imagine, feeling coming back.
         —*Not-I*

During the late 1950s, when I was in high school, German TV aired midnight specials, mostly foreign auteur films, experimental theater, and esoteric shows of all kinds. This was the occasion of my first encounter with Samuel Beckett's work. Mesmerized, I watched the airing of *Warten auf Godot*. Most likely it was a TV recording of the play's first staging in Germany at the Schlosspark Theater in Berlin in 1953. I had never seen anything like this play. I didn't quite know what to think of it, but it opened an entirely new world for me. Halfway into the play, however, my father appeared, watching for five minutes before he started berating me. I still see him standing there in the doorframe in his pajamas, already a Beckett character himself. "I think you have gone completely out of your mind now. What is wrong with you? This is the most boring thing I have ever seen. Nothing is happening! Why do you waste your time with this nonsense?"

Well, I have been wasting my time with nonsense like this ever since. For many weeks after watching *Waiting for Godot*, I couldn't get the play out of my mind. At odd moments, scenes or bits of dialogue emerged like flashbacks. The world had suddenly changed in a subliminal way. It had taken on an edge of dark humor, with Beckett characters lurking behind every corner. I wanted to know more about this mysterious Samuel Beckett, whose name I had never heard before. When my teacher told me he was an Irish writer and playwright, I asked in our school library and the local bookstore, but it was impossible to get a hold of any of his writings. After all, I lived in the predigital age in a small German border town at the edge of the Black Forest.

I'm convinced that Beckett's work played a major role in my becoming a literary critic. In 1969, I enrolled in the newly founded University of Constance, a reform university limited to thirty-five hundred students with an open structure and a focus on theory and interdisciplinarity. The literature professors there were focused on literary theory and philosophy and belonged to the Poetics and Hermeneutics group, whose philosophical work I had been reading with great fascination. Choosing the University of Constance was, I think, one of the best and most influential decisions in my life. Most important, it offered me the chance to work with Wolfgang Iser, one of the most prominent literary theorists and Beckett critics in Germany.

Just as I began writing my MA thesis, "Aesthetics of Response in Beckett's *Endgame*," under Iser's supervision, a cataclysmic event disrupted my life. My younger sister, Stefanie, who was the closest person in my life at the time, was diagnosed with an incurable uterine sarcoma at age sixteen. Devastated, I took a leave of absence for a year and moved to Freiburg, where she was hospitalized. With the unparalleled help and support of her doctors, I was allowed to live with her at the hospital, sleeping on a cot in her room. When there was no more treatment available, I took her home where, during the last year of her life, she lived with me and Harry, my partner at the time, who supported me and my sister in the most caring ways. This time became an endgame of an entirely different kind. At age twenty-three I had to learn how to take care of a cancer patient, administer morphine injections, and finally do hospice care. I was truly fortunate to find outstanding doctors and nurses to support me, some of whom became almost like family, joining us in Constance to help during my sister's final days. The earliest period of my thinking about life through the lens of Samuel Beckett's work thus became inextricably intertwined with my sister's illness and my first serious encounter with death. In many ways, this entanglement persists to this day.

By a strange yet utterly fortuitous coincidence, I found a therapist, Norman Elrod, who helped me process the challenges of caring for my sister and who happened to be an ardent Beckett admirer. The city of Constance suddenly became an environment saturated with Beckett. Apart from working as a therapist, Norman Elrod was also an occasional theater director who had staged *Endgame*, among other plays, at the Theater an der Grenze, a small but famous local theater in the Swiss border town of Kreuzlingen, located right next to Constance. I will never forget the ingenious way in which he was able to convey the difference between "silence" and "pause" in Beckett's stage directions. For pause, he had the actors stop for exactly ten seconds. For silence, however, he told them to stop until there was absolute silence in the audience. As it turned out, the pattern of audience response was always the same. As the break extended beyond expectation, the audience started to become restless, shuffling, coughing nervously or even whispering. The actors faced the agonizing task to stay silent. Then, inevitably a moment came when the audience, realizing that something utterly strange was going on, fell into a stunned silence. And exactly at that moment, the actors resumed the play.

Norman Elrod's staging of *Endgame* taught me something essential about the power of silence not only in Beckett but in the process of communication more generally. Understanding this generative power has helped me ever since, in my classroom, in my work as a psychoanalyst and, more generally, in listening to people and being mindful of the transitional spaces between utterances. It even helped me during my sister's final weeks when she no longer had the strength to talk while I was sitting with her, holding her hand in silence, feeling the vibrations of her vanishing life.

Elrod not only provided emotional support but also taught me to respect my boundaries and hold on to my own life. The latter included, most important, continuing to write my thesis about *Endgame*. In the hours I carved out between taking care of my sister, Beckett became sometimes a sanctuary, sometimes a curse. While it was often excruciatingly hard for me to find the mental focus to think about *Endgame*, Beckett also offered unexpected solace by helping me stare into the abyss of living and dying. During the final stages of my sister's illness, however, I had to put my writing on hold because I simply no longer had the energy for it.

After my sister died, I felt lost in my old world. I tried to adapt to a life without her, oscillating between periods of deep depression and manic defense. The latter helped me to prepare for my exams and finish my MA thesis during a phase of intense grief. Afterward, however, I couldn't bear the thought of returning right away to my student life to write a dissertation. Unable to face the gaping hole left by my sister's loss except by taking care of other people, I decided to begin a psychoanalytic training parallel to continuing my scholarly career. Taking on this double task was certainly part of what I earlier called my manic defense against going to the depth of pain that overwhelmed me after my sister's death. Immersing myself in challenging and rewarding work helped me cope and was a true alternative to succumbing to traumatic psychic numbing. It was during this time, at a conference in Milan, Italy, that I met Agostino Pirella, one of the leaders of the antipsychiatry movement in Italy. When he offered me a position as a volunteer therapist at his psychiatric hospital in Arezzo, I had only one hesitation: "I do not speak Italian," I told him. "That's good," he replied, "then your patients will have one advantage when they start working with you." Living near the border of Switzerland, I was fortunate to at least learn the basics of Italian from the Italian channels of Swiss TV. A few months later, I arrived at the *manicomio* in Arezzo, as the patients called it, laughing.

Working at the psychiatric hospital in Arezzo was in many ways like immersing myself for the first time in a truly Beckettian world. Beckett had amply prepared me for this experience. I felt instantly at home, drawn into connecting to the mental world of the people in this amazing community, just as I had been connecting to the characters in Beckett's world. I had a visceral sense that invisible ties I did not quite understand yet bound us together. Learning to relate to this alien world and the otherness of those that inhabited it also meant getting in touch with my own internal otherness. Looking back, I'm still in awe of the incredible amount of joy and love of life that was mixed into all the pain carried by the people who lived in this *manicomio*. It was in Arezzo where, for the first time after Stefanie's death, I learned to laugh again. More than anywhere before or after, I shared unfathomable pain, joy, laughter, even true ecstasy with the people around me. Strangely, and almost unbelievably, my six months volunteering as a therapist at Pirella's hospital belong to the happiest and most fulfilling times in my life. Part of the time, Harry joined me and offered to work there as well. Our evenings of sharing stories and experiences of the day and reading Beckett together created a rare closeness and intimacy. We laughed at the thought that we had become like Murphy, working in an asylum, albeit without ever finding anyone with whom to play chess.

Years after returning from Arezzo, Harry and I parted ways. We had gone through deeply traumatic upheavals together and in the process become more like siblings than partners. It was a very painful cut in both of our lives. When I proposed the separation, I felt like I was releasing him to his own life. Eventually we had families and lived on different continents, but we stayed close for the rest of our lives, visiting each other and occasionally traveling together with our families and children. Beckett was never far. I kept returning to Arezzo regularly during summer breaks until the year I was told that Rosa, the closest friend I had made there, had died. Afterward I returned only once more, almost thirty years ago, with my youngest son Leon and his father. Sadly, after the closure of psychiatric institutions in Italy, the hospital in Arezzo had become but a shell of itself. The beautiful buildings resembled an abandoned ghost town, most patients living elsewhere. But when I entered the main entrance, I saw Harry's favorite patient, Donato, appear behind the registration desk, almost like a spectral apparition. Having never been able to speak, Donato was reduced to communicate with gestures and sounds. And there he stood now, gesturing to us, almost as if to say: "Look what happened to our world!" I wish that Harry had been able to come with us and see his old friend Donato again. In one of my dreams, Harry and Donato appeared together, both deprived of speech, acting like ghost figures in Beckett's *Acts Without Words*.

When I wrote my dissertation, I realized I had to continue my work on Beckett. Iser's unequivocal support was crucial because many then still considered writing on Beckett to be overly esoteric. I heard responses such as: "Writing a dissertation on Beckett! I can only laugh when I hear this!" Or: "Writing on Beckett from a psychoanalytic perspective, that's outright academic suicide!" And the best of all: "That would be a risky topic even for a man, but for a woman it's madness!" With Wolfgang Iser's encouragement, however, I completed the dissertation on Beckett and was hired as the first female assistant professor in literary studies at the University of Constance. I will always be grateful to Wolfgang Iser for his trust and the unique chance he offered me, despite, as I found out later, the open resistance of many younger male colleagues who thought my position should have gone to a man who needed it to support his family.

Iser had published "Samuel Beckett's dramatische Sprache," an influential essay on Beckett's challenges to audience expectation. Realizing that Iser's entire focus was on cognitive structures, I knew I wanted to go in a different direction. What intrigued me about Beckett was that his writings engaged mental extremes, ranging from the most abstract thought to the deepest affect. I wanted to write about those extremes, including Beckett's mobilization of unconscious thought processes. Finally, I decided to focus my dissertation on Artaud and Beckett from the perspective of current theoretical debates in French and German theory. In this process, I became interested in engaging more deeply with psychoanalysis, and specifically in developing a psychoaesthetics of Beckett's work informed by a more general psychoanalytic theory of audience response. I wanted to address existential questions and explore how Beckett challenges philosophical notions of subjectivity, if not philosophies of the human and its boundaries. But I also wanted to understand Beckett's broad appeal to wide-ranging audiences across national, cultural, and even class boundaries. Moreover, the deepest interest for me personally was to understand why and how, as I was convinced, Beckett had changed not only my way of thinking but also my entire way of being in the world.

Despite my decision to focus on affect and unconscious responses to *Endgame*, I maintained the distance I put between my critical analysis and my experience of living with a play that resonated with so much of what I was going through, namely the sense of an ending, the feeling that I couldn't go on but then kept going, and the repetition of this cycle, again and again. I wish I had kept a journal of these years. Today I am stunned by the fact that there is no trace in either my MA thesis or my dissertation of the context that shaped my reading of *Endgame* during my sister's illness. What prevented me at the time from engaging the play's existential darkness and depth? The answer to these questions has a double edge. My feelings that resonated with and were modulated by *Endgame* were still too raw to address in a scholarly way, especially in German academia, where resistance against framing one's work in a personal context was pervasive and persists in milder form to this day. Moreover, as an adviser, Wolfgang Iser trained his students to translate their thoughts as well as their emotional responses into theoretical and philosophical abstractions. Finally, the imperative that scholarship had to remain free of personal responses was even more important if you were one of the very few women in academia in Germany in the 1970s.

But I also must admit that I colluded with this distancing imperative. In the vortex of grief, intellectual distance assumed a defensive function that offered at least superficial protection. The distance I created to Beckett's personal impact on my life was thus twofold, protective of both my professional recognition and of my own vulnerability regarding endings, loss, and mourning. Looking back at my thesis today, I can see that my writing was marked by a defense against what moved me most but was simultaneously also most painful to face in *Endgame*, namely the sense of living in the end times, the fear of death and dying, and the strategies we deploy and games we play to hold this fear at bay.

During my time at Constance, I also met John Fletcher, who taught there as a visiting professor. My many discussions with him over dinner at my house, mainly about form, style, and problems of translation, inspired me also to explore Elmar Tophoven's German translations of Beckett's work more closely. I knew that Beckett had visited Germany regularly since the 1920s and, given that his German was very good, he had worked with Tophoven on the translations of his work. Beckett had also been deeply immersed in German culture and stayed for extended periods of time in Berlin and Kassel. Tophoven's translations intrigued me because I found quite a few instances where the translations seemed too Germanic for my taste. High German tends to upscale Beckett's language to a more high-browed tone, especially in translating some rather colloquial phrases. I went out of my way, retranslating some of the lines and phrases, and eventually even composed a letter to Beckett in which I included my suggestions. However, I was completely paralyzed by the fact that I knew Beckett was meticulous at answering every letter he received. I couldn't bring myself to send the letter off, just as, years later, I couldn't follow up on Herbert Blau's invitation to join him when he visited Beckett in Paris. I guess I was too starstruck and too afraid of Beckett's legendary perfectionism. What if he thought my suggestions about the German translation or even my dissertation about his work were beside the point? What if my mind would freeze in awe of meeting him and I couldn't think of anything to say? There were other missed opportunities of meeting him. At the time there were few things I was afraid of, but I was truly afraid of not being substantial enough in Beckett's eyes. In hindsight, I also wonder if I unconsciously avoided meeting Beckett because I didn't want any intrusion of the real into my highly complex and difficult imaginary relationship with his work that had carried me through so many years, had grounded me while I was mourning my sister, and had inspired my therapeutic work with the people at various psychiatric hospitals. Most important, perhaps, Beckett's texts and plays had helped me face my darkest inner moods, including my fear of endings.

I had finished my MA thesis on Beckett in 1973 and then completed my PhD in 1976. In 1981, I published a revised version of my dissertation as a book titled *Samuel Becketts Endspiel mit der Subjektivität: Entwurf einer Psychoästhetik des modernen Theaters*. Most of my subsequent books contain what became an obligatory Beckett chapter, often included as a coda that gives the previous chapters a new turn. When I received the copies of my first book, I gave one to my parents. Even though they had opposed my academic career and never shown any interest in my work, I thought children owe parents a copy of their first book. On my next visit, my mother gave me the cold shoulder. "What did I do now?" I asked, not without a certain sarcasm. "Well, shouldn't I have known that, if my daughter ever publishes a book, it would be about parents sitting in a trashcan!" she exclaimed in righteous indignation. I consoled myself with the thought that she had at least read far enough to make it to my reading of the opening scene of *Endgame* with Hamm's parents, Nagg and Nell.

Teaching Beckett was always full of surprises. Students tend to get passionate in debates about his work. One unforgettable moment stands out. In an undergraduate class in the late eighties, I included *Imagination Dead Imagine* and asked students about their reading experience. One of them shared with the class that, having never read anything like it, she was at a complete loss. Unable to figure out what to make of this short text, she was nonetheless intrigued by Beckett's meticulously precise description of two bodies in space. Hence, she had the idea to do a drawing following Beckett's text, and to her surprise she discovered that together the two bodies formed the shape of the *I-Ching*. She brought the drawing to class, we pinned it to the blackboard, and reread the piece together to reconstruct its configuration of bodies.

I also cotaught classes with a focus on Beckett. The first one was with Albrecht Wellmer, a prominent philosopher of the second generation of the Frankfurt School, who published widely on aesthetics and taught at Constance during my time as an assistant professor. He became one of the friends with whom I could share a passion for literature and have extended discussions for hours, sometimes until late at night. Our main subjects included subjectivity, psychoanalysis, and Beckett. After Albrecht read my dissertation, he suggested we should coteach a class on subjectivity in philosophy and literature. We taught this class in 1981, and it became legendary with its completely amazing cohort of students, most of whom are now professors. They included Bettine Menke, Christoph Menke, Ulla Haselstein, Rebecca Habermas, Claudia Opitz, and Martin Seel, all of whom are now teaching either literature, philosophy, or history at different German universities. Beckett became undoubtedly a center of our debates, and, perhaps more important, the soul of this class. This teaching experience deeply impacted both Albrecht's and my future work, including my *Habilitationsschrift*, which contains a chapter on *The Unnamable* that I consider to be one of my most important pieces on Beckett. Albrecht Wellmer published *Zur Dialektik von Moderne und Postmoderne* in 1985, but at our last meeting shortly before his death he mentioned that even his later book *Endgames: The Irreconcilable Nature of Modernity* was still affected by our discussions in this class.

At the University of California at Irvine, I cotaught a class on Beckett with Wolfgang Iser, who regularly came to teach there for one or two semesters. By that time, I had become a close friend of him and his wife, Lore. Our Beckett class turned out to be a unique and amazing adventure. After years of conversations about our quite different approaches to Beckett, we decided to teach the class by presenting our readings of the same novel, play, or short piece in juxtaposition to each other. We did this with *Malone Dies* and *The Unnamable*, *Endgame* and *The Lost Ones*, and *Not-I* and *Imagination Dead Imagine*. These juxtapositions increasingly felt like point/counterpoint compositions and triggered vivid discussions with the students that Wolfgang and I often continued after class. One day, Wolfgang, who had always been squeamish about engaging with psychoanalysis, proudly announced that he had finally begun to systematically read Freud's work to get deeper into my psychoanalytic approach. Jokingly, I replied that he had his work cut out for himself, because after finishing with Freud, he would have to read Bion, Beckett's analyst. "Well, we don't have to get carried away," he laughed.

When Wolfgang eventually proposed that we write a Beckett book together, I was excited because I felt like two decades of our exchanges about Beckett, of our thinking together and against each other, would come to fruition in a collaborative work. We worked on this book for almost two years before we gave it up, often referring to it as our abandoned work. I did write a piece, though, that deals with Beckett's impact on Wolfgang Iser's work for a keynote at a conference in Wolfgang's honor at my home university in 1999. Titled "If Only I Were Not Obliged to Manifest: Iser's Aesthetics of Negativity," it appeared in print in 2000 in a special issue of *New Literary History*. A few years later I presented it in Bulgaria at another celebration of Iser's work and it appeared in a Bulgarian translation in 2004. This piece is on the silences in Wolfgang Iser's work, as well as the ways Iser both shaped and rationalized silence, including silencing the political, through his relation to the silences in Samuel Beckett's work.

Beckett also loomed large in my marriage with Martin Schwab. We had always had endless discussions about Beckett and when I wrote my book on *Endgame*, Martin faithfully read and commented on my drafts. But our real "Beckett phase" began when we saw Beckett's *Film* together in 1986 at a screening in the Arts Village at UCI. We ended up talking for hours, sharing our different ideas about the film. I was so inspired that the next day I wrote the draft for a short essay, "Transitional Spaces in Beckett's *Film*." After I gave it to Martin, he told me he wanted to write a response to my essay. As his response turned into a book on *Film*, I thought of Beckett's "From an Abandoned Work" and let go of my own essay. The happy ending came when Martin's "response" appeared in German as a book titled *Unsichtbares, sichtbar gemacht* (1996). Beckett remains a tie between us and always will be one.

It almost goes without saying that I introduced my children to Beckett at a very early age. I took my older son, Manu, to his first Beckett plays, *Acts Without Words I and II*, when he was barely four years old. The two mimes were staged at the Theater an der Grenze in Kreuzlingen, the same theater where Norman Elrod had staged his legendary version of *Endgame*. Two mimes seemed perfect to introduce a four-year-old to Beckett. I was utterly confident that Manu would get something from the experience, even though I had no idea what it would be. He was excited because special things such as going to plays, music performances, and art exhibitions had become our little adventures. We sat in the first row and the performance had barely started, with a man being flung backward onto the stage, when Manu already burst into laughter before anybody else had time to react. It went on like this throughout the rest of the two mimes. Manu's laughter came consistently a bit ahead of everybody else's. It took me a while before I understood that he didn't take any detours through thinking about the action that adult audiences commonly take. He reacted spontaneously and instantly to the slapstick actions, the whistle, and the objects hovering over the actor on stage. When a palm tree appeared from above, Manu whispered: "Did this tree grow in the sky?" When the man sat on the ground, staring at his hands, Manu stared at his hands. When three colorful cubes descended, he started clapping wildly. When the carafe of water remained out of reach for the actor, Manu commented that whoever was supposed to give it to him was mean. When it finally dangled in front of his face, Manu was puzzled: "Why doesn't he take it now?" He was even more excited about *Acts Without Words II*. He thought that the stick that appeared to poke the two men in their sacks was hilarious, and he was utterly amused by the endless repetitions of the actors dressing and undressing and getting in and out of the sack. He didn't want the mimes to end, and the next day asked me for a whistle, colorful cubes, a carafe of water, a sack, and a stick. For weeks to come he repeated his own version of *Acts Without Words*. Beckett has stayed with him ever since.

We saw a few more Beckett plays during his childhood, including a legendary staging in a theater in St.-Gallen of

Waiting for Godot in Swiss German, which got Manu hooked on this play for many years, even after we moved to California when he was five years old. He talked so much about the play that when he was about nine years old, I had the idea of writing a piece on Beckett's appeal to children. Over several weeks, I interviewed Manu about his thoughts on *Waiting for Godot* until he had perfectly outlined his take on the play. I presented from this collaboration at the annual MLA panel of the Beckett Society and the talk, "One daren't even laugh anymore: Samuel Beckett's *Waiting for Godot* for Children," triggered so much interest that an entire informal debate on Beckett and children continued for several years. I never published this piece, thinking that Manu was too young to give his consent. Sadly, it has since been lost in one of my many moves because I would otherwise have loved to include it in this volume.

Finally, in high school, Manu wrote his senior essay on "Jacques Derrida and Waiting for Godot." For me there was a certain irony in his choice because, unbeknownst to Manu, I had asked Jacques, then a colleague and friend at UCI, why he commented so much on modernist literature but never wrote about Beckett. Without any hesitation Jacques had replied: "This is easy to answer. It's because Beckett feels way too close." Years later, at a conference on Derrida's work, I ended my presentation with a poem composed as a collage of interwoven quotes from Beckett and Derrida:[1]

MURMURS AND SILENCES

> a voice without a mouth
> to speak of nothing
> that can leave a trace
> in the absence of others.

Nothing and no one moves
in the interzone.
But what does it mean
to be here, now?

WORDS AND SIGHS

Destroy, he said, destroy
I am at war with myself
a living being killing
its own protection,
cold war in the head
autoimmunity lost
something somewhere
that can leave a trace.

SHADOWS AND VOIDS

a gaze without an eye
knowing as seeing
the hidden traces,
the lost ones
proceed in the dark
eyes take over
the invisible form.
No shadow. Fancy is her only hope.

NAMES AND EYES

farrago of silence and words
this unnamable thing that I name
with excess of words

and I call that words.
If only I were not obliged to manifest
that is all I can have had to say
this murmur of memory and dream.

My younger son, Leon, became equally mesmerized by Beckett. We watched many of Beckett's plays on film, television, and eventually DVD. The most memorable Beckett experience with Leon, however, happened with a series of performances of Beckett's plays and short pieces by the Royal Shakespeare Company during the year we were in Munich in 1987–1988. Performed over a period of several weeks, these were easily among the very best performances of Beckett's plays I have seen. Leon was eight years old, and his excitement is hard to overstate. With the gift of memory children have at that age, Beckett's "wonderful lines," to echo Winnie from *Happy Days*, stayed engraved in Leon's mind. For days he was commenting on the world with Beckett lines. Or he came running through the house, exclaiming, "The buzzing, the buzzing in the ears . . . in the brain . . . the buzzing, in the skull."

A few years later, in 2000, we saw an outstanding staging of *Waiting for Godot* together, directed by Walter D. Asmus at UCLA's Freud Theater. It was a guest performance by the Gate Theatre of Dublin in which Barry McGovern played Vladimir and Johnny Murphy Estragon. I'll never forget the intensity of lighting in this staging, nor the opening scene with its long moment of absolute stillness, characters frozen under a copper sky. A still life of the entire play. A still life of Beckettian human existence. And there was the moon rising twice like an uncanny alien object, which reminded me of Winnie's line in *Happy Days* "asking for the moon." This is what Beckett does to us, he makes us ask for the moon.

Leon and I also saw an amazing performance of *Happy Days* together, this one staged in a small independent theater in Santa Ana, Orange County. Instead of a sand heap, Winnie was buried in a mount of shredded paper. It was a very intimate performance because the theater was so small that the audience sat extremely close to the stage. I remember having the feeling that I could viscerally grasp not only Winnie's agony but also the excruciatingly difficult discipline of the actress frantically repeating Winnie's "wonderful lines" in a confined state of imposed stillness. After the play we got a chance to talk to the local actors and director. They were all obsessed with Beckett, willing to do the hard labor of fundraising for a small theater. Just a few years later the theater closed, unable to compete with the brutal neoliberal turn in the entertainment world.

Last night Herbert Blau came to me in a dream, reading to me, as he liked to do in the past, from one of his manuscripts. In my dream he read what he wrote about his legendary performance of *Waiting for Godot* at the San Quentin prison. Herb was another friend with whom I shared a lifelong tie to Beckett. His and Kathleen Woodward's work on Beckett contributed to my excitement when I joined the faculty at the University of Wisconsin, Milwaukee for my first tenured appointment in 1984. I had read about Herb Blau's legendary staging of *Waiting for Godot* at San Quentin in Martin Esslin's *Theater of the Absurd* long before I first met him in person for my interview with the Milwaukee faculty. His many books, including the one on Beckett, *Sails of the Herring Fleet*, which includes interviews on the San Quentin production as well as an interview with Beckett not long before Beckett's death, are as unique as his theater. Herb and I remained friends until his death in 2013. I was living back in Constance during the year he died, and during the same year

I was also playing the role of Winnie in *Happy Days*, which Herb would have loved, had I still been able to tell him about it.

Ihab Hassan was also at UWM and became a close friend. His book *The Literature of Silence* includes one of the first treatments of Beckettian silence. I had met Ihab years earlier when he came to lecture on Beckett at the University of Constance during my time as a student. What I liked most in my exchanges with him during our Milwaukee times was the emphasis on playing with Beckett by writing creative responses to his work. Ihab did this, for example, in his hilariously funny experimental play "Joyce—Beckett: A Scenario in 8 Scenes and a Voice" in which he includes bibliographical entries such as "The Making of Beckett's *'End Game'*" by James Joyce and *The Borrowings of Dante, Bruno, and Vico from Finnegans Wake* by the Unnamable.[2]

Like the University of Constance, UWM provided an environment saturated with Beckett scholars and acolytes. Kathleen Woodward, another Beckett critic who directed the Center for Twentieth Century Studies at the time, had invited me to contribute an essay to the collection *Memory and Desire: Aging—Literature—Psychoanalysis* (1986) that she coedited with Murray Schwartz. Inspired by her own essay on transitional objects in *Malone Dies*, I had begun working on "The Intermediate Area Between Life and Death: Fantasies in Samuel Beckett's *Malone Dies*" shortly before I joined UWM. I have completely reworked and expanded the essay for this collection, adding readings of "The Calmative" and *Molloy*.

One of the most unique friendships I formed in which Beckett served as an imaginary mediator was with Indigenous artist Betty David. It was in August 1987 on one of those beautiful California days, full of sunshine and dry heat that fills your bones and lungs. I went to an Indigenous summer market at the mission in San Juan Capistrano with vendors selling jewelry, pottery, sage, and Indigenous music. There she was, in the middle of all these stands, Betty David, selling the most beautiful suede winter coats with thick warm fur inside and stunningly beautiful Inuit designs on the back. Betty and I had started talking, and she asked me: "What are you doing in your life?" "Apart from trying to raise a kid, I'm teaching literature," I replied. "Oh, I love literature," she said. "What do you teach?" "I'm actually teaching a lot of Indigenous literatures these days, especially Native American women writers." Laughing joyfully, she responded, "Don't we all love the things that come from far away? My favorite writer is Samuel Beckett. I am completely obsessed with him!" When I told her that Beckett was my favorite writer too, and that I had published a book on him, she pulled a chair up and poured us coffee. We spent the rest of the afternoon together, talking about the impact of Beckett on our lives. I did end up buying a beautiful brown coat with an inlay of black Inuit art, which is to this day the favorite piece of clothing I ever had. Betty and I heard from each other occasionally but never saw each other again. Ours became one of those inexplicable friendships emerging from an intimate connection that, once formed, is lasting, almost as if out of time. A few years ago, a last message came from her husband, who informed me that she had passed away. I performed a silent ceremony, reading from Beckett's short pieces in her memory.

I was always fascinated by Beckett's intense hold on the imaginary. Many people with whom I talked about Beckett shared that they had certain inexplicable yet insistent fantasies about him. The most stunning among them is one Danzy Senna, now a prominent American writer, shared with me. We had discussed Beckett in one of my classes, and I had mentioned Susan Howe, whom I had recently met after one of her unforgettable poetry readings. In passing, I said that Susan Howe appeared to me like the female version of a young Samuel Beckett. After class, Danzy asked if I wanted to go for coffee and then told me about her life. Susan Howe is her aunt, she said, and her mother is Fanny Howe, a writer whom she encouraged me to read as well. Then she added that her grandmother had had a brief affair with Samuel Beckett shortly before she became pregnant with Susan. Afterward the family nourished a persistent fantasy that Susan was Beckett's child. Completely fascinated by this story, I tried to imagine what it must have been like for Susan Howe to become a writer, thinking she was Samuel Beckett's daughter. A few years ago, I met Danzy again and we went out together after one of her own readings. She told me that, as soon as DNA tests became widely available, Susan was tested and, alas, she is not Beckett's daughter. It would have been too good to be true. As so often, fiction is better than real life. Unfortunately, this also includes our own fictions about ourselves. When I recently talked to Fanny Howe after one of her readings in Laguna Beach, she laughed and said the fantasy of her sister being Beckett's daughter still casts its ghostly shadow over the family lore.

The most telling fantasy of my own about Beckett remained unconscious until the day he died. Just before Christmas Eve 1989, the eventful year when the Berlin wall came down and my son Leon was born, I opened the newspaper and read about Samuel Beckett's death. I stared at the page in shock and disbelief. It is not that I hadn't known that Beckett had become frailer and frailer, but that was, as Patti Smith wrote so succinctly after Lou Reed's death, "a seemingly infinite knowledge."[3] At the moment when I found the announcement of Beckett's passing in black and white, I suddenly realized that I had unconsciously believed him to be immortal. It was, of course, his work that had instilled this fantasy in me. Everything is about the impossibility of ending, even the curse of having to go on. And yet, hearing about Beckett's death felt like an ontological rupture, almost akin to the betrayal of something sacred. How does one mourn someone whose complete work is about the inability to end? How does one mourn someone whose entire writing is an attempt to give birth to himself and who, in the process, helps giving birth to so many others? How does one mourn someone whose texts and plays are all a form of preemptive mourning? And how could I personally mourn a writer who continues to play such a central role in my life and whose work was so bound up with my grief about my beloved sister's death?

I should finally also mention my many conversations with German philosopher Dieter Henrich, Wolfgang Iser's colleague and best friend. Dieter Henrich and I became close friends when we started meeting for regular conversations during my visiting professorship at the Ludwig Maximilian University of Munich in the 1997–1998 academic year. We soon discovered that we were both interested in Beckett's unique ways of engaging psychic life. During our exchanges about experiences of abandonment in infancy and early childhood, we realized the deep impact of Beckettian images such as the mite who strains away, or the boy hiding behind a stone feverishly waiting to be found. As Donald W. Winnicott says, it is a pleasure to hide but a disaster not to be found. Meticulously playing with what remains unsaid in the speech of his characters, Beckett's work offers the rare gift of finding one in the inner spaces where one tends to hide. Many of the talks I had with Dieter Henrich over the years were about the unsaid between people, about how we tend to hide from others, yet crave to be "found" in indirect ways. Geoffrey Hartman once asked why we need the detour of literature to look at ourselves. Talking with Dieter Henrich, we both realized that

Beckett took us on such a detour. As we came to affirm to each other, Beckett contributed to shaping our very being in the world and with others. Beckett's obsession with the tragedy of an incomplete psychological birth also deepened our sense of being shaped by early life experiences. Years ago, Dieter sent me a draft of his recently published book *Sein oder Nichts: Erkundungen um Beckett und Hölderlin*. In his letter, Dieter also spoke about the urgency he felt of discussing with me the silences between him and his friend Wolfgang Iser about their immensely different, yet equally substantial responses to Beckett. Our conversations about Beckett continued into the strange space of our pandemic Zoom culture, until he passed away in December 2022.

One of my most exciting, albeit also most challenging, experiences with Beckett's work came in 2013 when I played the role of Winnie at the Studiobühne in Constance in a performance staged by Tessa Theodorakopoulos. Tessa had been the director at the Studiobühne since I was an actress there during my times as assistant professor. When Tessa heard that I would be back in Constance for a year, she recruited me for another play, bribing me by suggesting to stage Beckett's *Happy Days*, an offer I couldn't refuse. We did a highly experimental trilingual staging of the play with three actresses, weaving together Beckett's three languages, English, French and German. Each actress emphasized a different aspect of Winnie's personality, the Irish Winnie being the humorous one, the French the seductive one, and the German, whom I played, the philosophical and literary one.

We all shared the challenges of this extremely difficult role, with hours of sitting buried to the waist in a sand heap, and, in the second act, to the neck. Embodying Winnie in her tortured position made us merge with her discomfort at a corporeal level. As many of the actresses who played Winnie had complained, this is an excruciatingly hard role to memorize, and we came to share Winnie's terror of no longer remembering "those wonderful lines." By the end, however, we had internalized the rhythms and moods of Beckett's play, and with it came a rare form of hitherto unknown paradoxical happiness. We thus did have our "happy days" of merging with a theatrical experience utterly alien, yet uncannily familiar.

During the week *Happy Days* was staged at the Studiobühne, Harry, who had by then lost his speech to a crippling case of aphasia, took a train from Berlin to Constance. On what became his last trip to visit me, Harry attended every single one of our performances. Sadly, he could never tell me what he thought of our experimental way of staging the play. A year later I saw Harry again in a café in Berlin. I had gotten used to telling him stories to which he reacted with alert eyes and vivid body language, occasionally interspersing a text message. That day I told him I was going to see Beckett's *Footfalls* at the Schillertheater. In response, he typed: "Can I come?" That's how I ended up seeing *Footfalls* with Harry and his wife Rose. Happier than I had seen him in years, Harry sat next to me, absolutely mesmerized. Sometimes he squeezed my hand. Once, when I looked at him, I saw tears in his eyes. It felt as if he had finally become one of them, those Beckett figures we both loved so much.

The staging of the play at the Schillertheater emphasized its musical structure and timing. Uncannily, it is one of Beckett's most ghostly plays, dramatizing, as Beckett himself once stated, the difference between existing and living. Years ago, I had analyzed this difference and its link to Beckett's prominent themes, the incomplete birth and the transitional space between living and dying, in my reading of *The Unnamable*. Like May in *Footfalls*, many of Beckett's characters are haunted by the feeling that, having never been properly born, they are condemned to exist without living. May, in *Footfalls*, moves through life like a ghost of the woman she could have become, had she had a chance to be properly born. Sitting at the Schillertheater next to Harry, I wondered if he felt the resonances and dissonances to his own condition. While Beckett's characters are suffocating in a flood of discordant words they cannot stop, Harry had become trapped in a world without words. While Beckett's characters are ghosts condemned to exist without living because they have never been properly born, Harry seemed to be condemned to exist without living because the words that were the umbilical cord to his life had been taken from him. Did he feel any of this when he cried silent tears during *Footfalls*? Harry passed away on November 10, 2019. Once again it was Beckett who helped me mourn.

My latest engagement with Beckett came recently during the early phase of the Corona virus COVID-19 pandemic. From the very beginning I was struck by how the ways of living during the lockdown resonated with Beckett's world. In a piece I did for a special issue on the pandemic in the online journal *Foundry*, I described this experience as pandemic surrealism.[4] Day in, day out, we were condemned to play the same role in our own theater of the absurd. Suddenly Beckett gained new relevance in the context of the pandemic. Intuiting the connection between theater and the plague that Artaud described so succinctly, Beckett was once again out of time, in time, timeless. This resonance prompted my decision to return to Beckett's work and revise what I had written on him over the past decades in light of today's world. Inevitably, Beckett's short piece *Breath* came to mind, and I wrote about this and other pieces from within the experience of the pandemic. It is the coda that will conclude this collection of essays.

Like Beckett throughout his life, I suffer from insomnia. But when I fall asleep these days, I sometimes wake up with a jolt as

I hear a Beckett line in my dream. Recently, during my stay in Berlin, I went to a bar with the name Beckett's Kopf (Beckett's Head) located in Prenzlauer Berg. I had found out about it when I googled "Beckett in Berlin" and was intrigued, expecting to see photos of Beckett or posters from his plays, perhaps even a shelf with some of his books for people to browse. But the only thing displayed is one of the beautiful Beckett portraits in the window outside the restaurant. The restaurant and the photo have been there for seventeen years. When I told the owner that I had expected to find Beckett memorabilia inside, he said he had opted to focus instead on giving his bar a Beckettian atmosphere, minimalist and dark. He imagined his guests to enter with a sense of waiting for something that would never arrive. Then he laughed and quoted a few lines from *Waiting for Godot*.

Oh, those wonderful Beckett lines. Like Winnie, I find them everywhere and sometimes I can't turn them off when they occupy my mind. One day, I woke up at 4:00 a.m. with the ending of this introduction in my head: The buzzing, the buzzing in the skull . . . in the brain. I can't go on. I'll go on. Not-I?

POETICS OF THE END TIMES

Arguably, Beckett's deepest concern is with living in the end times, coping with death and the impossibility of ending as well as the specter of infinity. His work portrays not only the ending of individual lifetimes but also the ending of planetary life and the extinction of the earth. Images of characters imagining themselves to be the last humans reappear throughout Beckett's texts and plays. His characters are old, moribund, and preoccupied with their impending death, often harboring phantasms that they have already died and are forced to speak from the beyond or the grave. This state of mind becomes entangled with complementary phantasms of not being able to end or of being locked into a negative infinity.

Beckett's work confronts us with the most persistent philosophical questions about life, being, death, meaning, and language. It requires one to face irreducible otherness and radical uncertainty. At the same time, it touches and moves us at the deepest level, making us cry and laugh. The intensity of affect that Beckett's work generates is linked to its unique experimental aesthetics and form, its poetic images and stage settings and the lyrical quality and rhythms of his prose. Like no other author, he has offered us a poetics of the end times. As Beckett's work pushes the boundaries of language, literature, image and sound, genres and conventions, mind, and subjectivity, it summons us to expand our own boundaries toward the unthinkable and the unnamable.

It was Beckett who helped me face radical uncertainty, losses, endings, deaths, and mortality. It was Beckett who conveyed the inextricable entanglement of finitude and infinity as well as their discontents. It was Beckett who left me with the vision of a barren planet or cosmos without grand design or purpose. And it was Beckett who invited me to a balancing act on the tightrope of fragile emotions. As I return to Beckett, once again, on the way toward the end times of my own life, I am asking how he helps one face the manifold configurations of thinking the end times in the early twenty-first century. Rather than eschatological or chiliastic, most visions of the end times today are secular, born of ecological concerns and the frightful knowledge of impending environmental disasters. The latter include climate change, nuclear destruction, pervasive toxification of the planet, the acidification of the oceans, extreme weather conditions with droughts, fires, floods, and landslides, the dying of species and the so-called Sixth Extinction, as well as the onset of what virologists call a pandemic age. Add to this the economic devastation caused by global capitalism that leads to the increasing marginalization and disposability of peoples, to forced migrations, famines and abject poverty of masses and masses of people around the globe. These dire conditions make it easy to imagine a world populated by Beckett characters, evicted from their dingy abodes and temporary shelters, forced to migrate across the land, looking for scraps of food, hiding from other humans and telling themselves stories to fill the terrible void of catastrophic loneliness.

If you are living in a barren inhospitable world that does not offer you any livable design or space of containment, let alone the company of caring fellow beings, the only direction is to look inward. And inward Beckett's characters look. Most of his narrators are highly educated, sophisticated thinkers, philosophers, crafters of arcane words and poetic images. They are dreamers trying to find their way among the stars and observing the sky for comfort. Or, as Theodor Adorno says in "Trying to Understand Endgame," Beckett's characters are "those who dream their own death."[5] Yet they are also living in excruciating abjection, not shying away from naming the filth in which they live and the sores that afflict them. They freely expose their futile attempts at copulation, the scatological humor they enjoy, and even the murderous impulses that assault them out of the blue. As they explore the boundaries of the human, we can easily be tempted to see them as the precursors of a nightmarish future to come.

How then do they inhabit the end times they envision? What are the stories they are telling and what can we learn from them? What are the philosophies they discard mockingly and what imaginaries do they weave around their thinking about the end times? How do they challenge the secular end time visions formed in an era of ecological crises, mass extinctions, the Anthropocene and the Capitalocene?

As this book is going to press, we have been living through a pandemic for more than three years in a seemingly endless state of waiting, not knowing when it will end, how it will end. Moreover, the confluence of the coronavirus pandemic, the new upsurge of racism, and climate change with its devastating fires, hurricanes, tornados, and catastrophic floods generates a feeling of living in the end times, often surreally so. No author understood the end times better than Samuel Beckett, whose characters are, as Charles McNulty recently wrote, confined to "a narrow loop of existence."[6] Beckett is the perfect author to reread during the age of climate change and pandemics, especially since, while being obsessed with yet uniquely immune to aging, his work keeps aggregating new possible referential horizons in accordance with the changing times. Just as in the vortex of nuclear fears in the 1950s and 1960s, directors used the aftermath of a nuclear holocaust as a setting to stage *Endgame*, now they use climate change and perennial drought as a setting for *Happy Days*. Today we may also imagine the current Corona virus pandemic as a setting for a new staging of *Breath*.

Thinking in terms of living in the end times establishes a precarious relationship to time, future, and infinity. Catastrophic times thrive on negative hallucination. People tend to live in a mode of not wanting to see what is right in front of their eyes. While Beckett fully exposes and intervenes in the collective tendency to conceal, occlude, or openly deny catastrophe, the latter has always already happened in his work. In fact, it is the sense of catastrophe that fuels the psychic energies of Beckett's texts and plays. It was none other than Bion, Beckett's analyst, who said that neurotics suffer from premonitions

(*Ahnungen*) of catastrophes extrapolated from memory, and that they are driven to turn them into actions. One could say that Beckett's entire work is driven by using extrapolated memories of catastrophes and cataclysms to propel the imagined worlds of his characters. Yet, at the same time, his characters are stuck in a mode of waiting that marks their entire being.

Moreover, Beckett mockingly links this mode of waiting to the tradition of apocalyptic imaginaries, including most prominently that of the Judeo-Christian Apocalypse whose deepest truth about the end, according to Dietmar Kamper, is that there is no end.[7] Beckett's characters are living in a mode of waiting for an end that never happens, an impossible end. They can't go on, but they go on waiting for the end. Adorno says about the characters in *Endgame* that "phantasms of infinity" are their curse.[8] In this respect Beckett's entire work is an endgame.

Waiting for something that never arrives freezes one in a mode of perpetual deferral. Time before the catastrophe or the end seems to expand into infinity. The Greek *katechon* refers to this time of waiting before the apocalypse. But at the time nobody had the sense that this waiting would turn into an eternal deferral. *Waiting for Godot* and *Endgame* together reveal the paralyzing impasse this paradoxical temporality creates in the psychic life of those who are waiting. They also reveal that the laughter at death at the heart of the comedy of waiting for something that never arrives conceals a deep and pervasive melancholia. "Nothing is funnier than unhappiness," says Nell.[9] Beckett exposes his recipients to both, the laughter, and the melancholia laughter tries to mitigate by hiding it. Insistently refusing the reductive causality of either/or perspectives, Beckett always gives us both and nothing at the same time. He even refuses the alternative between more and less because in his aesthetics of persistent reduction and evacuation, less enhances the intensity of both effects and affects in the here and now.

During the current times of accumulated chronic crises, the sense of living in the end times is enhanced as well. More than ever, we depend on concord fictions that, according to Frank Kermode, offer us the illusion of a meaningful sense of ending.[10] Beckett's concord fictions refuse any consolation that comes from attributing meaning to the end. Paradoxically, however, it is perhaps precisely because of this that they can be strangely consoling. We know that we don't know anything about the end. But we do not want to accept this knowledge. Beckett offers us a training in radical uncertainty. Perhaps this becomes helpful in taking a few steps toward learning to accept the unknowable and unnamable.

Finally, one of Beckett's most unique and challenging contributions to thinking about living in the end times is that he offers us what I call a poetics of the end times. It is hard to imagine a more dire and relentless look at the world and the humans who live through the end times than Beckett's. Yet no other writer has looked at this world with such unfailing humor and, more importantly perhaps, no other author has described the end times in such mesmerizing, if not hypnotizing poetic words and images. It is the rare beauty of Beckett's works that characterizes their singularity. Even the novels and longer prose texts are replete with sentences that we commonly read only in poetry. It is this poetry that mitigates the gaze into the abyss.

One of Beckett's other unique achievements is to enfold extremes into each other, not only the beautiful and the ugly but also dignity and the abject, philosophy and scatology, or even the sacred and the profane. Straddling these extremes, Beckett's characters are outcasts living in basements, ditches, or stables, filthy and moribund. Yet they are highly educated philosophers who register the most minute details of other humans and their environment and keep protocol of their own struggle with death and the end times of their lives as well as their planet. They are writers who know the vicissitudes of writing and speaking, who are fully aware of, yet cannot but try to navigate the traps of manifestation, lies and embellishment. They are philosophical skeptics of the first order. They are psychologically minded beings who record the most minute nuances of their emotions and moods, including the numbing of mind and soul that inevitably marks living in the end times.

Trying to trace what this philosophical poetics can offer in our own times of perennial crises and disasters and the haunting from the future that marks the cultural imaginary of end times, I am proposing *Moments for Nothing* as a collection of essays that is timely in many ways. Like no other author Beckett speaks to living in the vortex of catastrophes. Celebrating his visionary anticipation of the existential conditions of living in the end times, the collection explores Beckett's particular sense of an ending with today's global challenges to planetary survival as a backdrop. While earlier versions of some of the chapters have been published before, I have rewritten, revised, and expanded them to highlight how they speak more specifically to the present, emphasizing among other things the paradoxical simultaneity of stasis and turbulence that marks living with a pandemic, including the seemingly endless times of lockdowns and restrictions.

In this introduction, I trace stages of my personal involvement with Beckett's work over half a century, showing how Beckett has shaped not only my work as a literary scholar and critical theorist but also important aspects of my personal life. The intensity of this encounter is symptomatic of Beckett's capacity to gain a profoundly existential hold on readers and audiences. Beckett has an uncanny ability to affect the molding of his recipient's lives, just as my first experience of *Waiting for Godot* transformed my life in subliminal ways that I only understood much later.

Chapter 1, "Moments for Nothing: *Endgame* and Its Discontents," presents a completely rewritten version of an earlier essay titled "On the Dialectic of Closing and Opening in *Fin de Partie*," originally published in *Yale French Studies* in 1984, and then republished in Steven Connor's edited volume *Beckett's Waiting for Godot and Endgame* in 1992. My rewriting for *Moments for Nothing* shows how the experience of living in an end time has not only informed my encounter with the play and with Beckett's work more generally but also continues to shape how I today read the entangled vision of personal and planetary end times. "Moments for Nothing: *Endgame* and Its Discontents" frames living in the end times with Hamm's story of a painter in an insane asylum "who thought the end of the world had come." When Hamm tries to show him "the loveliness of the world," the painter is appalled, since all he had seen was ashes. Seeing the ashes of apocalypse is, according to Hamm, the privilege of a madman. *Endgame* suggests that the characters are approaching their own end during the end time of the earth. When Hamm, indicating they might be the last survivors of a great disaster, declares "outside of here it's death,"[11] one can hardly evade the atmosphere of finality, decay, and apocalypse but soon learns not to take such pronouncements at face value. No symbols where none intended, as Beckett insists.

Beckett emphasizes "playing an endgame." The play's communicative structure with its recursive loops, iterative substitutions and double binds that sublate ending into play, complicate living in the end times in ever-new rehearsals. Rather than approach the end gradually, Hamm and Clov have always lived in the end times, just as they have always played their endgame. The end is in the beginning and life has never really begun. When Clov asks Hamm "Do you believe in the life to come?" Hamm answers with malicious glee: "Mine was always that."[12] Concomitantly, for them the earth has always been extinguished, as Clov suggests when he states: "I say to myself that the earth is extinguished, though I never saw it lit."[13] Here Clov also indirectly raises the issue of the rhetorical construction of the apocalypse, something the characters repeatedly expose in its fallacy. Through the characters' self-reflexive questioning of the adequacy of anything that can be said, Beckett's own performative language games tease the audience into a projective identification with the lures of apocalyptic images and stories—but only to reveal that words such as "life and death" or "beginning and end" can only ever be a form of catachresis. Throwing us back onto our own projections, Beckett triggers a self-reflection that reshapes the vicissitudes of apocalyptic cultural imaginaries.

Living in the end times is also the existential condition of old age. In chapter 2, "The Transitional Space Between Life and Death: "The Calmative," *Molloy*, and *Malone Dies*," I am exploring Beckett's staging of the black comedy of old age.[14] Displacing death in never-ending endgames, these texts explore aging and its discontents from the perspective of the paradoxical subjectivity of narrators that hover between I and Not-I as well as life and death. Often they even suggest that they speak from beyond the grave. "I don't know when I died,"[15] says the narrator of "The Calmative," locating his narrative beyond the end times. Temporality, however, is fluid and indeterminate in his story, because he also states that he feels older than "the day, the night, when the sky with all its lights fell upon me."[16] Was the cataclysmic event that caused the sky with all its lights to fall upon him the apocalypse in which the stars fall from the sky that John of Patmos describes in the Revelation? Are the characters awaiting their end at a time that coincides with the end time of their planet? Or has the death they are envisioning already happened during the fatal abandonment they experienced as children, as Beckett's analyst Bion suggests in his work on death? Has the earth's apocalypse in a similar way always already happened?

After this reading of "The Calmative," I turn to Beckett's trilogy. As if Beckett keeps being haunted by his own work, his characters keep being haunted by their earlier versions. Their porosity reveals the plasticity of a creative process precipitated by a sense of exhaustion and a paradoxical drive toward depletion, emptiness, and silence within the impossibility of ending. *Molloy*, the first novel of Beckett's trilogy, sets the stage for a series of narrators who, like the narrator in "The Calmative," describe living in the end times of their lives, already in the process of dying. Molloy is a writer who is lost roaming around on an earth that seems to be in the throes of cataclysm. Periodically, he lives with his mother in abject dependency. Both live in a transitional space between life and death, awaiting their end.

While Molloy affirms that he needs stories, he struggles not to talk about himself. His need for stories pushes him into the vortex of a struggle with language, with words and meaning, reflecting upon the end times of writing. Unable to find the serenity of composition, Molloy is seeking the "tranquility of decomposition," asserting that "to decompose is to live too."[17] Writing as decomposition marks the end time of writing for Beckett's characters, the unending gestures of qualifications, dismissals, and erasures. Molloy's world is haunted by murmurs and voices of others, including Moran's whose voice told him to write the report Molloy considers to be fraught with lies and embellishments. Eventually, writing as decomposition turns into a "long sonata of the dead."[18]

In *Malone Dies*, writing becomes a practice of displacing Malone's I from his decaying body onto a scripted eternal trace, thus diffusing his self, in a Kierkegaardian fashion, into eternity. A dying Malone is weaning himself from reality with the help of transitional objects, easing the fear of separation, loneliness, and death, and facilitating the passage to nonlife. The transitional space thus created is, however, always threatened by the intrusion of the real. Flourishing phantasms of the disintegrating body are used as images for the dissolution of the self in old age. With respect to both the body and the self, their function is ambiguous and polyvalent, serving simultaneously as defenses against, reactions to, therapeutic devices for, and artistic creations about the bodily fragmentations and deteriorations of old age, a process that is driven to its ultimate extreme in *The Unnamable*.

Chapter 3, "End Times of Subjectivity: *The Unnamable*" stages an endgame with an entire tradition of philosophies of subjectivity.[19] "Where I am there is no one but me who am not," says the Unnamable, thus creating a transitional space of speech between manifestation and nonmanifestation: "If only I were not obliged to manifest."[20] Playing with centuries of philosophical theories, Beckett tests their abstractions within the concreteness of a fictional life. Hovering on the boundaries between an empirical and a transcendental subject, the Unnamable performs a paradoxical subjectivity at its vanishing point. Entangled in the schizoid positionality of ontological insecurity, he produces a maniacal proliferation of imaginary selves. His trick is to take philosophical conceptions literally in order to mobilize radical epistemological doubt against both pathological ontological certainty and the stability of body images. Phantasms of the fragmented body manifest in alter egos such as Worm, an atavistic creature without being, whom Ruby Cohn describes as "a larva conceived but not quite born, a maggot buried but not quite dead."[21] Beckett uses these avatars as the basis of a philosophy of the Not-I, grounded in a paradoxical discourse that can't go on, yet goes on, locked in a phantasm of negative infinity.

Chapter 4, "'Laughing wildly inmidst severest woe': *Happy Days* and the Last Humans" presents a vision of the last humans on an earth that suffers from extreme desertification.[22] A woman buried to her waist in a sandy hill and a decrepit man in a hole live in an expanse of scorched land under a hellish sun that causes objects to burst spontaneously into flames. At the same time, the main character Winnie also invokes the other extreme, namely of living in a perishing cold. This is the apocalyptic scenery of Samuel Beckett's *Happy Days*. Performing an experimental abstraction of human adaptability to extreme conditions in the aftermath of catastrophe, *Happy Days* plays with an array of intertextual allusions to works that deal with the loss of paradise, the decay of empires and dynasties, or the sinking of human characters into madness and despair.

When *Happy Days* first appeared on stage, images of Hiroshima loomed large in the cultural imaginary, showing humans exposed to the hellish light of the atomic bomb. Today we may read *Happy Days* as a performative invocation and experimental exploration of destroyed ecologies such as globally spread toxicity, environmental devastation, depletion of resources, climate change and extreme weather conditions, the dying of species, the threat of a nuclear holocaust, and what scientists predict as the onset of a pandemic age.

The play's psychohistorical imaginary of disasters of apocalyptic proportion is doubled with references to literary figurations of world endings as well as self-reflexive exhibitions of the play's own theatricality. Ultimately, Beckett's tragicomic experimentalism uses Winnie's catachrestic language games to undermine the lures of an apocalyptic imaginary as well as the trauma fatigue that creates a protective shield against realist depictions of zones of disaster and deathworlds.[23] Perhaps Winnie's psychic automatism of inoperative citations and her clinging to a fake happiness explains why *Happy Days* might be the darkest of Beckett's plays.

In chapter 5, "Cosmographical Meditations on the Inhuman," I analyze Beckett's *The Lost Ones* from the perspective of Jean-Francois Lyotard's reflections on the question of whether thought can go on without a body.[24] Lyotard recalls imaginary "soulscapes," that is, uninhabitable spaces that extend the borders of Western philosophy from Aristotle to Kant. In response to a philosophically engendered profound ontological insecurity, these spaces induce a state of systematic madness, or *vesania*. Reading *The Lost Ones*, I argue, infects readers with a *vesania* that is symptomatic of living in the end times. Reminiscent of Dante's *Purgatorio*, *The Lost Ones* opens onto a cylindrical abode populated by an abject group of vanquished humans. Their naked bodies roam in futile search of other lost ones, while a disembodied narrative voice records an order invisible to human eyes. Many markers in the text evoke the sense of an ending, if not a future that announces the end of the human as we know it.

As an imaginary ethnography of the future, *The Lost Ones* embraces an ethics of radical epistemological doubt. Poetry alone seems adequate to envision a form of life familiar enough to solicit compassion yet alien enough to foreclose familiar categories of comprehension. What remains is the obstinate "resistance of the soul"[25] in a vanquished world and the lost ones' unfathomable attachment to the most minimal forms of being. Haunted by a vision of living in the end times, *The Lost Ones* anticipates and speaks to the catastrophes of the present time, that is, the viable end of the human species in the age of climate change, environmental destruction, pandemics, and an ever-increasing population of humans deemed disposable. Beckett's memory of the future opens a space for the most subliminal transformational use of literature—a form of soul-making that continually reconfigures the boundaries of the human and its primordial imprints.

The coda, "Beckett in the Pandemic: *Breath* and the Vicissitudes of Animation," is about reading Beckett in the years of the early 2020s after the onset of the pandemic. During the first year of the COVID-19 pandemic, which I call the Year of Breath, the sense of living in the end times emerged from the confluence of multiple catastrophes compounding each other. During the global pandemic people are suffocating because the coronavirus attacks their respiratory system. In the United States, a black man's strangulation by police triggers a worldwide movement against systemic racism, fueled by the slogan "I can't breathe." The merciless economic crash following the pandemic leaves no breathing space for the most vulnerable of people. Climate change causes raging fires across California, Oregon, and Washington, poisoning the already toxic air with microparticles that nest in people's lungs. Strangely enough, but not altogether surprising, in a world marked by catastrophes, many readers return to Beckett, seeking resonance and indeed solace and reprieve.

In "The Theater and the Plague," Artaud made the stunning observation that "the only two organs really affected and injured by the plague, the brain and the lungs, are both directly dependent on the consciousness and the will."[26] Linking the plague to its double, the theater, Artaud argues that the plague shakes off the asphyxiating inertia of matter.[27] In a similar vein, Beckett sweeps vulnerabilities and contradictions to the surface, confronting his audience with the essentials of life and death. Teaching us how to let go, the pandemic offers a lesson in the art of dying. Who in the theater but Samuel Beckett provides a better double for this hardest of all life lessons?

In 1969, Beckett wrote and performed one of his shortest and most elusive plays, *Breath*.[28] A meditative reflection on breathing, the most essential condition of life, *Breath* is uniquely attuned to the pandemic years of the breath. Victims of COVID-19 die because they cannot breathe. People's heightened states of anxiety during the lockdown makes them feel suffocated. They can't breathe because the age of climate change and raging fires fills the air with toxic smog. But people also meditate, using breath to ground themselves in this new alien world. This backdrop provides a new space of resonance for Beckett's *Breath*. Highlighting the brevity of life between our first and last breaths, the play's meditation on breathing confronts us with mortality. Perhaps the most minimalist of Beckett's pieces, *Breath* strips living in the end times of everything but the essentials of being, namely breath, life, and death. Ending with reflections on this short piece that contains the secret core of Samuel Beckett's work, *Moments for Nothing* moves the play into a perennial here and now in which breathing is the essence of life since time immemorial. Focusing his play on the short span between a human's first and last breath, Beckett once again offers his audience the strange gift of creating a space of containment, almost paradoxically, by helping to face the abyss and catastrophic loneliness.

1

MOMENTS FOR NOTHING

Endgame and Its Discontents

> *Infinite emptiness will be around you, all the resurrected dead of all the ages wouldn't fill it . . .*
>
> —Samuel Beckett, *Endgame*

The stage of *Endgame* opens on the bare interior of a gloomy room suffused in gray. Faint light falls on Hamm and Clov, the two main characters. Hamm sits in a wheelchair with a cloth covering his head, and Clov, staggering with stiff legs from one side to the other, performs a strange pantomime trying to climb a ladder to look out the barren room's two windows. They are placed on the wall way high up above eyesight, leaving the audience to wonder why. Did a taller race of men live here once? Or has Clov been shrinking, as Hamm suspects?[1] The only picture in the room is turned toward the wall, perhaps attuning spectators to become mindful of what remains invisible or is deliberately hidden from view. In front of the stage, we see two trashcans in which Hamm's parents, Nagg and Nell, are languishing in abject confinement. Is this more than a wicked metaphor for old age and the generation gap?

Given the characters' advanced state of bodily deterioration, they are presumably living in the end times of their lives, if not, as they later repeatedly suggest, planetary life. Clov is the only character still able to move, albeit with stiff knees and unable to sit down. Laughing heartily, Nagg and Nell like to remind each other of the story when they lost "their shanks" in a bicycle accident in the Ardennes. Hamm, lame, blind and bleeding, needs tranquilizers and suffers from a chronic cough. From its first lines onward—"Finished, it's finished, nearly finished, it must be nearly finished"[2]—*Endgame* evokes an ending world, albeit in a tentative mode of uncertainty. Apocalypse looms large, but it would not be accurate to describe *Endgame* as merely another apocalyptic fiction because Beckett uses the entire gamut of references to apocalyptic imaginaries as elements of a play that transforms them into more abstract algorithms of end time experiences.

Initially, however, the play's apocalyptic mood is generating intensities of affect that draw the audience into sensual apprehensions of endings. The play's entire atmosphere exudes morbidity, decay, and finitude. In tandem with their deteriorating bodies, the characters' material resources are dwindling as well. Calling their abode a refuge, Hamm states laconically "Enough, it's time it ended, in the refuge too."[3] There is no more natural growth and life in the desolate outside world. "Nature has forgotten us," says Hamm, whereupon Clov replies: "There's no more nature."[4] Seeds refuse to come up, he reports as he looks upon the desolate barren wasteland in front of the windows, indicating that they might be the last survivors of a great disaster of apocalyptic proportions.[5]

There is, as we hear, no cure for living on earth. From the very beginning, Hamm and Clov assert that they are waiting for the end, even abhorring the idea that life might continue, as

Hamm fears when Clov tells him he has a flea. With a sarcastic stab at evolutionary history, Hamm exclaims: "But humanity might start from there all over again! Catch him, for the love of God." The evolution and extinction of species is also on Hamm's mind when he performs his fantasies of escape from the refuge. "Let's go from here, the two of us! South! You can make a raft and the currents will carry us away, far away, to other... mammals!" Hamm's performative reference to humans as belonging to the species of mammals draws only a sarcastic "God forbid!" from Clov, and it doesn't take long before Hamm envisions them "sitting there, a speck in the void, in the dark, for ever."[6]

Finally, Hamm's musings about "if a rational being came back to earth"[7] might even suggest that other humans have relocated on a different planet. In *Endgame*, the world outside thus provides a perspective that extends beyond the end times to a vision of "the world without us."[8] Nothing seems more evident than to see this scene as a theatrical figuration of characters anticipating the accelerating decay of a dying world. The times of rational beings are over, as Hamm suggests, at least on this earth.

Relishing Clov's description of the outside world as a wasteland in which "nothing stirs," Hamm muses that beyond the wall is the "other hell."[9] Being prodded by Hamm to summarize what he sees, Clov chooses a single word, "corpsed."[10] Hamm later picks up Clov's allusion with the remark, "The whole place stinks of corpses," only to see Clov upstage him with a laconic "The whole universe."[11] Clov's use of the term "corpsed," of course, refers less to the wastelanding of the earth than to the dying of species in an unlivable environment. Moreover, in a play staged in a world still living through the traumatic aftermath of World War II and written by an author who was in the French resistance, it is hard not to think of a resonance with the corpsed world of the concentration camps. The ashes and the gray in Beckett's plays, as well as the repeated references to corpses, inevitably evoke the horrors of the time, the genocide, and the burning of those murdered in the camps, as well as the burned bodies and ashes of Hiroshima and the feeling that the atomic bomb has generated a pervasive sense of living in the end times. In this respect, *Endgame* certainly belongs to the writing of disaster in the aftermath of World War II. But in its unique form of theatrical figuration disaster appears, as in Beckett's work more generally, only via indirection and poetic abstraction. Badiou captured this quality of Beckettian writing of disaster well when he spoke of "the tender cadence of disaster."[12]

As I discuss in my reading of *Happy Days,* Beckett removed the concrete allusion to Hiroshima he had included in the initial version of his play, thus trying to prevent its reduction to a specific historical reading. Instead, he transforms the play's referential horizons into a more generalized sense of living through the end times in the aftermath of catastrophes. In "Trying to Understand *Endgame*" (published in German in 1961, four years after the first staging of *Fin de Partie* in French in Great Britain in 1957 at the Royal Court Theatre), Theodor W. Adorno insisted that in Beckett's plays, "form absorbs what is expressed and changes it."[13] This is also true about the resonances with the cataclysmic historical events of the twentieth century, the concentration camps, and the atomic bombing of Hiroshima and Nagasaki.

Emphasizing the resonance to the aftermath of the camps and Hiroshima as a general signature of the times, Adorno describes Beckett's translation of the event into an algorithm of the human condition: "Humanity vegetates along, crawling, after events which even the survivors cannot really survive, on a pile of ruins which even renders futile self-reflection of one's battered state."[14] In a similar vein, linking *Endgame* to the era of awareness of the Bomb, Stanley Cavell argues that what is new in Beckett's response is the "wish for unlimited surcease, and without the plan of redemption."[15] *Endgame*, for Cavell, is about thinking "it is right that the world end."[16] From this perspective, *Endgame* is also a play about the aftermath, that is, about what it means to live in the world after the Holocaust and the Bomb. It is a world without redemption, without the hope held out by an eschatological imaginary. In such a world, the end becomes an object of desire or in Cavell's words, "a wish for unlimited surcease."[17] If this wish is new, as Cavell argues, Beckett is certainly the writer who has most deeply explored its multifarious manifestations in the human psyche.

Also new is that the Bomb has shifted the sense of living in the end times from fantasy to viable reality. We know that humans have developed the potential to end the world and most planetary life, but the magnitude of this knowledge and the scale and duration of destruction transcend the limits of human imagination. Lacking any proportionate response, we resort, as Cavell points out, to the habitual reactions we know; that is, we use "forgetfulness, habit, hope against hope, humor, hysteria, fantasy."[18] "What I am suggesting," Cavell adds, "is that one dimension of our plight can only be discovered in a phenomenology of the Bomb. For it has invaded our dreams and given the brain, already wrinkled with worry, a new cut. And it has finally provided our dreams of vengeance, our despair of happiness, our hatreds of self and world, with an instrument adequate to convey their destructiveness and satisfaction."[19]

Is Hamm blind because of the horrors he has seen or because of the blinding light of the atomic blast? He can only hallucinate, never see the world, just as we can only hallucinate, never see the end. Living in the end times requires one to face radical epistemological uncertainty. Nobody, I think, provides a better training ground for being able to tolerate this condition than Beckett. "Art begins where explanations leave off, or before they start," writes Cavell.[20] Insisting on a radical uncertainty about living in the end times, Beckett not only shows fantasies and fictions of the end to be the characters' last resort, but he also engages the audience to respond by projecting their own fantasies of the end connected to the vast horizon of the play's possible referential meanings.

Most important, however, Beckett complicates and disrupts the play's possible referential horizons by consistently exposing its theatricality. This technique of theatrical self-reflexivity also affects the figuration of the end times as it becomes embedded in and entangled with the characters' endgame. Hamm, for example, expresses at least some ambivalence about ending: "Enough, it's time it ended. In the refuge too. (Pause.) And yet I hesitate, I hesitate to . . . to end."[21] Among other things, Hamm hesitates to end because, as he repeatedly asserts by emphasizing his role as the actor in a play, they are not living but playing a never-ending endgame. About halfway through *Endgame*, Hamm tells the story of a painter in an insane asylum "who thought the end of the world had come." When Hamm tries to show him "the loveliness of the world," the painter is appalled since all he had seen was ashes.[22] Seeing the ashes of apocalypse is, according to Hamm, the privilege of a madman. Yet seeing apocalyptic ashes is a sparing grace in a world that unfolds like a never-ending endgame.

The embers and ashes of the apocalypse are a signature of Beckett's entire work, and one could indeed also see this work as an endgame of writing or of acting in the theater. In response to the dark existentialism of the postwar years as well as the lures of surrealism and the theater of the absurd, Beckett offers us a series of endgames that strip living and writing to its essentials. Beckett's consistent self-reflexive exposure of his work's literariness and theatricality, however, challenges its recipients not to take referential pronouncements at face value. The communicative structure of *Endgame*, for example, with its recursive loops, iterative substitutions and double binds that sublate ending into play, complicate the notion of living in the end times in ever-new rehearsals. Beckett's language games tease the audience into a projective identification with the lures of apocalyptic images and stories, but only to reveal that words such as life and death or beginning and end, can only ever be a form of catachresis. Throwing us back onto our own projections, Beckett triggers a self-reflection that reshapes the vicissitudes of the apocalyptic cultural unconscious.

Nonetheless *Endgame* remains a highly self-reflexive theatrical meditation on living in the end times, and it gains new relevance and urgency at a time when the Anthropocene, the end times, and the world without humans have moved to the center of the cultural imaginary. Rereading Beckett today makes me realize that his entire work can be seen as a diagnosis of the impact that living in the end times has on both the theater and the psychic life of humans living, like the audience, in the "other hell" outside. *Endgame*, and Beckett's works more generally, are about what remains in the end times, life's embers and ashes, decaying bodies in pain, memories, stories, fantasies, visions, perhaps hallucinations. What also remains are daily routines, the tedium, the tantrums, the old questions and the words we need to think them even when words fail. And, finally, above all perhaps, laughter. "Nothing is funnier than unhappiness, I grant you that," says Nell.[23] But in Beckett's plays, a dark shadow falls upon this laughter, covering unfathomable psychic pain and catastrophic loneliness. Despite the carnivalesque aspect of this laughter at death, the mood of Beckett's work, however, lacks the celebratory aura of the carnivalesque tradition.

Frank Kermode called fictions of the end "concord fictions," arguing that they compensate for the fact that humans are unable ever to describe the experience of their own end.[24] Throughout the course of history, most cultures have produced and continue to produce fantasies and fictions about the end. While apocalyptic fictions abound and flourish in the cultural imaginary, Beckett is entirely unique in his portrayal of living in the end times, approaching the topic with algorithms of end time emotions and affects as well as at the highest level of a layered and condensed self-reflexivity.

Death forms the center of Beckett's work not only in the figurations of characters who imagine themselves in the process of dying but also in the indirect figurations through traces of the atrocious genocides and mass killings that mark the history of the twentieth century. Steven Connor emphasizes the centrality of death in Beckett's work in reference to repetition and the death-instinct: "The forms of repetition that proliferate in his work establish death not as the mere absence of life, but rather as a place where the natures of life, death, difference and repetition are concentrated and problematized."[25]

Beckett is also unique in the ways in which he faces and makes his readers and audience face the silence and darkness at the core of the trauma of inhabiting end times. Rhys Tranter argues that Beckett's work "engages with the status of writing and literary inheritance via a traumatic logic of belatedness, untimeliness, and deferral."[26] Looking back at my early work on *Endgame* today, I realize that this traumatic logic of belatedness has also shaped my own engagement with the play. The trauma of living with my sister through the end times of her life forms the silence and darkness at the core of my early reading. It is only now that I can, belatedly, recognize this silence.

Endgame is paradigmatic in embedding a traumatic logic of belatedness in its self-reflexive figuration of algorithms of end time emotions and affects. Moreover, the play's abstractions contain a paradox of sorts. While persistently exposing its own theatricality, the play nonetheless insists on the concreteness of the here and now, that is, the material conditions of the world on stage. Stanley Cavell spoke of Beckett's "hidden literality," linking it to the "wish to escape connotation, rhetoric, the noncognitive, the irrationality and awkward memories of ordinary language, in favor of the directly verifiable, the isolated and perfected present."[27] Abstractions, in other words, are embodied in concrete images, resonating with what Walter Benjamin called thought images, *Denkbilder.* The latter, I maintain, form algorithms of psychic life under end time conditions or imaginaries. They have, in Cavell's words, "the abstraction, and the intimacy, of figures and words and objects in a dream."[28]

Beckett's technique of using abstraction, however, also shapes its theatricality. As Herb Blau stated, "theater becomes conscious of itself as theater," unfixing cliches and idioms, defeating the implications of ordinary language, and confronting the audience with a "succession of demystifications and unveilings."[29] In this respect, *Endgame* marks a historically significant change in the nature of aesthetic response. The characters themselves repeatedly showcase their awareness of playing in front of an audience. While on stage they play being the sole survivors of a catastrophe, the moment Clov turns his telescope to the auditorium he reports seeing "a multitude ... in transports ... of joy."[30] Apocalyptic fantasies accumulate cultural capital and proliferate in a society of the spectacle. The spectacle of the world's ending, whether on stage or in life, may well draw "multitudes in transports of joy." This is, Beckett suggests, one of the more perverse absurdities of living in the aftermath and/or in the end times.

In the early 1960s, Martin Esslin launched a wave of reception that linked Beckett's theater to the theatre of the absurd.[31] Accordingly, critics read *Endgame* in an existentialist vein as a symbolic representation of the absurd life of dejected characters who are awaiting the end in an alienated world of decay. Moreover, the density of literary and historical allusions and possible references opens an entire range of intertextual interpretations. At first glance Beckett seems to offer a play decidedly rich in connotations. Literary critics have traced an entire array of allusions to literary, philosophical, biblical and cultural history: Hamm as Hamlet, as "ham" actor; his sheet as Christ's sudarium or a stage curtain; and so forth. Nevertheless, such connotations cannot be woven into the pattern of a coherent structure, let alone conclusive interpretation. With the continual fluctuation between offers of possible connotations and their mocking dismissal by the characters, Beckett insists on the play's plasticity of meaning.

This does not mean, however, that one cannot productively reduce this overcomplex plasticity by reading the strange and alien features of Beckett's play as signatures of an absurd world. But doing so deemphasizes both the play's particular theatricality as well as Beckett's strategies guiding audience response. The absurd becomes a stand-in category for interpretations that attempt to provide closure for the play's insistence on openness and undecidability, thus mitigating the impact of his radical epistemological doubt. I see such interpretive closures as coping mechanisms to escape the communicative dilemma of a double bind that *Endgame* creates to ensnare the audience. Beckett's "No symbols where none intended" is more here than a mere rhetorical warning against interpretive closures because the play's very atmosphere, its sensual imagery, and its mutilated plot undoubtedly invite symbolic interpretations. In fact, the very invitation to reductive referential or symbolic "misreadings" belongs to the play's main communicative strategies.

The double bind, in other words, provides the basis of a generative new type of engagement with the audience. One cannot but be affected by the play's suggestive symbolism, especially when responding spontaneously. But as soon as one follows the play's lead, the characters begin to mock any unequivocal symbolic construction of meaning. While Beckett undoubtedly lures the audience into imagining the apocalyptic scenario sketched out above, he only does so to complicate any conclusive vision of the end times. We recall here, of course, that seeing the end of the world approach is, for Hamm, the prerogative of a madman like the painter in the asylum who saw the world in ashes. The conflictual, yet generative communicative double bind thus becomes a crucial feature of the aesthetic response to Beckett's *Endgame*. We *ought* not to see any symbols, but we find it impossible *not* to see them. In other words, the central aesthetic experience of the play is anchored less in its possible referential meanings than in its strategies guiding aesthetic response.

A close reading may illustrate in more detail how this works. Replete with echoes and repetitions, Hamm and Clov's dialogues meander in endless feedback loops around the same old issues and questions: their past lives, their deteriorating relationship to each other, their daily routines, their dwindling resources, the world outside. But their actions prevent the audience from ever forgetting that they are performing their lives and routines, including their dialogues and stories, in a play. They even performatively expose their role within the kinship relations. Hamm and Clov model their relationship on a master/slave relation, albeit one in which the slave ultimately has more power than the master. But we also learn that Hamm took Clov in as a child, most likely adopting him as a son. He even plays with recalling times when Clov loved him before he made him suffer too much. In contrast to Hamm and Clov, Nagg and Nell share moments of tenderness, but even those have become a routine, performed during the repetition of daily rituals. Playing with these roles proves to be Hamm's favorite preoccupation, if not obsession.

Enacted through never ending and continually variable substitutions, Hamm and Clov's roles begin to resemble algorithms of kinship in the end times rather than figurations of spontaneously lived experiences. In this process, *Endgame* collapses the classical relation to finitude with the modern relation to play. We are not in the presence of characters living in the end times but in the presence of actors performing living in the end times.[32] This difference distances the audience from the immediacy of the characters' end time experiences. Clov's allusion to Zeno's heap of grains plays ironically not only with the viewers' own projections of their sense of an ending but also with their search for meaning in the end times. Thinking about the end in terms of a heap materializing from accumulated discrete moments of ending resonates with the audience's attempt to compile the play's meaning out of ever-new sequential repetitions and recursive loops of speech. The audience might well take Clov's allusion to "the impossible heap" as a hint that neither the sense of an ending nor the meaning of the play can be discovered by assembling fragments of meaning into a coherent whole. Instead of searching for a neatly circumscribed interpretation, the audience's attention is directed toward the iridescent plasticity of the play's characters, plot, words and actions. This also means becoming involved in the play's language game of endless substitutions, that is, a game in which fragmented units of speech appear to be randomly substituted for each other. The characters' strange yet often uncannily familiar dialogue is embedded in the play's language game with the audience. Familiar expectations of dramatic dialogue are undercut along with the very conditions for the functioning of dialogue. Neither is the dialogue situated in a clearly circumscribed context, nor does it derive from the representative or referential function of speech, let alone a coherent development of action.

Considering Beckett's consistent use of repetitive feedback loops, one may be struck by how easily the dialogue flows nonetheless. Most striking is the constant introduction of new topics and unexpectedly abrupt moves, accompanied by the recurrence of nearly identical sequences of dialogue, though sometimes with the roles of the speakers reversed. The characters seem to be involved in a language game in which speech units can be moved around like chess pieces, albeit a game that functions according to rules unfamiliar to the audience. An endless substitution of basic existential problems seems to control the subject of conversation. As it progresses with its preordained repetition of speech units, the game allows these themes to circle continually back on themselves. The existential content freezes into paradigmatic formulae that the characters toss to and fro like a ball, all the while performing circular movements of empty speech attuned to the rhythms of the end times. One might think of a shared private language game that no longer requires one to mean what one says but rather offers the freedom to play with the familiarity of old and empty words, phrases, and rules.

Seen from a Derridean perspective, Hamm and Clov seem to play with the superabundance of floating signifiers over and above possible signifieds, almost as if to thematize the character of this surplus itself. The resonances with Derrida's theory of the infinite play of language are so striking that one could even imagine Beckett's characters enacting this theory in the staged empirical world of *Endgame*.[33] As I will show in more detail in my reading of *The Unnamable*, this enactment of theory resembles, in fact, an aesthetic ruse that Beckett performs in many of his texts, namely playing out philosophical theories and concepts in an imagined empirical setting. The effects of this device include not only defamiliarization and estrangement but also a comical distortion that challenges the very concepts Beckett uses. When Beckett's characters perform the infinite play of language on stage, they cross the boundary between philosophy and comedy at the same time as they expose the ineradicable human need for fixity and meaning that freezes language into formulaic speech habits. In this respect, the defamiliarization performed by poetic language revitalizes the deadening effects of habitual speech.

How then are these self-reflexive games with philosophical legacies linked to the staged endgame that focuses on the vicissitudes and impossibilities of ending? Imagining the end times of one's life or the world commonly tends to generate the search for philosophies that mitigate the pain of ending by endowing it with meaning. Since the latter, however, is precisely what Hamm and Clov reject, they use familiar philosophical or mythological visions of the end as props in their own private endgame. In this process, they subtly shift the emphasis from philosophy or mythology to psychology. Clov, for example, knows how to gain advantage by threatening to violate the rules and terminate what is in principle an endless game. Similarly, Clov and Nell repeatedly threaten Hamm and Nagg with abandonment. In response, Hamm engages Clov in a dialogue about his incapacity to leave. Or does even the threat of breaking the rules belong to the game?

David Lapoujade likens Beckett's theater to an aesthetic of standstill. To stagnate, he argues, is "always to be in the vicinity of a limit, to occupy this vicinity, to hold oneself on a limit or near it, or in any case always in a polarized relation with it."[34] Invoking Beckett's crawling or immobilized characters "stuck in jars, lying on beds, paralyzed with aching joints or other pains," he states: "There are few stories in which one stagnates more than in Beckett's work. It is difficult to move less, to move worse, to stagnate more than in Beckett. Where others saw stagnation as a kind of bad will or passive nihilism . . . in Beckett it became a place of intense and vibrant life." The vibrancy of this (Beckettian) life emerges from what Lapoujade calls "feeling the vibration of the membrane of the limit."[35] Attuned to the most minimal vibration of life, Beckett conveys the intensity of feeling what happens when nothing happens, of life reduced to waiting for an impossible end.

Linked to the psychic economy of waiting for the end, Beckett's work from *Waiting for Godot* and *Endgame* to the increasingly shorter late plays and texts can be described in terms of its gradual approach to a limit of almost total dissipation. We could even push this further and say that his short texts and plays push toward a limit of total expiration. Beckett's shortest theatrical piece, *Breath*, which I will discuss in detail in my coda, comes closest to realizing this goal. Beckett, writes Lapoujade, "constantly sought to return to the limit of every possibility in order to be done with it, once and for all: to stop speaking, to stop writing, to return to the final white or the black, to end."[36]

The nature of playing this game of abandonment, ending and standstill in a theater of radical self-reflexivity makes it impossible to identify the characters unequivocally with their performed affects or dramatic speech. By alternately exchanging slightly varied sequences of stereotypical dialogue in this game of substitution, the characters undermine the familiar play of self-differentiation through speech. For example, Clov's question, "Why this farce, day after day?" has already been asked before by Nell, and Hamm's "Don't we laugh?" will in turn be taken up later by Clov.[37] The play with the substitution and repetition of speech units, in other words, undercuts the reduction of speech to self-presentation.

To aggravate matters, the characters continually vacillate between different levels of play. Thus, the boundaries between the "endgame" and the "games within the endgame" remain fluid. Moreover, Hamm self-ironically unmasks the seduction of the Other through self-stylization, thus undercutting the audience's expectation that dramatic characters are supposed to perform a presentation of self. Playfully exposing the role of a narcissistic artist, Hamm even parodies self-presentation as a mock fight for recognition. As if showcasing his dependence on Clov as his spectator, Hamm repeatedly urges Clov to ask him for his story, whereupon Clov immediately stages himself as a character who complies with this request. Hamm thus further exhibits self-presentation as a way of performing for the Other, openly demonstrating that such self-presentation can only portray a fictional self.

How are we to react to these language games? As the characters refuse mere self-presentation and even caricature the latent function of self-presentation inherent in speech, we may become unsure of how to relate to them. Where are the characters in their own speech? And how are we to respond to Beckett's strategic use of characters to set communicative traps and double binds for us, luring us into projecting our own sense of an ending, only to mock its inevitable inadequacy. The pervasive structure of negation, withdrawal and contradiction frustrates all partial investments of meaning and thereby fundamentally impedes every gesture of interpretation that strives for closure. Hamm and Clov thus present their dialogue as an imaginative game, replete with suggestive images, intertextual allusions, and symbolism, yet without pretensions to a fixable latent meaning. Just as Hamm's obsession with being placed in the center of the room/stage is a futile endeavor, so is any interpretation bent on centering the decentered play.[38] The dilemma becomes inescapable: in order to "understand" the characters, spectators must follow their lead, only to see that this very lead is set up as a trap for projections of a meaning the characters will later reject. Meaning itself becomes a target of mockery.

This refutation of meaning also affects the play's sense of an ending or, more precisely, its radical debunking of an eschatological imaginary. Through the characters' repudiation of the very possibility of meaning, Beckett undermines the eschatological idea that the last things on earth will have an order, a justification, a sense. Hamm and Clov's apprehension about the possibility of meaning something is a stab not only at the audience and their need for finding a meaning in the play but also at any eschatological hope the audience might project onto the play.

HAMM: Clov?
CLOV: (*impatiently*) What is it?
HAMM: We're not beginning to . . . to . . . mean something?
CLOV: Mean something! You and I, mean something! (*Brief laugh.*) Ah that's a good one!
HAMM: I wonder. (*Pause.*) Imagine if a rational being came back to earth, wouldn't he be liable to get ideas into his head if he observed us long enough. (*Voice of rational being.*) Ah, good, now I see what it is, yes, now I understand what they're at! (*Clov*

starts, drops the telescope and begins to scratch his belly with both hands.)[39]

As I mentioned at the outset, Hamm's suggestion that the world on stage is depopulated by rational beings, makes one wonder where they would come from if they returned to earth. From a different planet? As Beckett does in other plays and texts (for example in *The Lost Ones*), he smuggles subtle hints of worlds beyond the earth, if not elements of science fiction into the action. But at the same time Hamm treats the audience as if they too were from a different planet. Are we invited to look at the world as if we were seeing it for the first time? This would, of course, be a supremely artistic gaze and, given Beckett's insistence on exposing the theatricality of *Endgame*, we may safely assume that he uses the technique to tacitly foster his audience's artistic gaze.

The communicative dynamic outlined here is anchored less in *what* the characters say than in the very structure of the play, its dramatic language, and its positioning of the audience. Where the overabundance of connotations fails to provide unambiguous meaning and where possible interpretive projections are consistently mocked, the audience is deprived of its familiar relation to theatrical conventions and the functions of dramatic language. But seeing the world through Beckett's eyes as if for the first time already presupposes an intense involvement in the play. Ultimately, these different strategies of playing with the "overabundance of signifier, in relation to the signifieds" ensnare the audience in a double bind that targets language's "structure of double meaning."[40] Linguists have argued that a structure of double meaning is fundamental to the communicative dimension of language. Shunning a simplistic literal-mindedness, the manifest meaning of an utterance in a play commonly refers to a latent one, if not multiple latent ones. Especially if a play's manifest meaning is no longer evident, one cannot but suspect a hidden or latent meaning. Beckett teases the audience by mocking this very expectation, thus undermining one of the most basic and conventional receptive dispositions. Both the lure of interpretations and their failure are a direct result of *Endgame*'s strategy of guiding audience response. In this respect, we could almost say that *Endgame* becomes a training ground for the complex structure of negation that marks Beckett's prose texts, especially the trilogy *Molloy, Malone Dies,* and *The Unnamable.*

Beckett's strategy to expose the reductive character of any manifest referential meaning locates the play's purport in a transitional space beyond the manifest or latent dimension of dramatic speech. It almost seems as if the play's production of meaning tended toward an asemantic quality. Only when the audience foregoes what Beckett calls the "need for semantic succour" can they grasp what the play might be trying to convey.[41] Because of this shift in the process of reception, *Endgame* expands the engagement of the audience beyond the world on stage. Unsettling the structure of double meaning introduces complex differentiations into the play's relationship with its spectators, offering insight into the need for projective closures as well as the defensive qualities of communicative habits. In this process, attention shifts from the subjectivity of fictional characters to the subjectivity of spectators. Since the structure of double meaning is the linguistic basis of decentered subjectivity, playing with this form of expression that simultaneously shows and hides meaning gives the audience a chance not only to express but also to react to decentered subjectivity.

Beckett's singular presentation of characters extends this play with the boundaries of subjectivity. Rather than casting characters with a realistically portrayed decentered subjectivity, *Endgame* introduces stylized, condensed, and composite characters. Not unlike the figures who populate our dreams, Hamm and Clov are highly overdetermined characters who have absorbed meanings, signs, and even pure psychological or aesthetic functions as well as properties from other characters. No wonder that this complex and allusive overdetermination has occasioned an overabundance of speculative interpretations. Hamm and Clov have been seen as mythical characters in a mythical place. Critics have placed them within the tradition of the cosmological dialogue of the gods. They have been likened to Chronos and Mercury, to the sons of Noah after the flood, to Shakespeare's Hamlet, and also to Gloucester and Edgar in *King Lear*. Other critics have highlighted the manifold echoes to other Beckett characters in earlier plays and novels, Pozzo and Lucky in particular, as well as the Unnamable. On the other hand, *Endgame* has also been interpreted as an aesthetic differentiation of what is otherwise conceived of as a unity. Here the characters appear as components of a unified self or their room as a human brain whose various functions are divided up among the characters. Peter Brook characterizes Beckett's peculiar way of using symbols in a similar vein. "A true symbol is like Beckett's *Endgame*. The entire work is one *symbol* enclosing numerous others, though none of them are of the type which stand for something else; we get no further when we ask what they are supposed to mean, since here a symbol has become an object."[42]

Condensations are gestalt formations that mobilize unconscious productions of meaning. *Endgame* thus appeals on different levels and by different means to both conscious and unconscious dimensions of response.[43] While the play's mocking dismissal of referential interpretations generates a temporary frustration, this technique is often counterbalanced by the unconscious fascination of Beckett's alien world, its captivating poetic images, its condensed characters, and their strangely appealing dialogues. *Endgame*'s strongest appeal may issue precisely from what cannot be integrated into a clearly definable symbolic meaning, such as, for example, speech acts violating linguistic conventions, dramatic elements that disrupt the plot, or phrases and behaviors that seem to undermine the characters' psychological consistency. From the relative security of our status as audience, we can follow the endgame Beckett's characters are playing, becoming drawn into the play and temporarily affected, often unconsciously so, by the strange algorithms of characters living in their own private end time.

At the level of a more conscious response, coping positively rather than negatively with *Endgame*'s undercutting of projective interpretations opens a pathway to reflect upon the character of interpretive acts themselves. Unless the audience bails out of the play's communicative structure, it must engage the aesthetic double bind.[44] Several clues in the play such as, for example, direct references to the audience's situation, indicate that the way to escape the double-bind trap is by shifting to a metalevel and reflecting on one's own responses. *Endgame* thus pursues a double strategy of mobilizing first projections and later self-reflection upon their failure. Integral to the receptive process, self-reflection establishes both mastery of the induced frustration and insight into one's patterns of aesthetic communication.

Endgame thus entangles spectators both in the world on stage and in reflections on their own responses and projections. This dynamic, however, is only one of the disillusioning strategies aimed at inducing a meta-understanding or, perhaps more precisely, meta-experience. The audience experiences the act of projecting as an attempt to cope with, if not reduce, the play's inherently open horizon of meaning. But we might also see this effort at coping as a defense against the experience of the play's otherness. *Endgame*'s disillusioning strategies aim at making us aware of our interpretations as consoling concord fictions, and thereby altering our need to experience the play's sense of an ending, if not the end more generally, as meaningful. Like virtually all of Beckett's work, *Endgame* thus challenges us to cope with radical indeterminacy and epistemological insecurity. Just as we will never exhaust the meaning of *Endgame*, we will never completely understand what it means to live in the end times. But we will also never be able to stop creating fictions of the end. Only a madman like the one in Hamm's story will trust his own visions of the end with pathological certainty. The play thus becomes an endgame involving the boundaries of subjectivity and its entanglement with ending, mortality, and the concomitant need to create concord fictions.

Endgames are always fraught with ambivalence, releasing unconscious fears of the end and anxieties of disintegration, emptiness, abandonment, and catastrophic loneliness. While *Endgame* may mobilize latent fears of becoming inundated by the unconscious, unconscious responses can also become a source of delight. We derive pleasure from positive investment in the primordial, undifferentiated mode of being that has been largely relegated to alternate states of consciousness. The transgressive quality of *Endgame* is perhaps best documented by the isolated stifled laughter Wolfgang Iser analyzes as emerging spontaneously during the play's performance.[45] While Iser perceives the stifling of laughter as the result of a joke the play undermines, I see the audience's laughter also as the expression of an unconscious understanding or reaction. Laughter signals that the strangeness of *Endgame* is not so foreign after all. It arises spontaneously at the threshold of an unconscious understanding of something that is not yet understood consciously but experienced as uncannily familiar. As impenetrable as the dramatic action may seem, laughter indicates that there is indeed a hidden understanding. Moreover, laughter itself signals a pleasurable temporary breakdown of the boundaries of the self.[46] The seemingly insignificant spontaneous laughter physically anticipates the mobilization of the unconscious that has become one of the hallmarks of aesthetic response to contemporary art more generally.

By contrast, conscious experiences of a shift in or an expansion of the boundaries of subjectivity are more painful and have provoked defensive responses not only to *Endgame* but to many other experimental works of the time as well. The reception of Beckett's work shows that not only the open rejection of a work but also its projective appropriation can be a defense against its challenging otherness. Again, this is not to say, however, that projective interpretations are necessarily wrong. Many have produced elegant and insightful perspectives on the wide range of possible ways to respond to *Endgame* or, for that matter, many of Beckett's other works. Selective readings productively use defenses as a form of adaptation to the mind games Beckett's characters play with the audience. But *Endgame* mirrors our acts of and need for interpretation back to us. By exposing projective habits as selective operations that reduce the play's alien elements, *Endgame* activates our unconscious desire for the dissolution of boundaries, counterbalancing our frustrated need for meaning by making us shift to a metalevel. At its best, this strategy may offer insight into our encounters with otherness more generally.

While *Endgame* thus expands the boundaries of aesthetic response towards both the unconscious and self-reflection, it simultaneously works through the audience's dependence on constructions of meaning. The play thereby enhances the acceptance of, if not desire for open-ended structures and questions. The radical undecidability of Beckett's *Endgame* insists on tolerance for open-endedness. Openness means just this: to leave the end open. Beckett explores this as our basic existential condition. Since nobody will ever be able to fully know their end, we cannot but fall back on producing concord fictions of the end. Conveying yet another sense of ending, this insight is certainly one of the reasons why this particular play has become so successful as an "endgame" that plays with the boundaries of our subjectivity.

Strangely, it was *Endgame*'s insistence on open-endedness and the epistemological insecurity it generates that helped me temporarily to cope with the vortex of pain at the time when I took care of my dying sister. As I mentioned in the introduction, I had just started working on my MA thesis on Beckett's *Endgame* when my sister was diagnosed with terminal cancer. Continuing to work on *Endgame* seemed at first impossible, sometimes even frivolous. Yet I kept being drawn back into the play as its dialogues and sentences suddenly took on a new meaning in the context of my sister's illness. The imprisonment of Beckett's characters in their daily routines made me look differently at the imposed routines of care. They were all we both had to keep going. How often did I feel "I can't go on," yet knew I had to go on! Some of Hamm's monologues resonated in their desolation: "I'll close my eyes, perhaps have a little sleep, after that I'll feel better, and you'll close them."[47] "Then babble, babble, words, like the solitary child who turns himself into children, two, three, so as to be together, and whisper together, in the dark."[48] When my sister was little, we used to whisper together in the dark. Now we orbited around each other like solitary children, both isolated in our shell because we did not find a way to talk to each other about dying and the end. So we played our own ghostly endgame, filling our monotonous days with words to cover up our fear and pain. This made me extremely sensitive to the role language and dialogue play in *Endgame* as defense mechanisms against the agony of ending. Hamm's attempt to threaten Clov with an "infinite emptiness" that "all the resurrected dead of all the ages wouldn't fill" resonated with the haunting from the future of a world without my sister.[49] Years later, it was as if I found myself again in William Kentridge's painting "Her Absence Filled the World" that, for me, had a distinctly Beckettian feel.

Working on *Endgame* while caring for my sister had kept me attuned to the feeling of living in an end time, forced to face mortality. But at the same time, the play explored the challenges and vicissitudes of ending within the contained space of a play, thus allowing me to sublimate and modulate the rawness of pain. Epistemological insecurity was easier to bear than ontological insecurity. My sister's death destroyed all familiar coordinates that had oriented and grounded my life before. Without being aware of it, I involuntarily mimicked some of the defenses of Beckett's characters, especially when it came to neutralizing unbearable emotions. It was as if such emotions were always there and not there at the same time. Similarly, in Beckett's play, emotions related to ending, abandonment, and catastrophic loneliness are evoked and then transformed into abstract algorithms.

I wish I had kept a journal of this year, but I did not have the energy, and I even had to put my thesis on ice for the time being because my sister's care took every bit of my time and stamina. I only resumed my writing after my sister had passed away. What I did not know at the time but learned later was that, as S. E. Gontarski points out, much of Beckett's writing of what became *Endgame* "was precipitated by personal tragedy, the unexpected ending of his brother Frank's life on September 13, 1954. And so even the title of the new play proclaimed Beckett's overt preoccupation with eschatology, endings, final things, and the narratives that lead up to, shape, and explain them."⁵⁰ If the trauma of losing a brother shaped Beckett's *Endgame*, engaging with the play a decade and a half later certainly shaped my experience of losing a sister. But at the same time, this experience also shaped my reading of the play, albeit only in an indirect way that defended me against facing the pain. A brother's and a sister's deaths thus form the silent traumatic core of the play's composition and reception.

Beckett's transformational work in the contained space of the theater also worked for me at a deeper level. It felt as if, in a way that remained mysterious to me for a long time, Beckett's work contained and thereby modulated the experience of ontological rupture triggered by the radical uncertainties of facing mortality and death for the first time in my life during my sister's illness. I was twenty-three years old at the time, but my sister's dying pushed me back into a primordial psychic state of helplessness even as I did all the practical things needed to take care of her. I was haunted by the sense that what I felt was so raw and chaotic that it couldn't even be thought. The intensity of pain impinged on my mind, and it was extremely hard to metabolize intolerable thoughts about my sister's impending death. Often I would turn to reading Beckett, not only *Endgame* but also other plays as well as novels and short texts. I never quite understood at the time what eventually enabled me to use them as consoling objects.

Looking back, I think that Beckett's work provided a container space for my ontological insecurity and the intolerable pain of loss and catastrophic loneliness. It gave a form to what I was unable to tolerate in its raw state. Indirectly reading Beckett's texts thus contributed to containing the unthinkable experience of my sister's dying. It modulated my feelings, helped to momentarily reduce my fears, and gave me the strength to go on, even as I often thought I couldn't go on. Perhaps it even helped me to tolerate this very experience.

Experiencing the capacity of Beckett's work to serve as a container for unbearable pain might actually not have been a pure coincidence. Beckett had been in psychoanalysis with Wilfred Ruprecht Bion, whose theory of the containment of intolerable emotional experiences has become a cornerstone of psychoanalytic thinking. Part of Bion's concept of the psychoanalytic cure lies in mitigating the radical doubt and uncertainty that comes from encountering the limits of the knowable. Cure for Bion also requires increasing the tolerance for the unfamiliar. According to Bion, working with the unconscious is about intimacy with the unknown. Beckett's entire work could be seen as the creation of container spaces to explore the radical uncertainty of being and provide an intimate apprehension of the unknowable and unnamable. And it is precisely by fashioning such theatrical or textual spaces of containment that Beckett's works become transformational objects.[51]

This is where the sensorial aspects of Beckett's theater play such a crucial role. The lighting, the gray, barren stage, the sounds, including the sounds of the voice, all of these create an atmosphere that evokes primordial sensorial experiences of the world beyond language and speech. These theatrical techniques evoke spaces in which we know sensorially what cannot (yet) be thought. According to Christopher Bollas, one of the crucial functions of cultural objects and especially literature and the arts is to connect us to experiences of what he calls "the unthought known."[52] Such connections are transformational in a similar way as Bion's container spaces. By translating the unthought known into language, sound, color or form, they metabolize a sensorial form of knowing that cannot yet be thought or expressed discursively, thus making the experience accessible and communicable to others.

During the time of my sister's illness, our encounters often mobilized such experiences. We became like children again, clinging to each other to share a grievous psychic space of loneliness. We would have embraced any defense offered to us against the pain of knowing we would lose each other. However, I did not share my Beckett experience with my sister out of a sense that I wanted to protect her from his darkness. Gradually, and without my understanding what was happening, Beckett's algorithms of living in the end times became part of my mental functioning at the time. Often, I couldn't help seeing the world through Beckett's eyes. This way of seeing and being has remained with me to this day. Like Not-I's buzzing in the head, Beckettian phrases keep resounding in my inner ear with reliable regularity.

During the year after my sister's death, I volunteered as a therapist at a psychiatric hospital in Arezzo, Italy. Not surprisingly, it was Beckett's work that attuned me to this world of insanity and pain. I think I had intuitively chosen this hospital as a refuge to work through the inconsolable pain of my sister's loss. Many of the patients I worked with looked like Beckett's tramps, walking around the clinic garden in never-ending circles. Some lived in a state of abjection; some indulged in the pleasure of shocking others with obscenities. Some of them even had their own Beckettian patterns of formulaic phrases, repeating them again and again, sometimes in slight variations, during our daily group meetings. Rosa, one of the patients I became close to, would burst into monologues that reminded me of *Footfalls*. Others carried their meager belongings around in a bag like the one Winnie sports in *Happy Days*, taking them out and using them as consoling objects when needed. All the people living in the asylum were waiting, waiting in vain for someone to arrive or something to happen, to take its course. Some reminded me of the lost ones in their futile search for their missing other. One of the men, a painter whose work consisted of artistically composed phantasms of the fragmented body, uttered his existential musings in the style of pressed speech reminiscent of Lucky's monologue. I never asked him what he saw when he looked at the world outside. Perhaps he would have seen ashes like the painter in Hamm's story. During these years after my sister's death Beckett moved permanently into my inner world. His work would come to accompany me throughout my life, offering me ways to face the abyss of living on earth for which there is no cure and the infinite emptiness ahead of us. He also gave me the gift of understanding the endless defenses we need to be able to go on. "Old stancher! . . . You . . . remain."[53]

2

THE TRANSITIONAL SPACE BETWEEN LIFE AND DEATH

"The Calmative," *Molloy*, and *Malone Dies*

Strange task which consists in speaking of oneself.
Strange hope, turned towards silence and peace.
—Samuel Beckett, *The Unnamable*

Given that one of the most salient features of Samuel Beckett's texts is their saturation with literary images of the end times of life, many of the characters are aging or dying men and—more rarely—women who indulge in obsessively observing and taking inventory of their progressing decrepitude and corporeal decay. The grotesque disintegration of their bodies and minds, the deterioration of their often violent relationship to fellow humans, and the increasing depletion of the surrounding environment give rise to a black comedy of old age staged in exuberant speech performances.[1] Most of Beckett's texts and plays are framed as visions of old age, unfolding ever more artistic variations on the theme of death, yet endlessly displacing death in neverending endgames. Having started to work on Beckett while taking care of my dying sister, I held on to these displacements of death as much as Beckett's characters do. I avoided asking directly what it would mean to see their monologues or dialogues as voicing a process of dying. This structural defense is, as I tried to show in my reading of *Endgame*, built into the very form of Beckett's plays and texts. They are never simply "about" death. Refusing to be reduced to "representations" and defying symbolic or allegorical readings, they display strategies that invite us to project preconceived notions and philosophies of life and death, only to subsequently undermine those very projections in a complex process of transference between text and reader/audience.[2]

I want to open my reflections on Beckett's transitional spaces and imaginaries of the end times of old age with a close reading of "The Calmative," a story Beckett wrote in French in 1946 in the aftermath of World War II. While the French version was published in 1954, three years after *Malone Meurt*, the English translation only appeared in 1967. In many ways, "The Calmative" prepares the ground for *Malone Dies*. It is a mesmerizing text with haunting poetic images that contain Beckett's deepest concerns with living in the end times. Written under the impact of my first reading of "The Calmative," the following poem I composed with images found in this text illustrates some of the deepest concerns that pervade Beckett's work, forming the very core not only of "The Calmative" but also of later texts such as *Molloy*, *Malone Dies*, and *The Unnamable*.

"I NEED A LIGHT LESS GREEN"
(AFTER BECKETT'S *THE CALMATIVE*)

Among perishing oaks
on a distant earth
my first stumblings told me
I need a light less green
and another age to escape
the type of cruelty that smiles.

THE TRANSITIONAL SPACE

As in myth and metamorphosis
something has to happen
before I, who never wished
for anything except
for the mirrors to shatter,
vanish in the havoc of its images.

Sunk in a dream
I kept saying,
I'll go back, unbelieving.
A story to calm me,
words to carry away to my refuge,
to add to my collection.

The earth not the sky offers help,
perhaps a touch of tenderness,
I have my doubts,
nothing with me but my stone,
every step gladly the last,
as I hear footfalls die behind me.

All that remains,
a vision of two burning eyes.
Fallen into nightmare thingness,
I try to find my way in the sky,
still of this world
but paying the price.

All the mortals I saw were alone,
as if sunk in themselves.
This is not me, I said,
To one of my shadows flying before me.

I might as well not have existed
far from this terrible light.

How tell what remains
of those famished for shadow?
Slow swoon, light fading,
a cascade of paling colors,
as darkness falls into the same blinding void,
remembering still, the clouds.

"THE CALMATIVE"

"I don't know when I died."[3] Opening the narrative with its temporal location in the speaker's afterlife, this first sentence in Beckett's "The Calmative" features a narrator who tells the story of his life after he has already died, presumably as he suggests, when he was about ninety years old. Regardless of whether we take the statement "I died" literally, psychologically, or symbolically, temporality in "The Calmative" is fluid and indeterminate. The narrator also adds a statement about his geographical location: "this evening, alone in my icy bed, I have the feeling I'll be older than the day, the night, when the sky with all its lights fell upon me, the same I had so often gazed on since my first stumblings on the distant earth."[4]

How are we to think about the narrator's location, given that he uses the phrase "the distant earth?" He clearly speaks from an unspecified elsewhere, perhaps even from a distant star. Considering that the French original "Le calmant" appeared in a series of texts together with "L'expulse," we may wonder if the narrator has been expelled, like so many other Beckett characters, not only from his various homes but also from the earth. Is he a planetary migrant, expelled from his home planet? We may also recall a resonating image of the distant earth from *The Lost Ones*, a story Beckett had abandoned in 1966 and then completed in 1970, that is, three years after the publication of "The Calmative" in English. In *The Lost Ones*, the characters are confined in an abode that seems to float somewhere in outer space, since from it one can see the earth. These images suggest that Beckett was preoccupied at the time with stories or characters that look at the earth from a distance. It can hardly be a coincidence that 1966 is the year when NASA released the satellite photo of the sphere of Earth as seen from space that had a worldwide and ground-breaking impact on the cultural and geopolitical imaginary. People began thinking in planetary terms about ecology and social justice, if not in terms of species selves that share the destiny of living precarious lives on a vulnerable planet.[5] Beckett's use of images of the earth from the perspective of a planetary outside, if not a distant star, suggests that he drew on the cultural imaginary of the Blue Planet that fascinated people globally at the time and left a decisive imprint on scientists, artists, and writers.

But the narrator also alludes to a cataclysmic event that caused the sky with all its lights to fall upon him. What could be possible references for the use of this event? Was it the apocalypse in which the stars fall from the sky that John of Patmos sees in the Book of Revelation? Or one of the innumerable other references in the Bible to the stars falling from the sky? Is that also why the narrator now refers to "the distant earth?" Or is "the distant earth" merely a metaphor for the psychic distance he feels in the isolation of his room from the earth outside? The image thus condenses notions of the biblical end time, notions of the

Blue Planet, and notions of a psychic alienation and removal from the earth.

Enfolded in the description of the narrator's current state of being, psychic alienation, or more specifically the notion of death in life takes us to the core of the very end time of a life. We witness a narrator who, in his own words, is too frightened to "listen to myself rot." He waits for "the great red lapses of the heart, the tearings of the caecal walls," and the "slow killings to finish in my skull." Trying to counterbalance this final state of decomposition and "fornication with corpses" with an act of composition, he states, "So I'll tell myself a story, I'll try to tell myself another story, to try and calm myself." Just as it does for innumerable other Beckett characters, storytelling for the narrator in "The Calmative" becomes a way of mitigating emotional turmoil, that is, a calmative. But then he ends with an enigmatic statement: "Or is it possible that in this story I have come back to life, after my death? No, it's not like me to come back to life, after my death."[6] Where does this statement locate us as readers? Are we already inside the story or is the story about to begin? Suddenly it feels as if our own temporal location is in question. Moreover, how are we to imagine this narrator who uses the arcane medieval term "caecal" to speak of the tearing of his intestinal walls, or the late Middle English "capstan" to refer to the dysfunctional revolving cylinder on which he imagines himself sitting? Or the narrator who says: "Die without too much pain, a little, that's worth your while. Under the blind sky close with your own hands the eyes soon sockets, then quick into carrion not to mislead the crows."[7] Are we receiving the haunting voice of a deceased person, a voice, so to speak, that embodies the living dead? We are left with open questions and the sense of a haunting from the beyond.

The narrator speaks about living in ruins, moving from refuge to refuge, often "moving along in a dream. Yet, as soon as he invokes the city of his childhood, he states, again joining the ranks of many other Beckett characters: "All I say cancels out, I'll have said nothing." A narrator who tells a story in the end times and says nothing. Caught in the impossible temporalities of parallel narrative universes, he alternately states: "what I tell this evening is passing this evening" and "I'll tell my story in the past none the less, as though it were a myth, an old fable, for this evening I need another age, that age to become another age in which I became what I was." Impossible to locate in a proper age or time, the narrator is bending the boundaries of language and grammar to attune them to a vision impossible to voice otherwise: "Was I hungry itself?" "The fringe was near, a light less green and kind of tattered told me so, in a whisper."[8]

Whatever else this narrator might be, he is a supreme poet, finding poetry in decay, decomposition, ruin, pain and cruelty. I opened this reading with an assemblage of poetic images from the story. Perhaps even more so than other texts by Beckett, "The Calmative" had once again mesmerized me with its poetic images and rhythms, just as a long time ago, in the early seventies, it had become a container for my own pain, despair, and loss when my sister lay dying. Rather than serve as consoling objects, Beckett's texts perhaps function as containing objects, holding us while they open a glimpse into the abyss of the end times. When the narrator in "The Calmative" envisions, not to say wishes for, something to happen to his body "as in myth or metamorphosis," he adds "this body to which nothing ever happened, or so little, which never met with anything, loved anything, wished for anything, in its tarnished universe, except for the mirrors to shatter . . . and to vanish in the havoc of its images."[9]

It is hard not to think of the mirror phase that shapes the ego and the self in early infant development. We need to be mirrored by our environment to inhabit what the narrator calls the "age in which I became what I was." Yet, Beckett's characters are mirrored and thereby disowned by persecutory others who impose false images on them. We find an entire range of persecutory anonymous Others in Beckett's texts, most of the time simply referred to as "they," who impose false selves on narrators who, in turn, desperately try to prevent these selves from manifesting. This is why they need to cancel out everything they say and strive for having said nothing in the end. The narrator in "The Calmative" wants the mirrors to shatter and to vanish in the havoc of its images. On the other hand, he keeps invoking a faint memory of an earlier, more positive mirroring experience. It happened when, to calm him, his father used to read to him evening after evening the story of a lighthouse keeper's son. I see this narrative fragment as a beautiful illustration of literature's role, especially in childhood, to function as a mirror image that shapes the evolving sense of self. Later, the narrator also has erotic mirror experiences in a series of encounters with young boys, including the "young boy holding a goat by a horn," whom he calls "haunter of the waterfront."[10] Meeting him face-to-face in silence, the boy stirs a desire for a mirroring touch in him when their hands brush.

However, the narrator remains unable or unwilling to generate a sense of self through mirror experiences with others. In response to this existential lack, he resorts to storytelling. Telling himself stories is, of course, a practice of self-mirroring, but an impossible one in which the narrator wants to vanish in the havoc of images and aspires for each story to be the last. Seeking refuge and solace in the stars, he feels with certainty that he is "still of this world," a world in which all the mortals he sees are "alone and as if sunken in themselves," a world that needs stories as calmatives. Failing all attempts at self-mirroring as well as, paradoxically, the concomitant attempt at shattering all possible manifestations of self-mirroring, stories usually end with the recognition "this is not me," or "I might as well not have existed." Telling each other life stories equally fails at facilitating a mirror experience because the narrator is mortified at a stranger's request to tell him his life story. Yet there is the stirring of a "devastating hope" when the stranger begins "murmuring words so sweet that I went limp and my head fell forward in his lap." Of course, as so commonly in Beckett's work, not only queer desire but desire more generally is killed and vanishes in the instant it first manifests itself. Like the stories the narrator tries to tell, this scene of seduction and with it his queer desire end in an impasse. After the stranger asks for a kiss, the narrator's sensory apparatus shifts to the distancing operation of a dissecting clinical gaze: "His teeth shone. I listened to his steps die away. How tell what remains? But it's the end." He hugs the walls, "famished for shadow." Mirroring experiences have been replaced with shadowing experiences. Storytelling becomes a haunting by shadows, ghost selves that hover in a transitional space between life and death, unsure whether they are still of this world, alive or dead, yet always "back in the same blinding void."[11]

Commonly, storytelling generates not only a mirroring experience but also a transformational experience. Stories function as transformational objects, contributing to the continual shaping of self by connecting the storyteller or listener to sensorial experiences, affects and moods that resonate with earlier formative experiences.[12] Rather than an expansion or growth of the self, however, Beckett's narrators experience any sense of transformation as constituting the self as an alien object, a Not-I, a "blinding void." Instead of facilitating formative experiences, mirrors as blinding voids convey the *horror vacui* of someone facing the abyss of an empty self. Yet, at the same time, Beckett's characters paradoxically see a "mind at peace, that is to say, empty" as the only way to escape the haunting of the mind by the recursive loops of cascading alien images, stories and Not-I figures.

It is not surprising then, that the narrator in "The Calmative" becomes entangled with later Beckett characters, especially with the narrator in *Malone Dies*. Beckett wrote "Le calmant," the French original of "The Calmative," in 1946 and published it in 1954. During the time before the story's publication, he wrote *Malone Meurt*, published in French in 1951 and the English *Malone Dies* in 1956. Beckett's work on the two pieces and their translation must thus have overlapped at times and the resonances between them are significant. While *Malone Dies* was published in 1956, "The Calmative" only appeared in 1967. The entanglement of the two texts is a prime example of how Beckett keeps the boundaries between his texts and plays porous. Characters or their doubles and shadows routinely resurface in later texts. It is as if Beckett keeps being haunted by his own work, just as his characters keep being haunted by their earlier versions. The frame of a novel or a play never constitutes a space of containment. Rather, their porosity reveals the plasticity of a creative process haunted by a sense of exhaustion and a paradoxical drive toward depletion, emptiness, and silence within the impossibility of ending.

MOLLOY

Molloy, the first novel of Beckett's trilogy, sets the stage for a series of narrators who describe living in the end times of their lives, already in the process of dying. From his report that a man comes by and "takes away the pages," we may infer that Molloy is a writer.[13] One of his opening statements reads: "What I'd like now is to speak of the things that are left, say my goodbyes, finish dying."[14] Molloy, for one, has taken the place of his mother. He lives in her room and assumes that he must resemble her more and more. And when he is not in her room, he seems lost, gets picked up by the police, and, upon his release, resumes the long journey back to her. While he is roaming around outside his mother's room, Molloy is lost on an earth that seems to be in the throes of cataclysm. As the horizon is burning with sulphur and phosphorus, he smells the earth and eats grass, thinking of himself as "the last of my foul brood, neither man nor beast."[15]

Molloy's description of his relationship to his mother presents a spectacle of abjection: "we were like a couple of old cronies, sexless, unrelated, with the same memories, the same rancours, the same expectations." He describes his mother as incontinent, jabbering away "with a rattle of dentures." He communicates with her by knocking on her skull, first with his index-finger knuckle, then with thumps of the fist, but then he states, "My mother. I don't think harshly of her."[16] He lives with her in a transitional space of fluid boundaries. As he is gradually "becoming mother," he states that her charity keeps him imprisoned in the process of dying. It almost sounds as if his only sanctuary, his mother's room, has become a womb for the dying, a death chamber of sorts that holds mother and son in a deadly embrace. They both live in their own private end times, in a transitional space also between life and death with Molloy at times reassuring himself that he is still alive.[17]

The opening paragraphs of Molloy's discourse are replete with echoes of other texts and plays, especially *Endgame* but also *How It Is*. His fantasy that he perhaps has a son somewhere whom he might have helped recalls the relationship between Hamm and Clov in *Endgame*. Like Hamm, Molloy is going blind but is not sure if it's not all in his head. Unsure whether he is inventing, remembering, or embellishing things, he mentions two men in greatcoats, "two wayfaring strangers"[18] on a deserted road who not only recall the male figures in greatcoats from "The Calmative" but also Vladimir and Estragon in *Waiting for Godot*. Belacqua makes an appearance as well, testifying not only to the porosity of boundaries between novels, plays and poems in Beckett's work but also to the fact that each new character seems to be haunted by earlier characters who reappear like revenants.

Molloy also explicitly invokes the notion of "all that inner space," but it is not merely the space of psychic life but first and foremost a space created by corporeal caverns such as the brain and heart. Inhabited by "innumerable spirits of darkness," it is also a space "where thought and feeling dance their sabbath." Like the narrator in "The Calmative," Molloy observes the sky, asserting that "without seeing them I felt the first stars tremble."[19] However, soon after he adds "Let me hear nothing of the moon, in my night there is no moon, and if it happens that I speak of the stars it is by mistake."[20] In the second volume of the trilogy, Malone too will try to find his way in the sky, yet only to state: "I have studied the stars a little here. But I cannot find my way about among them. . . . The moon on the other hand has grown familiar. I am well familiar now with her changes of aspect and orbit."[21] Perhaps it is his characters' cosmic expansion of their uninhabitable space that leads Beckett to imagine an abode suspended somewhere in space beyond earth, as in "The Calmative" or *The Lost Ones*.

Unlike the Unnamable later, Molloy still affirms that he needs stories. He is a writer, after all, who is paid for the pages he fills.

But the fact that he struggles not to talk about himself, reveals that already for Molloy it is difficult to maintain the boundaries between self and Other. The need for stories, however, pushes him into the vortex of a struggle with language, with words and meaning, from which all of Beckett's characters suffer. Obsessively, he circles around questions such as whether it is better to obliterate texts than to blacken the margins, or "to fill in the holes of words till all is blank and flat." Dismissing his ruminations as "senseless, speechless, issueless misery," he "returns in spirit" to the other man whose story he wants to tell, only to blur the boundaries again and slide between the pronouns "he" and "I."[22]

Molloy is one of the writers and philosophers among Beckett's characters, thinking of the essence of systems and guiding principles of how to proceed. Unsurprisingly, he also reflects upon the end times of writing: "But it is only since I have ceased to live that I think of these things and the other things. It is in the tranquility of decomposition that I remember the long confused emotion which was my life." As a writer unable to find the serenity of composition, Molloy is seeking the "tranquility of decomposition," asserting that "to decompose is to live too."[23] Writing as decomposition marks the end time of writing for Beckett's characters, the unending gestures of qualifications, dismissals, and erasures. Molloy sums this up as follows: "Not to want to say, not to know what you want to say, and never to stop saying, or hardly ever, that is the thing to keep in mind, even in the heat of decomposition."[24] Writing as decomposition requires Molloy to be "living so far from words so long that his identity becomes wrapped in namelessness. As if living in the end times of a world of quantum physics in which waves and particles were all fading, Molloy states that "there could be no things but nameless things, no names but thingless names." It is, he writes, a cold and dying world in which "icy words" and "icy meanings" hail down on him, and in which he knows nothing but what the words know and the dead things. Writing as decomposition turns into a "long sonata of the dead."[25]

It is also a world of murmurs and voices of others, including Moran whom Molloy assumes to be the carrier of a voice that tells him to do things. The novel ends with Molloy imagining that while he had not known what the voice wanted, in the end he finally understood this language, adding that it doesn't matter he might be wrong.[26] It is Moran's voice that told him to write the report he wrote, a report full of inventions, embellishments and lies even though he paradoxically also thinks that nothing can be invented. He ends his report, and Beckett ends the novel, with the statement, "Then I went into the house and wrote, It is midnight. The rain is beating on the windows. It was not midnight. It was not raining."[27]

MALONE DIES

Like Molloy, Malone lives in a transitional space between life and death. Like Molloy, he plans to use his end time writing and making an inventory of his possessions. Compared to Molloy's, Malone's obsession with his impending death, however, has gained in intensity. Presenting one of Beckett's deepest explorations of the end times, *Malone Dies*, the second part of Beckett's trilogy, opens with the statement, "I shall soon be quite dead at last in spite of all."[28] Of course, we expect Malone eventually to cancel or question this statement, and indeed, some forty pages later, he projects an alternative scenario: "There is naturally another possibility that does not escape me, though it would be a great disappointment to have it confirmed, and that is that I am dead already and that all continues more or less as when I was not."²⁹ This statement establishes a resonance with "The Calmative," written in French in 1946, that is, about a year before he began working on the trilogy. Beckett finished *Malone Meurt* in 1948 and published it in French in 1951. His entire body of work at the time was thus returning repeatedly to the vision of endowing the (presumably) dead with a narrative voice. Malone's end times, during which he initially imagines himself being nearly a century old, are haunted by the notion of speaking from an indeterminate beyond of life.

Malone's world is a comatose world, a world of gradual decomposition and losses, a world in which he tries, without succeeding of course, to amuse himself with inventing events marked by loss. The loss of consciousness, for example, about which he says that "it was never any great loss" leads him to state, "I have lived in a kind of coma." Haunted by the sensation of speaking from beyond the grave, he proclaims, "The truth is, if I did not feel myself dying, I could well believe myself dead."³⁰ Like Molloy, Malone is obsessed with decomposition. In Malone's mind, the decomposition of the body happens in tandem with that of the soul. "I am far from the sounds of blood and breath, immured. I shall not speak of my sufferings. Cowering deep among them I feel nothing. It is there I die, unbeknownst to my stupid flesh.... Somewhere in this turmoil thought struggles on.... It too seeks me, as it always has, where I am not to be found."³¹ Feeling nothing, he perceives himself like the living dead. Contemptuous of his body, his "stupid flesh," he ponders the question Jean Francois Lyotard posed in his sketch of a planetary philosophy: "Can Thought Go on Without a Body?"³²

Malone can only conceive of such thought as a futile struggle in pursuit of an ever-evanescent self. Above all, thought struggles on in Malone's attempt to tell stories while waiting for the end, stories about which he says, "they will be almost lifeless, like the teller."[33] Unlike Molloy, Malone is no longer a paid writer but a lonely storyteller without an audience who tells himself stories or writes them down in his exercise book. In the stories he invents about himself, he finds himself alone or abandoned in the dark, in a world that is shapeless and mute, full of "incurious wondering, darkness, long stumbling with outstretched arms, hiding."[34] He imagines storytelling as a game, which he also calls "the losing game," after having stated, "I never knew how to play," and adding, in one of his paradoxical turns, "I shall never do anything any more from now on but play."[35]

As a reprieve from the losing game of storytelling, he engages in equally futile attempts at making an inventory of his possessions. Trying to list the objects in his possession serves as a repeated deferral of telling the story of his life. The thought of writing his memoir does occur to him, yet only to be dismissed as a joke that emerges in his thoughts like a Freudian slip: "When I have completed my inventory, if my death is not ready for me then, I shall write my memoirs. That's funny, I have made a joke. No matter."[36]

In an essay on *Malone Dies*, Kathleen Woodward compares the objects and symbols Malone creates to face the pain and suffering of dying to Donald W. Winnicott's transitional objects.[37] Transitional objects are created in a space between reality and fantasy. Like the dream, the so-called transitional space knows no contradiction or paradox. It is designed for the perpetual mediation between self and environment and for the redrawing of the boundaries of the self in the process. Malone gradually withdraws meaning from the last remains in his environment until he eventually concentrates on the final possession, his exercise book, which he uses as a transitional object. Woodward writes, "The exercise-book is the place of both the I and the

Not-I. And as Malone is increasingly alienated from his disintegrating body . . . the I comes to exist in the book itself."[38]

Yet this displacement of the I into language or, more precisely, into a speech that is used as a transitional object does of course not leave the I unchanged. While the I deliberately renounces the fiction of being clearly delimited, continuous, and differentiated from the outside world and from others, it does so only by transmuting itself instead into the paradoxical I of the transitional space. With an I that is always also Not-I and vice versa, the speaking subject can play the game of presence and absence (*Fort-Da*) with the first-person pronoun, thus abstracting the I into a linguistic dimension or an epistemological problem.[39] This is the very point at which *Malone Dies* ends and *The Unnamable* begins. "I, say I. Unbelieving," or "I seem to speak, it is not I, about me, it is not about me."[40] Is this statement still connected with the fiction of a "living" voice? Nothing seems less sure with a narrator decidedly denying the security of such a connection. Instead, one of the most obsessive fantasies that Malone and the Unnamable share is the impossibility of defining a self between the boundaries of life and death.

As for so many Beckett characters, the notion of death is inherently linked to birth, giving rise to prenatal and postmortem phantasms and evoking the paradoxical image of a very old being already in the process of decomposition whose foremost task is to be born. Malone, for example, sees himself as an old fetus that shall never be born and will therefore never be dead. Similar phantasms of incomplete birth, a topic that was central to the two years of Beckett's psychoanalysis with W. R. Bion, abound in Beckett's texts. Jean-Michel Rabaté goes so far to argue that a new turn in Beckett's work was initiated by the sense that he had never been properly born. "If this was the case, then he would never really die either—such an insight allowed him to go on writing. . . . He had found his main theme . . . that death itself is not a catastrophe: it is the impossibility of dying that is catastrophic."[41]

Freed from their ontological foundation, the categories of life and death ultimately tend to function as pure elements in a language game that playfully investigates their linguistic possibilities. Yet, contrary to the characters' declared intentions, the categories "life" and "death" never cease to assume psychological connotations, because even in their abstract artistic form they resemble familiar phantasms and metaphors of the self. As such, they interfere with a transitional speech performance that hinges upon refusing *any* representation of the self.

For both Malone and the Unnamable, this game is achieved, however, with only intermittent success. The transitional space of old age is a refuge that is always already threatened by the intrusion of the real. In the case of Malone, the real takes the form of his disintegrating body reasserting its claims. But at the same time, Malone is also disturbed by the irreducible autobiographical implications of his writings because they threaten to refer his words back to himself.[42] For the Unnamable, the threat is even more abstract: it is the principle of representation itself that brings too much of the real into his transitional speech. Behind this, of course, hovers a notion that Herbert Blau identifies as one of the most prominent desires in postmodern thought, namely the desire for "presence with no illusion."[43] Knowing it can only be an illusion, the Unnamable, however, has long given up the desire to establish such a presence. Yet, while he himself does not desire presence with no illusion, he perceives this desire to be an impossible task anonymous others impose on him because they want to "snap him up among the living."[44] The Unnamable thus seems less obsessed with a presence without illusion than with the illusion of absence.

Thinking in terms of an epistemological unconscious, one could perhaps say that, as long as one can hide in the transitional space of speech, death cannot get one, because it is always out there in the realm of the real where one is not.

The obsession Malone and the Unnamable share about existing in a form of nonbeing, a Not-I condemned to hover in the transitional space between life and death, earth and elsewhere, is intimately tied to their generative paranoia of being haunted and colonized by others whose voice has invaded them and taken over their stories. Of these persecutory anonymous shadow figures Malone says, "they have abused me ever since I was born."[45] Who speaks? Is it the paradoxical voice of others that cannot but manifest as the illusion of an I? The impossibility of ever disaggregating the voices of an illusionary I and its others undermines even the ease of using such basic categories as life, death, time, language, self, and other.

According to Winnicott, one of the primary functions of cultural objects is to provide a space for the continual restructuring of the boundaries of the self. Characters like Malone challenge us to envision a transitional space of the end times used to imagine the conditions and possibilities of the unimaginable end. Thinking of the narrator in "The Calmative" as well as Molloy, Malone, and the Unnamable as "transitional characters" created by a "transitional area of speech" challenges one to explore how this mode of being in the transitional space might relate to a specific experience of old age. Winnicott insists that the fear of death is indissolubly linked to the earliest experiences of loneliness and separation. For Winnicott, fearing death therefore is the fear of a catastrophe that has already happened. In a similar vein, Jean-Michel Rabaté argues that Beckett's work stages a catastrophe that already happened in the past: "we have to survive the worst by the dark humor deriving from the notion that there has been even worse; we will live by facing an ancient catastrophe that has already happened, and this awareness keeps a certain panic active while muting what would have been pure horror or disabling terror."[46]

Winnicott links the catastrophe that has already happened to the catastrophic loneliness infants feel in response to a total abandonment they experience as death. This resonates with the catastrophic loneliness of most Beckett characters and their recurring memories of themselves as abandoned children. The narrator in "The Calmative," for example, asserts that he always remembers himself as an abandoned child. Significantly, the transitional space of infancy is created to cope with separation anxieties and to master the transition into reality, while in old age we must prepare instead for the transition out of reality and thus cope with the anxieties of an ultimate separation from the world. Reactivating the modes of being of the transitional space might help with the transition from life to death, easing the way *out* of reality as they once eased the way *into* reality. In old age, the "transitional space" might again absorb more and more of everyday life, providing a sanctuary where one can learn to cope with the menacing dissolution of the body.

Seen in this way, the speech of Beckett's transitional characters can be understood as a symbolic object in the psychoanalytic sense created to wean themselves from reality, the body, others, and even a lingering sense of self. All humans presumably need psychological crutches to face the facts of aging and dying, the fear of solitude, decrepitude, and death. While the original transitional objects of infancy were rooted in the infant's need to cope with presence, absence, and separation,[47] the creation of transitional objects and spaces in old age serve to wean from their world those who prepare to die. Beckett's texts look in the abyss of old age's catastrophic loneliness, scrutinizing the impossible ways and ultimate helplessness to find a voice that helps to ease or even defend against the unnamable pain of the ultimate separation we face when imagining the world without us. But Beckett makes his readers gaze into this abyss through the lens of characters who have already killed the awareness of this pain. They have numbed and trained themselves to think they would gladly die if only they could. Rereading these texts during the current pandemic, however, they deeply resonate with the fear of separation, catastrophic loneliness, and death of victims of the pandemic who are completely isolated from others, dying in abject seclusion in homes for the elderly or hospitals.

Death haunts the transitional speech of virtually all of Beckett's characters. If, however, commonplace notions such as life, death, time, and self, lose their validity, following the trajectory of Beckett's characters eventually requires one to give up the coordinates that commonly serve as a grounding of ontological security. Even if we imagine his characters in the process of dying, their voice undercuts any conventional notion of the end times, let alone death. Yet it is less the experience of old age than the preconceived images of aging that Beckett's texts undermine. Instead of being presented with a fixed image of old age or the end times more generally, we are provided with individual characters' singular experiences of old age, transformed into a speech that intentionally explores the paradoxes of a speaking voice in the transitional space between life and death.[48] It is this very otherness that has caused Beckett's work to be among the most influential and provocative works for times to come, resisting any reduction to familiar stereotypes of aging and living in the end times. By gradually familiarizing ourselves with Beckett's radical otherness, we allow it to work upon and eventually even to reshape the boundaries of our own subjectivity.

One paradoxical effect of the recursive loops of Beckett's characters derives from the fact that their discourse is a form of literary speech. The image of old and dying characters in their end times fades behind that of narrators who, with skilled perfection and artistry, refuse to allow any self to materialize in speech. This is where Beckett anchors his poetics of the end times, translating his characters thoughts and ruminations into philosophical and poetic images of rare beauty that couldn't contrast more starkly with the material conditions of their ending lives. Beckett, more than any other writer, has composed a true poetics of the abject that is at the same time a poetics of decomposition, corporeal and linguistic. As readers we cannot but participate in a paradoxical ambiguity: the most sophisticated versions of the self-reflexive subjectivity of literary characters presents simultaneously one of the grimmest yet most playful and hilarious practices in the art of dying. Or, inversely, what we could read—if we focus our attention on the situation of a dying narrator—as a practice in the art of dying can be seen as a paradigmatic expression of subjectivity in the end times. This indissoluble ambiguity, and the fact that Beckett's texts undermine any reduction to *one* exclusive meaning, while at the same time inviting an entire gamut of proliferating provisional constructions of meaning, is perhaps one of their greatest achievements.

Living in the transitional space of old age, Beckett's characters dissolve the constraints imposed by secondary processes. They recuperate primary-process functions without giving up the function of judgment or the reflectivity of the secondary process, thus undermining the reductive stereotype of aging as a second childhood. Cultural stereotypes of old age tend to see all forms of undifferentiation or dedifferentiation in terms of regression. Indeed, the very forms of old age that most Western societies produce have a debilitating function. The elderly we find in homes or psychiatric hospitals provide us with a distorted image of what old age could be or what it might look like in the psychic life of those living it. A culture socializes its elderly as much as its children. In his analysis of mental hospitals, the Italian psychiatrist Franco Basaglia argues that we cannot know what mental illness is, because what we see is only mental illness *plus* the effects of isolation, discrimination, and hospitalization.[49] The same is true for the elderly. This unavoidable internalization of the gaze of the Other that carries the norms of socialization up to old age might account for the powerful role persecution by anonymous others plays in Beckett's text. These anonymous others, to whom Beckett's characters mostly refer to simply as "they," are the transindividual instances of a paranoid cathexis of the real. But often the paranoia of Beckett's characters is a "creative paranoia."[50] The characters give way neither to the notion of total absorption by the gaze of the Other, nor to that of a possible freedom from it. Beckett thus uses the mental alertness and hyperreflexivity of his characters' voices to free the gaze on the end times from petrifying stereotypes of old age. At the same time, his unconventional voices of old age undermine conventional notions of aging and its impact on subjectivity by exposing the very exclusions that tend to ignore early childhood *and* old age in the conceptualization of subjectivity.

Thus, the characters' speech performances in the transitional space between I and Not-I, the real and the imaginary, life and death or not-life, body and disembodiment, time and timelessness, or speech and silence become more than simply a weaning process. Beckett's works express aspects of subjectivity that, while they tacitly pervade all manifestations of subjectivity, tend to remain confined to the transitional spaces of play, poetry and art. Beckett thus also reveals a potential in and of old age itself that one usually does not see and might never experience. Among other things, he reveals the full potential of the creation of subjectivity through language. Exploring the paradoxes of the transitional space and finding a voice in old age that transcends the narrow boundaries of the I might be a task that helps to better inhabit the transitional space of the end times or even reveal some aspects of the "old heart's wisdom."[51]

3

END TIMES OF SUBJECTIVITY

The Unnamable

"At the end of my work there's nothing but dust—the namable. In the last book—*L'innomable*—there's complete disintegration. No 'I,' no 'have,' no 'being.' No nominative, no accusative, no verb. There is no way to go on." While this was Samuel Beckett's response to *The Unnamable* in his interview with Israel Shenker in 1956, the Unnamable's last words appear as a scathing rebuttal to his author: "I can't go on, I'll go on."[1] Almost seven decades after its publication, Samuel Beckett's *The Unnamable* still marks the cutting edge of contemporary explorations of language and subjectivity in the spirit of the sense of an ending where there is no way to go on. Beckett probes the very limits of dissolution, disintegration, decomposition, and ending while firmly rejecting an apocalyptic philosophy of depravation and extinction. How can we read this exhaustion of a literary subjectivity obsessed with visions of the end without reducing it to the fictional life of an undefinable character living in the end times, if not to a referential phenomenology of decay?

There is hardly any contemporary conception of either subjectivity or the end times—be it literary, philosophical, or psychological—for which *The Unnamable* does not present a challenge. Beckett's text has a striking capacity to incorporate the most diverse theories and conceptual models without remaining caught in any one of them. Echoing numerous other literary texts—not the least of which are Beckett's earlier novels, especially the first two of the trilogy, *Molloy* and *Malone Dies*—*The Unnamable* invokes centuries of philosophical thought, both Eastern and Western, and finally contemporary, especially psychoanalytic, theories of language and the subject. I see the subversive power of Beckett's intertextuality rooted less in a practice of quotation than in a practice of deconceptualization. Indeed, one could argue that one of Beckett's main concerns is to explore the limits of conceptualization. Just as his characters, his texts ultimately resist and mock all attempts at being swallowed up by any specific concept. "The thing to avoid, I don't know why, is the spirit of system,"[2] says the Unnamable laconically, amid his endless series of hopelessly systematic self-conceptions, each of which is rejected as soon as it materializes. Recalling that in *What Is Philosophy?* Deleuze and Guattari famously defined philosophy as "forming, inventing and fabricating concepts,"[3] we could argue that *The Unnamable* plays an endgame not only with subjectivity but also with the very activity of philosophizing. Alas, readers and critics become themselves entangled in the Unnamable's irresolvable paradox: "What am I to do, what shall I do, what should I do, in my situation, how proceed? By aporia pure and simple? Or by affirmations and negations invalidated as uttered, or sooner or later?"[4] Or, as he states later: "First I'll say what I'm not, that's how they taught me to proceed, then what I am, it's already under way, I have only to resume at the place where I let myself be cowed."[5] Most likely, our response to the Unnamable's question of how to proceed will echo his repeated incantation: "I can't go on, I'll go on."

END TIMES OF SUBJECTIVITY ☙ 97

LITERARY SUBJECTS, EMPIRICAL WORLDS, AND PHILOSOPHIES

One of the central questions the Unnamable asks with supreme irony is: "But can that be called a life which vanishes when the subject is changed?"[6] This philosophical statement pertains to both literary and real life. The Unnamable mocks literary fictions with characters built according to the conventions of literary realism by exposing them to the light of philosophical models of subjectivity. But the inverse is also applicable, for he forces the most basic philosophical assumptions to collapse by testing them within the concreteness of both a fictional and an empirical life. It is impossible to confine this protagonist to any clearly delineated fictional world or philosophical model since he merely traverses them to play them off one another. By constantly contradicting his own utterances and self-projections, he evokes the fleeting notion of a subject at the vanishing point. The medium of fiction grants him a space for probing epistemologies and ontologies that would be unavailable to either an empirical or a philosophical subject. Having left behind a literary tradition that evokes the illusion of an empirical world with empirical subjects, his referential systems always retain a theoretical and philosophical dimension.

However, the theories evoked in *The Unnamable* are also embedded in the concreteness of a fictional world. The narrator thus gains the peculiar status of a literary subject located in the liminal space between an empirical subject and a transcendental subject of philosophy.[7] Exploring the aporias of any imaginable concept of the subject, the Unnamable blames anonymous others for implanting alien concepts in his mind and for forcing him to speak about himself. But in so speaking, he endlessly asserts that he can neither speak of himself nor keep himself from speaking about himself. A never-ending chain of affirmations and negations withdraws the ground for any utterance at the very moment it threatens to become even minimally assertive. His statement "If only I were not obliged to manifest" names the core desire that propels his paradoxical speech acts.[8] In order *not* to manifest himself, he would have to be silent, but since he cannot be silent, he needs to speak endlessly, yet only to continually erase whatever becomes manifest. Speaking, the Unnamable refuses the position of a speaker by perpetually denying the validity of his speech. From this perspective, the very notion of attributing an "I" to this speaker becomes paradoxical.

How to describe the subjectivity that manifests itself in this speech—if subjectivity is still the right word? A striking feature is the peculiar merging of empirical and theoretical perspectives within the Unnamable's discourse. From a logical perspective, *The Unnamable* simply commits epistemological errors by confusing different levels of abstraction—the empirical, the philosophical, and the literary. But at the same time, the text playfully uses such errors to challenge established epistemological complacencies. At one level of abstraction, of course, the Unnamable's literary subjectivity gains a privileged status over empirical, philosophical, and psychological models of subjectivity. However, the literary subject constitutes itself precisely by undermining the conditions of subjectivity defined in both philosophical notions of subjectivity and psychological theories of empirical subjects. Subjectivity in *The Unnamable* thus constitutes itself paradoxically by effacing precisely that level of literary abstraction that distinguishes it from other conceptions or modes of subjectivity evoked in the text.

Despite this deliberate conflation, it is nearly impossible for readers *not* to distinguish different levels in the Unnamable's discursive self-projections. It seems hard to read otherwise, even as one becomes increasingly aware of the fact that each specific reading reduces the text's play with ambiguities and incongruencies. We may realize after a few pages, for example, that familiar features in the Unnamable's subjectivity—be it Cartesian skepticism, existentialist paranoia, or Kierkegaardian sickness unto death[9]—are only mock invocations that form part of the Unnamable's sarcastic practice of negation and rejection. At the same time, however, one tends to respond with delight to every new philosophical allusion. This might create the feeling of being caught in discursive traps, if not double binds, resembling the ones embedded in the communicative structure of *Endgame*. Once we realize, however, that this is precisely what the Unnamable's discourse is all about, we may accept that, if we are willing to follow the maze of this narrator's mind, we have no choice but to proceed, like the Unnamable, "by aporia pure and simple"—which means that we must mobilize, against our better judgment, all available concepts of subjectivity to expose them to Beckett's challenge.

The Unnamable's invocations of diverse philosophical conceptions of the subject are pointedly approximated to symptomatology. As Beckett critics have convincingly argued, the ways in which the Unnamable projects himself as the subject of his imaginary world have strong affinities to psychological dispositions of ontological insecurity or even a psychotic disintegration of the self.[10] Translated into the textual world of a literary character, such dispositions, however, undergo decisive transformations. Features that remind one of schizoid or paranoid structures of experience emerge primarily when the Unnamable speaks under the compulsion of negating each manifestation of a possible self. In speaking of himself, the Unnamable tries obsessively to keep himself free from any positive attribution. Constant qualifications and negations of his utterances initiate a dynamic of increasing disintegration in his discourse. This disintegration appears to go hand in hand with a disintegration of the self. Utterances that the Unnamable constructs to preempt his own self-projections and reverse all manifestations gradually threaten instead to revert to manifestations of an empty self. One can hardly ward off the impression that the Unnamable speaks as if he felt a metaphysical *horror vacui* in confronting his own emptiness. This at least might provide a motivation for his maniacal replication of self-images that have to be destroyed as soon as they are produced. Yet, an empty self seems to be as threatening as a full self. Therefore, the Unnamable must produce ever new images at the same time as he prevents them from becoming stable or constant.

Two reasons seem to move him to maintain this discursive strategy of accelerated negations: first, each act of negation is supposed to mark an unbridgeable difference from any self-image, and second, the proliferating negations are designed to protect him from being appropriated by anonymous others who impose their own images on him. All these rhetorical gestures of withholding are supported by fantasies of being intruded on if not devoured by others, as well as visions of an implosion or a petrification of the self. From a psychological perspective, these fantasies create the impression of a schizoid subject threatened by disintegration and loss of reality in a paranoid world. Obsessed with the idea that even his own speech has been disowned, the Unnamable tries to escape the alien voices that speak through him. Psychologically, the frantic production of imaginary bodies and selves is commonly interpreted as an effort to fight self-dissolution. However, the Unnamable also explicitly voices a desire for dissolution and unboundedness. His discourse is not motivated by contradictory wishes for either the stabilization or disintegration of his self but by a desire for the constant oscillation between the two. Insisting on this tension, the Unnamable produces a discourse that hurls itself against the very boundaries of subjectivity.

In *The Unnamable*, notions that resonate with a schizoid and paranoid subject, however, are related not only to psychological but also to philosophical concepts of subjectivity. These philosophical resonances transcend fictions of pathological subjects in the empirical sense. Some of these philosophies are drawn from theories that assume an absolute ground of being, such as Plato, Descartes, Leibniz, or Fichte. Others insist on the irrevocable contingency and embeddedness of all being in the world or in textuality, such as Hume, Wittgenstein, or Derrida. We can, for example, easily find striking affinities with Wittgenstein's *Philosophical Investigations* (which incidentally appeared in the same year as *The Unnamable*) or with Derrida's work, which Beckett seems to anticipate. *The Unnamable* shares with all these philosophies the sense of a problematic relationship between language and subjectivity. Am I what I say, or can I be outside of my discourse? Playing upon diverse variations of this question, the Unnamable insists on a fundamental undecidability between the two alternatives.

Similarly, his discourse seems to exhaust a whole tradition of metaphysical questions. Am I in my body or in my mind, and can the two be separated? Am I what the gaze of the Other wants me to be—be it the gaze of anonymous others or concrete others, like Basil? Am I a windowless monad? Does my individual substance encompass infinity such that it cannot be encompassed itself? Can I be identical to myself only in pure reason or in silence? Is individuality or mediated textuality the condition of my self-consciousness? Am I an endless process? Is my I generated by symbolically mediated interactions with others? Do I have to give up my particularity to conceive of myself as a timeless subject of pure reason, or does such a timeless subjectivity dissolve me into nothingness? Do I speak or am I spoken by others, or even by a language that is alien to me? These questions form the philosophical horizon of this last novel of Beckett's trilogy. They emerge from direct allusions or quotations, or they are evoked by similar figures of thought. The Unnamable seems to carry them around like a burdensome transgenerational philosophical legacy.[11]

But while these questions resonate throughout the Unnamable's discourse, his mocking tone suggests that he no longer poses them with philosophical earnestness. What then happens to the invoked philosophical conceptions of the subject? With a sarcastic sense of humor, the narrator transposes them into the imaginary shapes of his own subjectivity and envisions them under conditions of a quotidian world that undermines and decomposes their rigorous conceptual shapes. Translated into the fiction of an empirical world and thereby snatched away from the aloof abstractions of a philosophical system, the conceptual consistency of these philosophies often dissolves into absurdity. The Unnamable's trick is to take literally philosophical concepts such as solipsism, dualism, and monism and philosophical assumptions such as the objectification of the subject under the gaze of the Other, the unrepresentability of a subject-in-process, or the self-transparency obtained through mystical silence. By taking such concepts literally, he exposes their deepest aporias. Subjecting philosophical abstractions to the conditions of empirical concreteness, Beckett thus produces a literary subjectivity that is subversive to both philosophical and empirical notions of the subject. Not even a literary subject can incorporate a dualistic Cartesian subject or a solipsistic Berkeleyan subject under empirical conditions without running into aporias pure and simple.

Significantly, we are once again confronted with the fact that these difficulties resemble those encountered by persons who suffer from incomplete or problematic individuation or from schizoid or psychotic dissolutions. At times, it looks as if *The Unnamable* lays bare the inherent paranoia of entire philosophical traditions. Allen Thiher interprets this coincidence as a trademark of the postmodern schizo-text: "This view of the separation of language and self is a schizo-comedy that takes desperate delight in its own impossibility. In this respect Beckett's work ushers in the era of the schizo-text that is perhaps the postmodern text par excellence."[12] By merging the two horizons of philosophical conceptions and schizoid dispositions, the discourse of the Unnamable equivocates the epistemological premises of the cultural heritage of (mostly) Western philosophies with the symptomatology of schizoid disturbances. Is this more than a highly sophisticated and artistic endgame with Western philosophies?

Resonances with debates about cultural schizophrenia seem at first glance to support philosophies that proclaim the death of the subject. But what exactly is the status of the Unnamable's schizo-discourse? How can we describe the literary subjectivity that emerges against all odds? Proclaiming that he is suffering from unwanted self-images imposed by Others, the Unnamable produces ever more proliferating alternative configurations of subjectivity. From whatever perspective one may approach this subject, one will inevitably become entangled in paradox. Often the same utterance appears either as the expression of a subject suffering from intolerable social and psychological conditions (if one chooses the perspective of an empirical subject) or as the willful play of a philosophical subject who roams through its cultural heritage in search of a fitting frame for its mock projections of subjectivity. From a third perspective, one could even assume a literary subject whose ontological insecurity results from its fictional status, but who is free to use an entire heritage of philosophical models in order ironically to expose the impossible conditions of both philosophical and empirical subjects in relation to language. Or, to use another formulation by Allen Thiher: "The schizoid suspension of logic allows the unnamable to live his narrative project as an experimental critique of language theory."[13]

The Unnamable is replete with echoes of classical philosophical texts that deal with the relationship between language, subjectivity, and the precarity of embodied human life. The beginning, for example, is full of resonances with Plato's simile of the cave.[14] Like Plato's cave dwellers, the Unnamable seems to live in a cavelike space, unable to move or to see his own body. Like them, he must apprehend the world and the self under conditions of sensual deprivation. But in contrast to them, he has inherited the concept of a three-dimensional world. Given his philosophical erudition, we might even suspect that he knows Plato's simile and plays with it by questioning the adequacy of both a two- and a three-dimensional model of the world or the self. These abstract mind games reveal that he possesses a conceptual sophistication the cave dwellers lack. But it is precisely his philosophical erudition that opens the abyss of ontological insecurity. Here, the lack of ontological stability has epistemological rather than psychological roots. The traditional philosophies the Unnamable draws on presuppose the notion of a finite, spatiotemporal, causal world. His fantasies of an unbounded, infinite subjectivity, however, would require a four-dimensional spacetime continuum. Without it, he, like the cave dwellers, would lack the conceptual tools to describe his world. In both cases, this lack of tools accounts for the necessary aporias of all projections of world and self, aporias of which the Unnamable is fully aware since he suffers from hyperconsciousness and must continually expose the inadequacies of all available means of thinking and speaking.

It is tempting to link the Unnamable's epistemology of doubt with the tradition of metaphysical philosophies. Since Aristotle, the infinite and the unrepresentable have appeared as negative metaphysical definitions of individuality. From this perspective, the discourse of the Unnamable may sound like a postmodern version of voicing the paradox of individuality. The Unnamable indeed evokes philosophical notions of a pure I that reach as far back as antiquity and mysticism. Such a pure I would be beyond space and time, but also beyond thought and speech. In playfully pursuing this notion, the Unnamable effaces all traces of self-consciousness and challenges even the illusion of an I. Paradoxically, however, the very project of imagining oneself as a nonconceptual I is itself a new conception. As such, the project already enfolds its own failure. Since, for Beckett, failure is inevitable, it becomes a question of "failing better," as he says. Trying to escape prescribed false images and therefore compelled to undermine any concrete manifestation, the Unnamable's recursive loops of compulsive negations, however, entraps him in his own discursive spirals because each utterance leads to new definitions and differentiations, thus establishing new boundaries that he must subsequently remove again. The Unnamable thus remains caught in the paradoxes of endless affirmations and negations, until he begins to shake the foundations of language itself. Only a literary subject can self-reflexively incorporate such an epistemological position. The level of abstraction at which the Unnamable performs his epistemological games makes it possible to imagine a purely literary or textual subjectivity, almost like an ironic echo of the old metaphysical notion of a pure I. This notion, however, seems as hard to conceptualize as the Unnamable himself.

NEVER BORN AND BURIED BEFORE TIME

In principle, a purely literary subject could be imagined as completely freed of a body. And yet, the Unnamable demonstrates how hard it is to maintain the notion of a disembodied subject. He finds it as impossible to sever himself from the notion of a concrete body as to invent himself as pure consciousness. "It is well to establish the position of the body from the outset, before passing on to more important matters," he declares after numerous unsuccessful attempts to precisely do that.[15] He can neither take his body for granted, nor can he maintain an internalized body image. As a result, his own corporeality becomes an object of investigation to which the Unnamable turns with the meticulous obsession of a pedantic philosopher and the fantastic inventiveness of a writer. Even the mere existence of a human form with familiar organs is questioned. Suspending the idea of a conventional body, he uses diverse and changing imaginary bodies as artificial constructs for temporary incorporations.

At first, the Unnamable retains the notion of a stationary, semihuman form with rudimentary sensory organs whose existence he deduces by self-observation. Since he hears voices, he concludes that he must have an auditory passage of sorts, and since he perceives his immediate surroundings, he assumes he has eyes. He speculates that he must also have hands because he is writing, but, at the same time, he is convinced that he cannot lift them from his knees. Soon, however, he has worn out the reliability of feigned self-observation as evidence of the body and replaces it with deliberately unrestricted inventions of the most bizarre bodily shapes or functions. He muses about the disappearance of certain body parts and imagines himself without legs, nose, and sex: "Why should I have a sex, who have no longer a nose? All those things have fallen, all the things that stick out, with my eyes my hair, without leaving a trace."[16] The body turns more and more into an elastic form that can be molded at will.[17] The Unnamable hardly conceals his uncanny pleasure in fragmenting and recomposing his imaginary bodies or in presenting them as obscene objects, often afflicted by infirmities. Finally, he abandons anthropomorphic forms altogether and envisions his body in the form of geometrical abstractions.

These phantasms of the body, in conjunction with imaginary reorganizations of organs or projections of organless bodies, question the very conditions for representing the body in literature.[18] Often they even violate certain cultural norms—as, for example, when the Unnamable indulges in artificial conceptions of intimate bodily acts or functions. He produces phantasms of insemination, incarceration in the womb, and incomplete birth: "You'll never be born again, what am I saying, you'll never have been born."[19] Or: "I alone am immortal, what can you expect, I can't get born." At the same time, he is obsessed with phantasms of amputated limbs, a decaying and decomposing body, and a premature burial. These images are interspersed with de-eroticizing descriptions of the sexual organs and functions, or with neutralizing abstractions of the common affective cathexis of corporeal functions. Like the Lacanian phantasms of the fragmented body, the Unnamable's imaginary bodies abound with severed limbs and reconstructed body parts or organs that have become autonomous. He even envisions a form of organless hearing and speaking: "Without an ear I'll have heard, and I'll have said it without a mouth."[20] By transcending any notion of a functioning human body, these geometrical abstractions or condensations of bodily shapes, along with their vanishing, decomposing, and recomposing organs, evoke the notion of a literary subject who freely plays with and then disposes of a series of highly artificial bodies.

There is, of course, a whole literary tradition of carnivalesque literature that uses grotesque bodies to violate taboos regarding the human body. From this perspective, the phantasmatic bodies in *The Unnamable* appear as epistemological echoes of the grotesque bodies in carnivalesque cultures. Their bold conceptualizations, however, reach far beyond a mere violation of cultural taboos related to embodiment. Rather than fantasize bodies as grotesque distortions of empirical bodies, the Unnamable tries to break with the notion of a given empirical body altogether. By stylizing grotesque bodies as literary phantasms (such as an organless ball that speaks without a mouth or a flat surface without interiority or emotions), he carnivalizes phantasmatic bodies. Instead of directly exposing or subverting social codifications of bodies, Beckett thus uses his literary images to solicit the unconscious effects of such codifications of corporeal phantasms. The carnivalization of social conventions of the body is replaced by the carnivalization of an unconscious spectacle of the body whose agents are imaginary bodies and body phantasms.

Deleuze and Guattari have read Samuel Beckett's characters as models of the figure of the schizo and the body without organs.[21] They see the organless bodies in *The Unnamable* as resulting from a sort of autopoiesis, a self-production that disturbs all cultural codes, arguing that, like the schizo, the Unnamable incorporates the illness of our epoch and figures as a universal producer, inseparable from his products.[22] Noncompletion is the imperative of this production, which is haunted by the fear of closure. Accordingly, the goal is no longer to produce a product—for example, the I—but rather to produce a dynamic of endless production. Without the illusion of an identity, the agent of this production continually reproduces him or itself in moments of pure intensity, void of any formal definition. Unwilling to assume the balance of a systemic entity, such an agent would then traverse an unlimited number of stationary or metastable positions in which the distinctions between I and Not-I or inside and outside are no longer meaningful.

Undoubtedly, the Unnamable voices similar dispositions. But rather than reproduce the basic features of a schizo, the Unnamable seems to amalgamate the philosophical concept of the schizo as one among many other philosophical concepts, only to reveal its internal aporias. The Unnamable projects his humanoid as well as his organless bodies without turning them into a foundation for a subjectivity—not even for the unbounded subjectivity of a schizo. To the extent that he empties his imaginary constructions of the stereotypes of human corporeality, his principles of forming and shaping become more and more autonomous. "All that matters is that I am round and hard, there must be a reason for that,"[23] he remarks before wishfully assuming the form and consistency of an egg, or indulging in fantasies of being a big talking ball, a cylinder, or simply a geometrical surface: "Perhaps that's what I am, the thing that divides the world in two, on the one side the outside, on the other the inside, that can be as thin as foil. I'm neither one side nor the other. I'm in the middle, I'm the partition. I've two surfaces and no thickness."[24] Playfully mirroring, once again, in abstract form the conditions of Plato's cave dwellers, the Unnamable projects himself as a two-dimensional geometrical border creature within a three-dimensional space—a surface without outside, inside, or depth. But in *The Unnamable*, such fantasies are always open to multiple frames of reference. Apart from the Platonic allusions, this vision of the narrator also recalls numerous other philosophical conceptions such as the traditional theory of two worlds (Descartes and Kant) or the notion of the self as a worldless boundary (Husserl and Wittgenstein).

At the same time, the discourse also recalls psychological notions of the self as depth, and of the I as a surface—as in Freud's formula of the I as the projection of a surface.[25] From a psychological perspective, geometrical phantasms of the body are creative artifacts produced by the I to ward off its dissolution.[26] The recourse to a simple order is commonly interpreted as an attempt to contain the onslaught of a complexity that threatens to revert into chaos. By creating very simple geometrical shapes as self-figurations, the subject tries to regain control by reducing unbearable complexity to primary structures. The image of the I as a surface, for example, neutralizes a depth that threatens the subject from within. Without interiority, the I can maintain itself as the projection of mere surface.[27] If one adapts this perspective to the conditions of literature, one could also say that the Unnamable envisions himself as surface to neutralize the symbolic depth of a literary character and thus assert the two-dimensionality of a textual being.

While his early fantasies about his body are still inspired by stages of the decay or mutation of a conceivably empirical human body, the geometrical phantasms play with intricate imaginary equivocations between body and self. For the Unnamable, such geometrical shapes provide the lure of a seemingly inherent neutrality. They can both work against the dissolution of the I and prevent the stabilization of a definite form of the I. This irreducible ambiguity fundamentally shapes the Unnamable's literary subjectivity. Shunning conventional forms of the human body, his imaginary bodies also refuse the illusion of a physical ground for an I. We are thus faced with the paradoxical result that, even though the delineated geometrical forms provide the clear boundary of a material shape, the Unnamable prevents them from ever becoming reliable projections of either his body or his self.

Once again, we are returned in a recursive loop to the disposition of a schizo. As Melanie Klein and others have convincingly argued, in schizoid and schizophrenic productions of mechanistic or geometrical body images, the body as machine or simple form ambiguously expresses both the threat of psychotic disintegration and the "will to form" that tries to counteract it. While the Unnamable's phantasms undoubtedly resonate with the conditions of psychotic disintegration, his concrete projections complicate and transcend this framework. In his discourse, the flourishing phenomena of dissolution generally result from the explosive complexity of his ever-changing provisional creations of body and self. This implies that they are not induced by a lack or a decrease of differentiation, but, on the contrary, by overdifferentiation. The explosion of complexity is a function of the narrator's rejection of any stable form or conceptualization. For the Unnamable, even the most minimal notion of a bounded body or self appears as too much of a fixation. He therefore does not use his imaginary bodies to ground a self, but to ground the paradox of the impossible, yet inevitable, manifestation of an I.

His mind released from the fixations to an organic body, this first-person narrator thus projects himself on the boundary between I and Not-I. But a subject without a self and a body cannot project an imaginary life because the very categories of birth, life, and death seem to depend upon the notion of an embodied subject. This explains why, rejecting the boundaries between life and nonlife, death and undeath, the Unnamable envisions himself as unborn yet buried before his time. For one never born, it does not make sense to project a life between birth and death. Endless fantasies of one who has never been born and therefore cannot die—interspersed with images of a prenatal or postmortal existence—engender the Unnamable as a fictional character beyond those boundaries of a lifetime. "I can't get born" is the underlying theme of numerous fantasies, such as those of a dry sperm freezing in the linen of a bed, a lifeless creature who yearns for his impossible ending, or a fake human upon whom others try to impose the status of a living being, only to expect his paradoxical death.[28] Other fantasies evoke the notion of "one buried before his time."[29] A paradoxical dynamic of endless autogenesis and autopoiesis, maintained only by continuing dissolutions of every manifested form, creates a paradoxical existence in which it is impossible either to live or to die. Imaginary self-figurations become the representational analogies of a limitless nonbeing.

Yet, at the same time, these self-figurations assume changing and provisional, but nevertheless concrete, forms. They may, for example, temporarily materialize as a new character named Worm who is born out of a condensation of prenatal and postmortal phantasms. Worm is an atavistic creature without being, or, as Ruby Cohn writes, "a larva conceived but not quite born, a maggot buried but not quite dead."[30] The Unnamable describes Worm as follows: "He the famished one, and who, having nothing human, has nothing else, has nothing, is nothing. Come into the world unborn, abiding there unliving, with no hope of death, epicentre of joys, of griefs, of calm. . . . On the outside of life we always were in the end."[31]

Worm himself is, however, only one of many immortal frames for the non-selves that temporarily assume form in the discourse of the Unnamable. Paradoxically, Worm's form is formless. As a nothing on the outside of life, Worm does not appear to have a body, even though the name links him with the Unnamable's prenatal and postmortal phantasms. If we can talk about the form of Worm at all, it is only in the sense that the Unnamable creates a discursive form for him by naming him and speaking about him. But even this cannot be stated without qualifications since it never becomes clear in the text if or when the Unnamable is speaking about Worm or about himself. To use the name "Worm" would logically presuppose a minimum of difference between the two, but the Unnamable performs his discourse about Worm as a mere mirror reflex of his own situation, so that the logic of difference crumbles under the nauseating spirals of his reflections:

> I'm like Worm, without voice or reason, I'm Worm, no if I were Worm I wouldn't know it, I wouldn't say it, I wouldn't say anything, I'd be Worm. But I don't say anything, I don't know anything, these voices are not mine, nor these thoughts, but the voices and thoughts of the devils who beset me. Who make me say that I can't be Worm, the inexpugnable. Who make me say that I am he perhaps, as they are. Who make me say that since I can't be he I must be he.[32]

PARADOXES OF AN IMPOSSIBLE AND UNAVOIDABLE SUBJECT

If we follow the Unnamable's assertions that his I can no longer be grounded in a body or a self while he nevertheless continues to say "I," one question becomes more and more urgent: the question of the possibility or impossibility of the I as pure textuality.

How can one talk about oneself without presupposing a speaking I? "I, say I. Unbelieving" is the Unnamable's very first utterance.[33] Is this an utterance about himself? Or does the Unnamable put into question that he possesses a core of unchallenged certainty about himself, a so-called epistemic self-consciousness?[34] Does he merely doubt the linguistic function of the personal pronoun of the first person singular? Paradoxical phrases proliferate in self-propelling loops around an impossible I: "He who I know I am, that's all I know, who I cannot say I am."[35]

The sober analytic language philosopher would, of course, diagnose a wrong use of language, arguing that "when the word 'I' is used significantly it is not possible that the entity referred to does not exist or "since I cannot doubt in my own case that I employ the word 'I' significantly, the self-evidence from which Descartes proceeded arises—*cogito (loquor) ergo sum.*"[36] The Unnamable's post-Cartesian mediations, however, start with suspending any evidence of a *cogito (loquor) ergo sum*. The utterance "I, say I. Unbelieving" is both a problem of language and a problem of subjectivity. What kind of subjectivity and what use of language do we have to presuppose if we want to understand the Unnamable's discourse as meaningful?[37] Émile Benveniste insisted on the close link between subjectivity and the functioning of pronouns in a linguistic system. At times, the Unnamable's discourse sounds like a literary echo of such linguistic theories. But at other times he seems to parody the general skepticism toward pronouns in contemporary theories of language, found not only in Benveniste but also in de Saussure, Lévi-Strauss, Lacan, and Barthes: "It's the fault of the pronouns, there is no name for me, no pronoun for me, all the trouble comes from that, that, it's a kind of pronoun too, it isn't that either, I'm not that either."[38]

A widespread theoretical consensus maintains that subjectivity is linked to the functioning of the I within discourse. But in *The Unnamable* an "I" speaks about itself and establishes so much distance to itself within its discourse that it doubts the very possibility that the pronoun "I" could refer to a speaker or express a self-identification. The I itself becomes a paradox. Since the Unnamable uses the pronoun not only to refer to himself but also to mark the distance to himself, the linguistic I is simultaneously a Not-I.[39] This is another dimension that the analytic language philosopher would have to exclude from the sphere of meaningful communication: "The talk of a 'not-P' is an absurdity, since as Aristotle already pointed out singular terms cannot be negated."[40]

Samuel Beckett, however, not only uses the term, but he also develops a philosophy of the Not-I and even chooses *Not-I* as the title of one of his prominent plays. Paradoxical formulations such as "I seem to speak, it is not I, about me, it is not about me" or "one who is not as I can never not be" or "where I am there is no one but me who am not"[41] are typical of this paradoxical discourse, which tries to establish itself on a boundary between I and Not-I. From time to time, the Unnamable intimates that all these boundaries along which his discourse moves without acknowledging them—be it the boundary between I and Not-I, life and death, differentiation and undifferentiation, or self and other—are produced as an effect of self-reflexive discursive acts without ontological foundation. The self-relationship of the Unnamable thus turns increasingly into a problem of speech. Or, more precisely, the problems of this speech seem to result from the deliberate confusion of different levels of self-reference. The Unnamable feigns the unhappy consciousness of a language philosopher who knows that the pronoun "I" only refers to the speech act in which it occurs, and who therefore pursues the paradoxical project to speak as an I beyond language—which, in turn, keeps him imprisoned in unending self-reflexive spirals. If the use of "I" alone is already a self-referential speech act, the Unnamable exaggerates this unwarranted self-referentiality by reflecting the difference between the pronoun I and the I of the speaker, thus building an abyssal self-reflexive distance into his own discourse. But since the difference between the pronoun I and the I of the speaker results from the abstract quality of linguistic signs and syntactic functions, the Unnamable must undermine the foundations of language if he does not want to be trapped within a merely rhetorical problem.

Consequently, the relationship between language and speaking subject itself becomes paradoxical. The Unnamable rejects both the idea of a subject outside of discourse and the notion of an identity between speaking subject and discourse. Remaining deliberately unresolved, this impasse becomes the discourse's generative force. How can a speaker mark the difference between himself and his speech without at the same time constituting himself *ex negativo* on a different level of abstraction as the one who marks the difference? How can one document one's absence from one's own speech without saying I? It seems impossible to speak of oneself without assuming the position of an I. The Unnamable's playful attempt to blame everything on the pronouns and subsequently refrain from saying I clearly demonstrates that avoiding this pronoun is no option. "I shall not say I again, ever again, it's too farcical," he declares—only to end up with the very same problem of differentiating between I and Not-I on a higher level of abstraction. The pronoun "he," which he decides to use instead of the "I," soon becomes indistinguishable from the he that he had reserved for others such as Worm.

The threat of forming with those others an unwanted identity—even if only the identity of a shared pronoun—eventually drives the Unnamable back to using the "I," which then breaks forth in his discourse with a vengeance. The paradox of an impossible and unavoidable I thus also becomes foundational for the very conditions of speech in *The Unnamable*.

INVENTING AND BEING INVENTED

Without a clear distinction between I and Not-I, it is impossible to establish a relationship to others. And yet the Unnamable tenaciously clings to a notion of anonymous others who force him to speak of himself, who determine the rules of his language games, who impute a self and a voice on him, and who want to define him as a living being. At times he fantasizes that he is indebted to them, expiating a crime unknown to him. There are also concrete others, mainly characters from the earlier works. At the beginning, the Unnamable mentions that Malone passes by him, though not without immediately qualifying that it could also be Molloy with Malone's hat. Since he mistrusts his sensory organs as instruments of reality testing, he doubts that these characters even exist outside of his imagination. He remains equally undecided about whether a cry he hears comes from himself or from another definitely not human creature, thus implicitly doubting his own humanity.

At that stage he still perceives others as figures who are at least temporarily differentiated from him. But the same dynamic that marks his self-relationship also marks his relationship to others. As soon as the pure form of an Other manifests itself, he must efface it again. His constant oscillation between differentiation and dedifferentiation also erodes the boundaries between different characters. He even inverts the logical possibility of understanding the entire textual world as his own projection by claiming that he has been invented by other characters. Eventually his spiraling doubts erode the boundaries between inventing and being invented. The most tangible modes of relating to self and other are also the most extreme poles: paranoid rejection on the one hand and dedifferentiating fusion on the other. In the case of the Unnamable, even the latter is marked by paranoia. His fusions are never symbiotic unions that create a sense of primordial oneness, but involuntary fusions induced by the logic of his own discourse or calculated acts of mimicry intended to deceive the others: "I'll put myself in him, I'll say he is I."[42] Or: "He speaks of me, as if I were he, as if I were not he."[43]

The process of this self-undermining genesis of self and Other is intrinsically endless. Any self-genesis requires the differentiation from an outside. Since the Unnamable acts under the compulsion retrospectively to negate any form of differentiation, the emergence of other bounded characters would be tantamount to the respective delineation of himself as a bounded character. Therefore, he must maintain the uncertainty of boundaries between himself and all other provisional characters. While his discourse begins formally as an impossible linguistic self-definition of a first-person narrator, it moves toward a universal dedifferentiation of imaginary subjectivities. Once again, the Unnamable moves along a boundary: he remains between self and other or differentiation and undifferentiation without ever being one or the other.

At the most basic level of textual self-reflexivity, the diffusion of boundaries between self and Other appears in the form of a question of who invents whom.[44] Hyperconscious of his own fictionality and obsessing about being invented by others, the Unnamable nonetheless systematically dismisses any historical convention of distinguishing between the real and the imaginary. Yet the question of the real seems to reappear through inversion when the Unnamable begins questioning even the fictionality of fiction. Beckett writes at a time when the fictionality of the real begins to emerge as one of the most powerful contemporary epistemological configurations that affects all disciplines. His insistence on questioning the fictionality of fiction adds an unsettling dimension to this episteme. While most contemporary theories tend toward challenging strict distinctions between the real and the imaginary, Beckett's diffusion of boundaries is more radical. Instead of simply assuming a dissolution of boundaries and a respective revaluation of the real as an "absent cause" (Althusser/Jameson), as an "effect of structure" (Lacan), or as a "simulacrum" (Baudrillard), Beckett's texts suggest a complete reorganization of the relationship between reality, fiction, and subjectivity on a different level of complexity and abstraction. The virtuosity with which the Unnamable ultimately avoids both the differentiation from and the fusion with others while also dismissing the definition of his fictional status as either real or imaginary, indicates that instead of passively suffering from a diffusion of boundaries, he actively practices and reflects such a diffusion. He makes a true art of inventing ever more complicated diffusions to subvert traditional epistemologies, not just to reverse or reject them. At the same time he probes the possibilities and limitations of higher and more complex differentiations.

Yet, even though he stages everything from the very outset as a problem of discourse and textuality, the necessity of differentiating between reality and fiction is not removed, because it reappears on a higher level of abstraction as a problem of the reality of fiction within fiction. One of the most cherished poststructuralist rhetorical figures, the *mise-en-abime*, is here not the end point but the starting point of a discourse that, instead of eliminating the questions of reality, the subject, and individuality as the obsolete legacy of an old humanism, grounds them differently by pushing humanist traditions from Cartesianism to existentialism beyond their own boundaries. The *esse est percipi* serves both as a starting point for endless fictions of subjectivity and as the opening of an endgame with philosophies of subjectivity. Basil, for example, under whose gaze the Unnamable seems to assume the form that Basil has invented for him, embodies the persecuting and petrifying gaze of the Other. Basil mobilizes the Unnamable's existentialist heritage. In trying to escape Basil's gaze, the narrator traces the self-referential spirals of the existentialist philosophies of Kierkegaard, Sartre, or Laing—including the postexistentialist spirals of Lacan—to a point where they disperse under the illusion of infinity.

The determination of the subject by the gaze of the Other is, however, only a starting point. Translating this problem into its textual equivalent—the determination of the subject by the voice of the Other—the Unnamable envisions speaking in alien voices. Yet it remains unclear whether others have disowned his voice or, vice versa, whether he has disowned the voices of others. He keeps inventing literary characters who seem to speak from within him or whose voices he speaks—and whose invention he claims he might be. The inversion of the creative act, in which characters invent their author, a core problem of literary self-reflexivity explored in its most basic form by Pirandello and Borges, for example, is brought to its extreme in *The Unnamable*. A mere inversion would still maintain the boundaries between I and Not-I. Hence, the Unnamable must problematize the inversions as such. The problem of inventing or being invented no longer obeys a logic of "either . . . or" but a paradoxical logic of "both . . . and." Embracing this paradox, the

Unnamable stylizes himself as the creator of literary characters who invent him.

The telescoping of inverted acts of invention ultimately feigns the disowning of another voice: that of the author, Samuel Beckett, who by inventing the Unnamable is in turn invented by him. One must only prolong this endless perspective of inversion far enough back into the past to arrive at an ironic invocation of the God of the Old Testament as the original creator. The Unnamable, of course, immediately rejects the idea of such a creator god as another perspective imposed by others: "They also gave me the low-down on God. They told me I depended on him, in the last analysis."[45] The God of the Old Testament who, like the Unnamable, refuses to be named, possesses the very self-identity of an "I am who I am" from which the Unnamable removes himself further and further in his discursive spirals. Absolute self-identity with one's own speech, without *différance*, however, is the Other of the Unnamable's discourse, its tacit obsession.[46] Due to the paradox of feigning self-identity as the Other, the Unnamable transforms the "I am who I am" of the Old Testament into his endless chain of paradoxical counter-formulas such as "I am he" or "Where I am there is no one but me who am not."

Self-identity or fictionality of the subject, differentiation between the real and the imaginary, speech as a medium of realization or fictionalization of the subject—these are the obsessive questions that repeatedly force the Unnamable's discourse back to reiterations of the old metaphysical questions and their reformulations in contemporary theories of language and subjectivity. The Unnamable demonstrates that, driven toward their extreme implications, they can be reformulated only as a paradox. While he probes the paradoxes of both absolute self-identity and self-presence of the subject in discourse, he at the same time indirectly questions the possibility that a literary subject can ever *not* be identical with his/its discourse. Deliberate shifts between the positions of a philosophical versus an empirical versus a literary subject inevitably create epistemological ambiguities and paradoxes. If a literary subject feigns being an empirical subject while simultaneously insisting on its pure fictionality, the subject of the discourse becomes entangled in the paradoxes of different levels of abstraction. But this is true only if one assumes that the literary subject's pure textuality creates an irrevocable difference to the empirical subject position. The Unnamable, however, collapses the very distinction between inventing and being invented. Philosophically, this position also exposes the aporias of deconstructionist definitions of the subject as pure textuality and the related insistence that a subject has no depth or metaphysical dimension.

The fantasies of the Unnamable that collapse the distinction between inventing and being invented resonate with deconstructionist definitions of the subject as pure textuality and the related insistence that subjects have no depth or metaphysical dimension. Beckett, however, complicates this position as well: he posits a literary subject as textuality that posits itself as transtextual and thus generates an epistemological problem that adds a new dimension to the philosophical controversies. While textualist theories reject the idea of a subject that could situate itself outside its own discourse, the Unnamable organizes his entire discourse precisely under this premise. He aspires to the philosophical notion of a unity of self and other while at the same time insisting on their irreducible difference. In this process, he draws on a long philosophical tradition that has defined such a unity as the ineffable. Following this tradition, the Unnamable sets out to demonstrate that the paradox of representing the unrepresentable is the ultimate paradox of subjectivity—for empirical, philosophical, and fictional subjects alike. At the same time, however, he refuses to let go of the notion of absolute self-identity. In fact, he demonstrates that it is intrinsic to the very notion of the unrepresentable, since only the dream of an absolute identity of the subject with its self-representations can engender a notion of unrepresentability.

This awareness leads to yet another manifestation that inverts familiar premises: the more the Unnamable refuses any illusion of representability, the more he indirectly asserts his singularity and individuality. The latter appear as what is truly unnamable but, at the same time, as what determines the very forms of the Unnamable's discourse. As Manfred Frank argues, individuality in this sense would be without its double, it would not know any interior alterity.[47] From this perspective, one could interpret the Unnamable as a literary character who produces a paradoxical discourse because he tries to do the impossible, namely, to name the unnamable, the ineffable. At the other end of his paradoxical spirals of thought thus emerges an increasing awareness that, because absolute self-presence in discourse is impossible, the subject is faced with the choice of either continually producing new self-projections or renouncing every attempt at self-presentation. The choice of endless self-productions leads to a hermeneutic of the subject, the choice of renunciation, to a mystic philosophy of the subject. The Unnamable moves between these two poles—between the extremes of an endless hermeneutic circle of self-production and an unattainable self-presence through mystic silence, between absolute and irreducible individuality and an existence beyond individual forms. His discourse settles neither for the one nor the other, even though he extends it toward both extremes. "*The Unnamable*," writes Ulrich Pothast, "has left individuality as a form of 'life' behind."[48] But one can also argue that, for the

Unnamable, attaining individuality in his discourse is as impossible as attaining mystical self-presence in silence. Contemporary literature and theory share a desire to open language toward both extremes. Modern and postmodern attitudes toward language dispel the dream of metaphysical presence. Following a logic of "imagination dead imagine," the Unnamable, however, is haunted by the old dream in his eternally self-negating autopoiesis.

The two poles of discourse, endless self-exegesis and mystic silence, both maintain the notion that there is something beyond language. If one understands irreducible individuality as what is unrepresentable and cannot be translated into meaning, the movement of hermeneutic self-interpretation would strive toward a form of representation beyond meaning. But this would also imply a turn against any philosophy which maintains that we cannot meaningfully speak about what resists meaning. Rather, the Unnamable demonstrates that since we cannot meaningfully silence what resists meaning, we must voice it in paradoxical speech acts. Rather than a Sartrean hermeneutic of silence (still understood in existentialist terms), the spiraling discourse of the Unnamable thus constitutes a hermeneutic of paradox within which categories such as I and Not-I, subject and object, or absolute individuality and irrevocable mediation by Others collapse into each other. Silence therefore remains forever unattainable.

SPEAKING TOWARD SILENCE

Even though the Unnamable can never embrace the notion of mystical silence, his spirals of representational negativity often seem to follow a secret teleology of ultimate silence. This places his discourse within the series of Beckettian endgames that move toward increasing reduction, minimalism, and visions of the end. But here even the notion of living in the end times that frames my readings of Beckett falls short because the Unnamable is incapable of envisioning the end of one who has never been born yet buried prematurely. Silence forms an imaginary end point, if not the last myth, of this tortured discourse. But simply ending the discourse would not suffice to reach mystical silence. The Unnamable intimates that a mere renunciation of speech would not grant the peace of an empty mind; rather, it would provoke a metaphysical *horror vacui*. Silence, however, also appears as the only possible space of an impossible self-presence. While speaking, the difference between the subject and its speech cannot be transcended. Only silence could possibly erase this difference. Since a first-person narrator is condemned to speak by definition, he can at best use his discourse to project himself toward silence.

With this project, the Unnamable follows the traces of Kierkegaard's sickness unto death. In his speaking toward silence the Unnamable seems to be afflicted by all three variations of the Kierkegaardian sickness at once: he is "in despair at not being conscious of having a self" (Kierkegaard's "uneigentliche Verzweiflung," translated as "Despair Improperly So Called"), "in despair at not willing to be oneself," and "in despair at willing to be oneself."[49] The Kierkegaardian subject is a self-conscious synthesis of finality and infinity, and the sickness unto death is an imaginary despair of infinitude. "Imagination is the reflection of the process of 'infinitizing,'" according to Kierkegaard. "The self is reflection, and imagination is reflection, it is the counterfeit presentment of the self, which is the possibility of the self." The Unnamable, who cannot define himself between the boundaries of life and death, reveals obvious traits of a reflection that creates infinity. Endlessly dealing with ending and not being able to end, his "speaking toward silence" moves toward an "evaporation in the infinite. "The self thus leads a fantastic existence in abstract endeavor after infinity, or in abstract isolation, constantly lacking itself, from which it merely gets further and further away."[50] The infinite discourse of the Unnamable is thus stylized as the speech of a nonliving being who fantasizes mystic silence as an unattainable teleology: "Strange task, which consists in speaking of oneself. Strange hope, turned toward silence and peace. Or: "My mind at peace, that is to say empty."[51]

The infinite spirals of discourse reveal the structure of a secularized, profane negative theology. Just as negative theologies attempt to clear consciousness of every trace of a representation of God to approach God as pure nothingness, the Unnamable tries to clear his consciousness of every trace of a representation of his self to experience himself in silence as pure nothingness—hence his dream of ultimate silence and an empty mind at peace. His dilemma, however, results from the compulsion to put this attempted progression toward silence into language. To speak of himself while at the same time obliterating every trace of the self, becomes a paradoxical task that resembles solving a *koan* in Zen Buddhism. In fact, the Unnamable deliberately plays with such affinities to mysticism and Eastern philosophies. His desire for a complete emptiness of mind and his fantasies of death and rebirth have absorbed some of the assumptions of Eastern philosophies.[52] Yet to fully adopt a mystic philosophy would mean for the Unnamable to define and manifest himself in a way he tries to avoid. He thus evokes notions of mysticism only to assert that they remain as alien to him as all the other philosophies that have imposed their traces on his mind.

Silence and infinite discourse are the two poles of a contemporary obsession with transcending the conditions of representation and the symbolic order. Negatively or positively, all these attempts rely on the figure of self-presence and struggle with irreducible difference and imaginary self-formation. The dream of a pure speech that would allow for self-presence while retaining absolute individuality has a long tradition within mysticism. We find it, for example, in the notion of an Adamic language in both Christian and Jewish traditions. Contemporary philosophies revitalize this notion as a problem of self-realization versus mediation or self-alienation by the symbolic order. The Unnamable shifts the focus from the phenomenon of self-presence within discourse to the paradox within the notion of self-presence as such. If the experience of self-presence is ineffable, its philosophical representation is haunted by paradox. The Unnamable, however, shows that such a paradox is necessary and relevant for any self-reflexive presentation of subjectivity.[53] Instead of cherishing a new myth of absolute self-presence, the Unnamable plays with the mythological and historical roots of contemporary philosophies of presence. The dream of mystic silence is therefore not an end point, but an unattainable counterpoint of his discourse.

Since the Unnamable takes it for granted that he can neither be silent nor attain self-presence in speech, he performs a paradoxical act of speaking against language. This seems to be the only way of speaking while avoiding any manifestation of the subject within speech. To speak against language, he increasingly tries to empty language of its semantic content. The changes in the forms of his discourse might be read as a progressive fulfillment of this goal. Since the Unnamable negates all self-determination in speech, we are reduced to focusing on the ways in which he materializes himself in the forms of his discourse. What happens to this speech, once the Unnamable withdraws more and more semantic crutches? At times it seems as if he had won a new freedom from those symbolic mediations he rejected as impositions from anonymous others. But then again, it seems as if the singularity of his speech catches up with him and makes him assume an unwanted identity. Or does he find a way also to establish distance from the *forms* of his speech in this endgame with language?

DISCOURSE AND FORM

The compulsive structure of negation that marks the Unnamable's discourse increasingly reduces what can still be said, and, at the same time, requires ever more complex forms of negation. Initially, this discourse still obeys the basic rules of secondary-process speech. Moreover, the richness, sophistication, and eccentricity of the Unnamable's vocabulary, as well as his abundant philosophical allusions and the complexity of his reasoning, testify to an unusually high linguistic competence, a solid and broad philosophical education, and a hyperreflective mind. However, the very rules of discourse and the philosophical erudition he displays so eloquently belong to a cultural tradition and symbolic order he rejects.

Given its intrinsic complexity, the discourse of the Unnamable seems to unfold at the opposite pole from the primary-process language of a text such as *Finnegans Wake*. But the structure of negation indirectly subverts the conceptual organization of speech. The constant use of negation indicates a hyperactive function of judgment,[54] but this function is driven to such an extreme and to such a level of philosophical abstraction that its practical effects are undermined. From a purely linguistic point of view, the use of negation would indicate a speaker who can distinguish between I and Not-I and whose discourse operates within the symbolic order. Primary process does not know a logic of negation. The Unnamable, however, inverts the original function of negation. While psychogenetically negation provides the basis of the capacity to say "I," the Unnamable uses negation to undermine this very capacity.

This strategy reveals a general tendency of the Unnamable to draw subversive energies from within specific norms of speech or traditions of thought. By driving certain cultural or linguistic practices to their extreme, he generates paradoxes that are latent but immanent within the system. Ultimately this strategy of subversion undermines the very means it uses. "Yes" and "no" are commonly used to stabilize a discourse and to exclude contradictions, but the constant oscillation between affirmation and negation in *The Unnamable* produces the opposite. A consciousness whose function of judgment is so exaggerated that it subjects every experience to the most scrupulous epistemological and ontological doubts can no longer work with a binary logic of affirmation and negation. It will instead maintain an undecidability and an insistence on paradox and contradiction. Instead of revealing that he lacks critical judgment, the Unnamable demonstrates that the extreme use of judgement disperses all those propositional certainties that usually ground what we call self-consciousness. By driving his self-projections to the extreme, the Unnamable loses any ground that would allow him to distinguish discursively between self-consciousness and fictions of the self. "It drags on by itself, from word to word, a labouring whirl, you are in it somewhere, everywhere."[55]

The structure of negation also has formal consequences. Since the whole discourse circles around the problem of I and Not-I, the negations of the Unnamable inevitably and repeatedly return to the very premises he had previously rejected. But as the discourse keeps spiraling around the same problems, its rhythm accelerates centripetally—with the effect that the spirals become narrower and narrower. Despite its general tendencies toward dissolution, the discourse possesses a precise inner structure, which at first follows the dynamic of a hyperactive mind but then assumes more and more an internal dynamic of accelerated speech. The traditional function of negation—namely, to provide a criterion for judgment and differentiation—is discredited. Instead, negation is used to mockingly subvert the very foundations of language and subject. "With the yesses and noes it is different, they will come back to me as I go along and how, like a bird, to shit on them all without exception."[56] The subversion has a double edge: by negating the very strategy of negation, the Unnamable performs a double negation, which ordinarily converts into an affirmation. His negations, however, operate at different levels of abstraction, and therefore fail to be affirmative, becoming instead the foundation of a self-reflexivity that uses the most basic operations of speech to put the subject in question.

This has the paradoxical effect that, on a merely formal level, the Unnamable indeed circumvents complete absorption by his speech. In other words, he also escapes the disowning of the subject by its speech. But as we recall, formally he also maintains the incompatible norm of self-presence. His insistence on these two incompatible attitudes toward language makes it nearly impossible to define his relationship to his discourse without becoming entangled in contradiction or paradox. One possible resolution is to read the formal qualities of discourse as symptomatic of the status of the subject. The high degree of reflexivity alone can be taken as a signal that the Unnamable does not simply succumb to a regressive dissolution of speech—not even when, toward the very end, he increasingly abandons the discursive mode in favor of sounds and babbles that draw on primary-process utterances. But instead of resulting from a regression to linguistic undifferentiation, these dissolutions by contrast turn out to be a product of the most extreme differentiation. With the ever more complex refinement of his thoughts, the

Unnamable has reached a point where further differentiation can no longer be translated into greater precision.[57] The loss of precision creates the impression of secondary undifferentiation. Instead of founding an "I," which, for the Unnamable, would require a reduction of complexity, he performs an implosion of complexity that results in a diffusion of the I. Instead of passively succumbing to primary process, he thus radicalizes this mode of speech by generating it from within the secondary processes. The goal, as Floyd Merrell writes, is not an archaic pleasure in using primary process but a secondary pleasure in controlling it: "Beckett goes a step further; he desires to bring the primary process under his domain, to make words, creativity, laughter, and *aporia* possible when two or more ordinarily incompatible domains are intersected."[58]

Speech in this process remains irreducibly ambivalent: on one hand, the Unnamable denounces it as an instrument of reducing complexity; on the other, he uses language against the conventions of speech to increase complexity. If language can ground the subject, this function can also be inverted. The Unnamable produces paradoxes of subjectivity from within a dynamic of linguistic subversion. After all, we need language even to think the paradox of "I am Not-I." To probe this paradox in all its possible implications, the Unnamable exaggerates the most complex linguistic operations to the point where language itself becomes paradox. This enables him to develop a subtle critique of language within his speech. But at the same time, nearly inadvertently, the difference between subject and language begins increasingly to vanish. Since the Unnamable produces his paradoxical subjectivity from within language, he pushes the assumption of a subjectivity beyond language *ad absurdum*. These linguistic endgames with subjectivity would be inconceivable without the very language he deems so inadequate. The result is a unique kind of language subjectivity. Instead of announcing the end of the subject, *The Unnamable* reveals the insistence of the subject in language—albeit against the subject's own will.

For the Unnamable, the unavoidable subject effect of language appears as a coercion—an imposition of a symbolic order that is Other. But, as J. E. Dearlove has shown, such a rejection of the power of language can only be motivated if we concede that there is a nonverbal core of the self: "On the one hand, he [the Unnamable] is the formless, fluid speaker who rejects all that is alien to the nonverbal core of himself. On the other hand, he resides in the fixed shapes and external orders of his spoken words."[59] Yet the Unnamable also reflects himself as a fictional character for whom the very idea of a nonverbal core of the self is a paradoxical contradiction. It is precisely this tension between a linguistic subjectivity and its nonverbal core that drives the Unnamable to invent himself as a paradox in language. Far from effacing the words and silencing the voices that haunt his mind, the Unnamable performs his inseparability from language precisely when he strives to locate himself outside the symbolic order. Instead of dissolving his subjectivity into nothingness, he infinitely expands it through operations based solely on language. In the Unnamable's paradoxical discourse, the notion of a subject freed from language thus appears as reductive as the notion of a language freed from the subject.

RHYTHMS OF EMOTIONS IN LANGUAGE

Since the Unnamable can become neither identical with nor different from his discourse, he oscillates between the complementary fictions of a nonverbal core subjectivity and a discourse without subject. This oscillation regulates the shifting distance to his own utterances as well as the rhythm and affective dynamic of his discourse. As all fictions about the self, the fictions of the Unnamable, too, reveal a certain affective cathexis. However, it is difficult to weigh the affective distance the Unnamable possesses to his own discourse. It becomes increasingly impossible to distinguish when the Unnamable is controlling his discourse and when he is losing himself in it. Beckett thus ends his trilogy of novels by reiterating the complex dynamic between master and slave (which commonly characterizes the relationships between Beckett characters) as a dynamic between language and subject. As we have seen, the Unnamable uses negation to prevent himself from being subsumed by language, but the further he drives this process and the more complex it becomes, the more he is in danger of becoming identical with his discourse. Negation turns into negative fixation.

This dynamic can also be traced within the rhythms of speech. Initially, the discourse remains segmented by passages with short sentences that obey conventional rules of grammar and punctuation. Even the spirals of argumentation can be followed without too much difficulty. Increasingly, however, passages of speech and sentences dissolve into rhythmical fragments. Ever longer, uninterrupted sentences finally merge into a flood of paratactical sequences. The affective cathexis of speech seems to increase proportionally to the decrease in its designative or semantic definition. This much, at least, we could conclude if we read the formal and rhythmical elements as expressions of affect. We would notice the accelerated rhythm, the repetition of highly affective core words such as "silence" or "I," and the emancipation of formal qualities from semantic connotations, often exaggerated to the point of playful linguistic nonsense. "Nothing but emotion, bing bang."[60] The more the discourse begins to resemble the primary process, the more its energies seem to increase, which would confirm Freud's hypothesis of a decrease of energy in the secondary process.[61]

But things in *The Unnamable* are never as straightforward. If there was indeed an increasing affective cathexis of language, it would indicate decreasing distance between the Unnamable and his discourse. Initially, this rapprochement is still countered by repeated assertions of a complete nonidentity between speaker and speech. We could, of course, interpret such assertions as a defense. But even if they were defensive, reflexivity as a medium of distancing would begin to erode and collapse into entropic diffusion. The collapse of reflexivity actually happens precisely when the Unnamable deliberately activates primary forms of distancing in his regressions to linguistic nonsense: "I'll laugh, that's how it will end, in a chuckle, chuck, chuck, ow, ha, pa, I'll practice, nyum, hoo, plop, pss, nothing but emotion, bing bang, that's blows, ugh, pooh, what else, oooh, aaah, that's love, enough, it's tiring, hee, hee . . ."[62] Such an asemantic conglomeration of sounds resembles the spontaneous production of glossolalia, that is, a form of linguistic nonsense that supposedly indicates a breakthrough of the pleasure principle in language.[63] The Unnamable, however, only mimics this original discharge of affect. In announcing his glossolalia as "inarticulate murmurs, to be invented,"[64] he reveals them to be fully conscious and intentional utterances. If he must "invent" archaic forms of language, their function does not unfold spontaneously. Instead, they are used in a calculated way to void the semantic content of discourse. The assertion "I'll practice" makes it clear that the Unnamable does not produce linguistic nonsense in a spontaneous game with words and sounds. Rather, he uses nonsense as one of the possibilities to subvert his discourse even further and to enhance his paradoxical delight in controlling the pleasure principle. Pushing language back to play with its most archaic roots, the "bi(n)g bang of language," so to speak, only enhances the performance of pleasure.

The Unnamable practices yet another form of regression when he uses foul language to spice up the phantasms of his body. The sarcastic pleasure he takes in obscene and scatological utterances only enhances their ability to undermine the potential philosophical gravity of his reflections. Significantly, these interspersed vulgarities emerge whenever his discourse threatens to assume conceptual density or reach a level that smacks of philosophy. He particularly likes to fall back on them when his hyperconscious reflections collapse under their overcomplexity. As in the case of the glossolalia, the affective cathexis of these obscene images of the body is broken. They are not, as one might expect, used as a spontaneous assertion of the pleasure principle against the dominance of the reality principle and the cultural exclusion of the organic drama of the body from language. Rather, the Unnamable uses artificial phantasms and obscene images of the body as well as scatological invectives in a calculated way as an aggressive rhetorical strategy against the civilizing forces in language. Once again his subversion is not figured as a spontaneous regression or a lapse into anarchy but as a reflected and controlled act of speech.

At one level, the recourse to the archaisms of primary process, to nonsense or to the obscene is just a further step in the Unnamable's endgame with philosophy. More generally, the dynamic of form in his discourse is governed by shifts in rhetorical strategies that target philosophical conceptualization. Such shifts are necessary because the Unnamable wears out each strategy by overusing it. The strategy of negation, for example, threatens to become a systematic philosophy of negativity, but for the Unnamable, the "thing to avoid is the spirit of system."[65] A philosophy of negativity could after all still be interpreted and ideologized as the negative self-definition of a paradoxical subject forced to reject any self-manifestation. We can thus conclude that, paradoxically enough, the Unnamable deliberately uses rhetorical strategies like nonsense or obscene language not only to mock reflection and self-consciousness but also to defer the failure of his self-reflexive spirals. He then indeed manages to have it both ways: he undermines conceptual self-definition, but at the same time he neutralizes any traceable affective cathexis of his discourse. What appears at first glance to be an expression of affect turns out to be only a willfully deceptive mimicking of affect. Disguised affective abstinence then becomes just another strategy of speaking without manifesting himself.

This strategy thus consistently counteracts the initial impression of an increasing affective cathexis of language. Since at the semantic level affects are only mimicked, the last resource for measuring the Unnamable's distance toward his speech is its changing rhythms. There are no signals in the text to indicate that the Unnamable deliberately controls these rhythms. One could therefore assume that the more he tries to distance himself from all semantic manifestations, the more he inadvertently inscribes himself into the rhythms of his speech. This perspective would account for the accelerating formal dissolution of language. Due to longer and longer paratactical sentences, speech becomes increasingly leveled. Repetitions of core sentences, words, and syllables make the discourse more rhythmical but also more monotonous. The rhythms of speech begin to dominate over the semantic content, especially since their uniformity and redundancy undermines the sparse reminders of narrative tension. The text eventually gains a stronger equilibrium toward the end, but it appears to result from textual entropy rather than from a figuration of the narrator's mental balance. The Unnamable seems to have eventually succeeded in emptying language of semantic content, but this does not help him in finding the "peace of an empty mind."

With his repetition of sounds and rhythms toward the end of his discourse, the Unnamable activates an ancient technique of separating language from meaning, which has been used in the most diverse cultural contexts. Children love to keep repeating a word until its meaning disappears behind the sound. Eastern meditative practices use the repetition of internally spoken mantras to transcend conscious thought. All these practices use sound and rhythm to detach language from meaning and endow it with spiritual if not magic power. Evidently, however, the Unnamable does not use language like a mantra or a playful nonsense game. Despite his proclaimed dream of the meditative peace of an empty mind, his frenzy to avoid semantic manifestation ties him negatively to semantics. His hyper-suspicious if not paranoid awareness of the semantic traps of language is maintained until the very end. Instead of moving toward silence, his discourse moves away from it. After a deceptive transitory period of rhythmic stabilization, his rhythms become increasingly hectic and ruptured. As Bruce Kawin writes, "The literature of the ineffable, in contrast to the language game of *Om*, accepts the conditions of time and fragmentation."[66]

We may conclude that even the ultimate recourse to rhythm and sound is marked by the Unnamable's fundamental ambivalence toward language and subjectivity. The rhythms of speech form a countermovement to silence. Behind all suspicion, they reveal a deeply rooted negative fixation to language. This might appear as the ultimate curse of a writer or a literary character. If the Unnamable's speech were indeed a speech toward silence, its emptiness would have to be both semantic and affective. The forms of discourse, however, suggest that silence is at best a superficial teleology, an impossible dream performed by the

Unnamable in full knowledge that it can never be attained. Silence as the declared goal of speech is counteracted by the practice of speech. This tension is also mirrored as a tension between syntax and semantics. The further the Unnamable proceeds in dissolving syntactic units, the harder it becomes semantically to evoke the cherished notion of silence: "I want it to go silent, it wants to go silent, it can't, it goes for a second, then it starts again, that's not the real silence, it says that's not the real silence, what can be said of the real silence . . ."[67]

The Unnamable, who never wanted to occupy a space within language, seems to dissolve into the forms of his discourse. He, who wanted to renounce the use of the pronoun "I" to destroy the illusion of an identity with his speech, ends up producing a discourse more prolific in the use of I than any other conceivable text of the same length. *The Unnamable* ends as it began: with a paradox. The dream of silence, dream silence, generates an encompassing spiral of utterances that leads the speaker back to the impossible origin of his unending speech: "Before the door that opens on my story, that would surprise me, if it opens, it will be I, it will be the silence, where I am, I don't know, I'll never know, in the silence, you don't know, you must go on, I can't go on, I'll go on."[68]

AESTHETIC EXPERIENCE

The fundamental ambivalence toward the spirit of system in *The Unnamable* also marks the aesthetic experience of reading this last part of the trilogy. Samuel Beckett's texts fascinate and threaten with experiences of primary undifferentiation. They elicit deeply rooted, often unconscious memories of such experiences. The fact that *The Unnamable* is a novel that deploys an inordinately high level of self-reflection without succumbing to the traps of consciousness, and is at the same time so close to the primary process without becoming entrapped by the unconscious, accounts for this text's insistent appeal to both a conscious and unconscious level of reception.[69] This effect is enhanced by the text's inherent openness, its seemingly endless number of possible interpretations, and its resistance to being fully understood from any one philosophical or theoretical perspective.

It is the dissolution of language and subjectivity in *The Unnamable* that has provoked the strongest reaction in readers and critics. As the Unnamable is turning familiar psychological configurations into abstract figurations of subjectivity, strategies such as the deployment of his unbounded imagination, his play with cultural artifices and philosophical concepts, his hyperconscious abstractions, his black humor and biting self-irony or his pleasurably pedantic obsessions, all remove this dissolution of the subject from its psychological grounding in primordial experiences. At a conscious level, the reader must follow the Unnamable's paradoxical reasonings as he performs his balancing act on the boundary between I and Not-I with the artistic skill of a pedantic perfectionist. The more the first-person narrator undermines the notion of an I, the more the reader, in order not to lose all imaginary ground, feels compelled to cling to whatever becomes manifest in the discourse. Almost paradoxically, it is now the reader who begins to lose distance to the Unnamable's speech. It seems impossible to maintain an aesthetic distance in relation to a text or a narrator that can never be fully grasped. The absorption of the reader by the text becomes a condition of its reception. Whoever resists this dynamic will not be able to follow the Unnamable into the abyss of his endless language games of dedifferentiation.

The pains and pleasures of this first-person narrator might truly overwhelm the reader in an initial attempt to follow his acrobatic mind games. One can hardly avoid the full force of this text's explosive complexity that always threatens to fall into a secondary undifferentiation. Initial responses might suddenly mutate into their opposite: the pleasures or pains of order might turn into pleasures or pains of chaos—which appears as the inverse of pedantic order. By generating chaos from within order and order from within chaos, the Unnamable polarizes them to a point where the difference between them is harder and harder to discern. As we have seen, he also collapses other deeply ingrained cultural oppositions, such as that between I and Not-I or self and other. Even collapsing the difference between "I am I" and "I am Not-I" will begin to draw readers into a vortex of ontological and epistemological insecurity and nonbeing. As Floyd Merrell states "'I am I,' then, can be referred to *either* as *identity* or *difference*. It makes no *difference*. If *identical*, there is no discrimination—at one level—and if *different*, there is *nothing but* discrimination. . . . Both 'I = I' and I # I are simultaneously right *and* wrong, at the deeper level."[70]

These plays with diffusions and dissolutions of boundaries, undecidabilities, and paradox provoke highly ambivalent reactions, since they break away from an order that defines opposites as incompatible with each other. To the extent that the Unnamable oscillates between differentiation and undifferentiation, he cannot be perceived as a bounded literary character. And since the boundaries between Beckett's texts remain porous to begin with, the reader must follow the Unnamable's paradoxical strategies to avoid the traps of subjectivity. Following this self-reflexive flight from the self entangles the reader more intricately with the Unnamable than if he were a bounded literary character. The diffusion between I and Not-I requires a closeness to the Unnamable that results less from empathy or fascination with undifferentiation than from a loss of distance due to lack of orientation and certainty. The reader must at least temporarily adapt to the conditions of this text—with the hope of perhaps reducing its complexity retrospectively in a more distanced aesthetic reflection. *The Unnamable* thus produces its most profound initial effects more through its elaborate form than through the depiction of an imaginary world. Narrative voice and forms of speech counteract temporary semantic manifestations and prevent the reader from forming imaginary identifications. In other words, closeness is established as an effect of structure.

In fact, there are two different forms of closeness to the text: one results from its hyperreflexivity, the other from its affinities to primary processes and its respective appeals to the unconscious. But these two entangled strategies of establishing a closeness between reader and text are also inextricably tied to distancing strategies. The narrator's negations compel readers to establish a self-reflexive distance to their own interpretive acts. One aesthetic device in *The Unnamable* particularly underscores this activity: the self-reflexive metalevel at which the text exposes its own fictionality. Granting readers a certain distance from the overly complex reflections of the Unnamable, this metalevel allows them a temporary reduction of complexity. But, at the same time, the metalevel shifts the focus from the subjectivity of the Unnamable to the aesthetic devices that have produced this subjectivity.

In this complex receptive process, *The Unnamable* engenders a peculiar aesthetic experience of the genesis of a literary character. As we have seen, the first-person narrator performs his literary autopoiesis in contrast to the psychogenesis of the subject on the one hand and to philosophical foundations of subjectivity on the other. By fusing these two cultural formations of the subject, he creates a paradoxical subjectivity that can only be lived by a literary subject. His core problem, the relationship of the subject to its speech, changes with varying perspectives. The status of this relationship depends upon whether we assume that this subject is the fiction of an empirical subject, of a philosophical subject, or of the self-reflective fiction of a literary subject. From a purely logical point of view, a literary subject cannot possess any subjectivity distinct from its textuality. In other words, a literary subject confirms undisputedly what theories of textuality claim in general: that there is no subjectivity beyond textuality. But we can just as easily read the whole discourse of the Unnamable as an attempt to undermine this certainty along with all the others.

What then is the aesthetic experience of the Unnamable's textual subjectivity? Because literary texts are concretized only in the reading process, the subjectivity of the Unnamable is to a certain extent an effect of aesthetic experience. The Unnamable can only constitute himself as a subject in interaction with a reader. But if we take this position seriously, he would no longer be protected from transtextual or paratextual interferences. The latter include projections made by readers, that is, those anonymous others from whom he is trying all along to escape. Inadvertently, readers are thus interpellated into the position of the anonymous Others the character tries to escape. And what if he were conceived as a literary character whose subjectivity becomes manifest first and foremost in these projections, but who also tries continually to undermine them?

From this perspective it becomes crucial to determine to what extent the text invites such projections and to what extent it tries to control or prevent them. One of the most striking characteristics of *The Unnamable*, as I demonstrated earlier, is that this text can be successfully linked with almost any philosophy or theory of the subject in relation to language. But characteristically, it can never be completely subsumed by any one of them. As soon as we try to attribute a familiar subjectivity to the Unnamable, we involuntarily assume the role of the anonymous others. Like them, we seem to disown him with our alien projections. Only by renouncing such unequivocal attributions can we escape the dubious role of the Other. But if we could give up such projections altogether, from a cultural perspective we would have overcome our habitual ethnocentric or anthropocentric patterns of appropriating otherness. In principle, those patterns can be activated in the reception of a literary text just as they are in the encounter with cultural otherness. The Unnamable's insistence on his irreducible difference to all conceivable confining conceptualizations and the text's resistance to interpretive closure can thus also be read as a protection against the negation or appropriation of otherness.

The only problem with this perspective is that the text thus resists a basic operation of interpretation as such—namely, the hermeneutic mediation of otherness through familiar patterns.[71] With his insistence on irreducible otherness and singularity, the Unnamable challenges the basic norms and conventions of interpretation. In resisting its reception, if not appropriation according to familiar terms, the text may convey the necessity of developing new modes of dealing with and retaining otherness. If readers meet this challenge, the aesthetic experience of *The Unnamable* can indeed become a strong form of cultural interaction. The text would no longer be reduced to the status of a passive object used to confirm what readers already assume. Reading would instead become an encounter with a true literary subject—character and text—able ultimately to challenge and transform the boundaries of our own subjectivity.

THE UNNAMABLE AS A TRANSITIONAL CHARACTER

One of the most important cultural functions of the transitional space of literature is to transform the subjectivity of readers. In *The Unnamable*, transitionality is also a central strategy of presentation by which the text deploys what is perhaps the most radical contemporary literary subjectivity. The blurring of boundaries between I and Not-I, or the imaginary and the real, indicates a change in the transitional space of cultural objects and in the cultural formations of subjectivity. In tandem with the widespread cultural theoretical revaluation of subjectivity, new forms and functions of literary subjectivity have emerged. *The Unnamable*'s reception initially unfolded at a time when controversial debates about the death of the subject and the end of literature had ignited between those who celebrated the end of the bourgeois subject and those who saw proclamations of the death of the subject as a further step in its overall cultural colonization.

The excruciating trials of subjectivity in Beckett's text address core issues and epistemological implications of these debates. We have seen that the Unnamable constitutes himself as a transitional literary subject by fiercely resisting cultural and textual appropriation. How can an invented literary subject assert a subjectivity against the author who invented it under the auspices of the literary canon and the rules of the transitional space? And how can this subject escape its appropriation by the cultural norms of the time? From this perspective, the transitionality of the subject functions as a privileged strategy of cultural mediation.

The Unnamable's position between I and Not-I, life and death, body and disembodiment, time and eternity, speech and silence, reality and imagination resonate with the position the subject assumes during the psychogenetic formation of the transitional space. From this perspective we could see the Unnamable as a transitional character *par excellence*.[72] Furthermore, if we follow Donald W. Winnicott in locating literature in general within the transitional space of culture, the transitionality of a literary character also entails a further self-reflection of its fictionality. As a transitional character, the Unnamable is a successor of the transitional objects in the transitional space. As such he also performs a literary equivocation of the basic function of the imaginary for the constitution of the subject. The tenacious insistence upon his own fictionality thus also reflects the imaginary constitution of subjectivity in general.

At the same time, however, the Unnamable violates the taboo that regulates all activities in the transitional space: he asks the question of the real. According to Winnicott, the distinction between reality and fiction is suspended in the transitional space. "Do not challenge" is the most crucial attitude toward all activities during this transitional mode of experience. The Unnamable clearly breaks this rule. His obstinate insistence on questions concerning the reality of events and observations, or the notion of a true self, works against this rule that is basic to the transitional space. It works equally against its aesthetic equivalent—namely, the convention of accepting the status of a literary character with willing suspension of disbelief. This violation of the rule, however, only illustrates the importance of the imaginary as a cultural force. The anthropological function of the imaginary in the transitional space and its contribution to the constitution of the subject—a function of which we commonly remain unaware—is brought to the surface of this fictional presentation of subjectivity. In this process, the function of the imaginary is simultaneously emphasized and problematized. The negated manifestations of subjectivity in *The Unnamable* reflect and deflect a social norm that requires the exclusion of the imaginary from one's relation to oneself. The text shows that even though it is impossible to fulfill this norm, it nevertheless brings about a split in the subject. The Unnamable's feigned attempts to avoid all imaginary attributions always turn out to be the opposite of what they are supposed to be on the surface: instead of approximating a hypothetical true self, they undermine its very possibility.

This epistemological skepticism of a fictional subject creates a conceptual affinity with contemporary theories that assume an imaginary and inaccessible dimension of subjectivity. As demonstrated in the Unnamable's discourse, the process of voicing such a subjectivity depends upon facing the paradox of representing the unrepresentable. For this purpose, as we have shown, the Unnamable chooses various forms of dedifferentiating language. This again recalls similar moves in theories that deal with the ineffable. Theoretically, dedifferentiation of language might be induced by a hermeneutic or a phenomenological model of reflection with the infinite regress of a self-reflexive hermeneutic circle. They might also be induced by a (Lacanian) model that follows the traces of the unconscious in the signifier or a textualist model that assumes the principal undecidability of linguistic disseminations. In all these cases conventional forms of reading are questioned, if not overturned. Moreover, the development of new models of reading helps one to understand the implications of contemporary literary subjectivity and the cultural change in the status of the subject. Dieter Henrich, for example, interprets the self-reflexivity in contemporary fiction as a cultural reaction to the awareness that we cannot grasp "the ground of our own subjectivity."[73] While many critics focus on the effects of self-reflexivity, poststructuralism and deconstruction are more interested in the effects of the unconscious on speech that occur against the intention and beyond the reflexivity of the speaker.

The fact that *The Unnamable* encompasses both extremes—the unconscious as well as self-reflexivity—turns the text into a prime paradigm of subjectivity in contemporary fiction. Self-reflexivity reveals the imaginary ground of subjectivity as well as its formal and material structures. The textual self-reflexivity in *The Unnamable* appears as an attempt to gain access to the inaccessible ground of subjectivity. The Unnamable's relentless questioning of his own strategies of formal presentation—or what Dieter Henrich calls "the effort of form against itself"[74]—is the material condition for his speaking against an I. The form of this speech is turned against itself to prevent a fictional I from stabilizing within a discursive formation.

Challenging basic assumptions about subjectivity in such different spheres as literature, philosophy, psychology, and the empirical world, *The Unnamable* uses primary-process energies and modes of production to play across the boundaries between the conscious and the unconscious. Beckett has constructed a character for whom those boundaries are suspended, but who nonetheless sees himself forced to speak against his own alien discourse that presupposes them. In this sense, too, he is a truly transitional character. The transitional space of *The Unnamable*, in other words, circumvents the familiar dynamic between consciousness and the unconscious that is nonetheless inscribed in all the loops of its discourse. The paradoxical fictions of the Unnamable draw on the imaginary but can no longer be derived from it, just as his negations can no longer reduce uncertainty to doubt. There is, in other words, no way to escape the Unnamable's paradoxical recursive loops.

Beckett's transitional character is both an inhabitant of the new transitional space of postmodern epistemologies and a cartographer who draws an imaginary map across the boundaries of philosophical, psychological, and linguistic legacies. Ultimately, the Unnamable invites us to "grow new organs,"[75] organs adaptable to the conditions of the arid space beyond the illusory certainties of logical conclusions, binary oppositions, linear narratives, teleological trajectories, and bounded bodies or selves. He thus becomes the catalyst for traversals of ever more imaginable and unimaginable boundaries within the transitional cultural space—with all the ambivalence that those traversals entail. By pushing further and further the very limits of a literary mediation of subjectivity and language, the Unnamable walks on a tightrope toward the impossible, suspended across time and space. This is how the text becomes part of Beckett's monumental effort to teach readers about inhabiting and living in the end times.

4

"LAUGHING WILDLY INMIDST SEVEREST WOE"

Happy Days and the Last Humans

> *... asking for the moon.*
> —Winnie in Samuel Beckett, *Happy Days*

Imagine an expanse of scorched grass in a wilderness where nothing grows, a hellish sun creating a heat so intense that objects and bodies are expanding and spontaneously burst into flames. Or, conversely, imagine an earth that has lost its atmosphere and persists motionless in an everlasting perishing cold. Imagine an eternal dark, a black night without end. Now imagine two human beings, a woman and a man, in this otherwise lifeless world, the woman buried to her waist in a sandy hill and the man living in a decrepit state in a hole behind it. This is the apocalyptic scenery of Samuel Beckett's *Happy Days*.

Performing an experimental abstraction of human adaptability to extreme conditions in the aftermath of catastrophe, *Happy Days* plays with a large referential horizon. An array of intertextual allusions and citations from works that deal with the loss of paradise, the decay of empires and dynasties, or the sinking of human characters into madness and despair, is woven together to evoke a psychohistorical imaginary of possible end time scenarios. The play's allusion to disasters of apocalyptic proportions is consistently doubled by references to literary figurations of world endings, mostly from a Western canon. But rather than cite these texts as genealogies, Winnie, the main character, invokes them as remnants of a ruinous language that no longer fits her current world. Detached from their original meaning, her quotations of "wonderful lines" assume a life of their own, producing a proliferation of meaning. They are running on empty, hollowing metaphoric images out from within. The latter belong to Winnie's mnemonic arsenal of speaking in "the old style." It is as if the remainders of a wasted language proliferate endlessly, almost comparable to the proliferation of nuclear waste. In this respect, Winnie's monologues resemble a frantic effort to ward off the effects of the disaster of nuclear language. Yet, repeatedly throughout the play, she reiterates its core refrain: "another happy day."

In *Civilization and Its Discontents*, Freud poses the question of the purpose and intention of human lives. What, he asks, do humans "demand of life and wish to achieve in it?" The answer to this question, he continues, "can hardly be in doubt. They strive after happiness; they want to become happy and remain so."[1] While Freud's answer provides the foundation for his concept of the pleasure principle, he hastens to argue for the necessity to moderate claims to happiness by substituting the pleasure principle with the reality principle.[2] Beckett's *Happy Days* leaves these choices behind. In Winnie's world, any recourse to something resembling a reality principle seems obsolete. At the level of the play's imaginary life world, the entire sphere of *bios* has been reduced to the conditions of a dying planet. The environment is a hostile place in which the last humans are living under extreme weather conditions, threatened by hypothermia due to the perishing cold or by a merciless sun that extinguishes all life.

Within this framework, Winnie seems to have no choice but to perform the role of one clinging to the pleasure principle and its hallucinatory suggestion that this will have been yet another happy day. The end time scenario of *Happy Days* is, however, doubled by self-reflexive exhibitions of the play's own theatricality. Winnie productively occupies a transitional space where the binary oppositions between life and theater, the real and the imaginary, language and meaning, being and nonbeing, life and death, happiness and despair have been undermined. Life and theater have merged to the point that life is theater and theater is life. Almost as if language becomes, as in Burroughs, a "virus from outer space,"[3] Winnie is infected by the unavoidability of obsolete metaphors, condemned to speak in the "old style," in a mode of "as if." As old metaphors proliferate along positive feedback loops, any attempt to adapt them to Winnie's current world becomes a trap, for both Winnie and the audience. Just as her body is trapped in a heap of sand, her mind is trapped in a heap of metaphors. As audience we witness a unique ecology of mind and language. Operating like a totalized catachresis, language infects the mind with the proliferating waste of literary and philosophical remainders of a bygone civilization.

From the outset, *Happy Days* defies conventions of theatrical realism. The play opens with a scene in which the spectators see Winnie buried to her waist in a mound of sand, and, as they realize in the course of the play, she is gradually sinking deeper into the ground. In the second act, Winnie is buried up to her neck, deprived of any mobility except the movement of her eyes. How did she get there? Who buried her? Why did Willie, her husband who lives in a hole behind Winnie's mound, not dig her out? Why is he himself not sinking into the ground? And most strikingly, how can both characters live day by day without food and water in a searing heat that has, as Winnie suggests, destroyed life on the planet? Such questions remain, of course, bound to the conventions of theatrical realism. And yet, it is impossible not to ask them because Beckett teases his audience with those very conventions, inviting interpretive projections only to introduce new elements and twists into his language games that expose their inadequacy.

Questions of the real, including affects and thoughts of existential depth, are impossible to suspend completely, if only because the play abounds with existential metaphors and displays an astounding adaptability to a wide range of possible life scenarios. In Beckett's "endgames" the real is always there, looming darkly, albeit as an absent cause. Any effort to mobilize theatrical conventions and existential habits of thought to glean the play's meaning is doomed to fail. Just like Winnie, the audience thus becomes trapped in a condition of impossibility to which the only mode of adaptation is an adaptation to inevitable failure.[4] Through Winnie's speech performances, Beckett challenges the audience to see that in language, among the many proliferating (nuclear) options, only failure seems worth pursuing.

This is significant because Winnie explicitly addresses human evolution and adaptation to changing environmental conditions. Moreover, beyond invoking evolutionary biology, adaptability is also a central strategy of communication in Beckett's play. It offers itself as a projective screen onto which Beckett invites us to transfer our own concerns, phantasms, desires, and philosophical/theoretical legacies, albeit only to have them unsettled and defamiliarized. Adaptability thus becomes first and foremost adaptability to failure and catachresis. Beckett uses the projective screen, in other words, as the site of a "theater of cruelty" designed to entrap the audience in a double bind, that is, a productive impasse that exposes the partial and constricting nature of every single referential attribution. To "speak in the old style" by invoking the proliferating waste of "wonderful lines" that are imposed on Winnie is the only way of speaking, albeit one in which failure and catachresis are inherent. Ultimately, speaking in the old style throws us back onto the basic existential questions and presuppositions that mark and delimit our being in the world.

At the theatrical level, on the other hand, we have been trained to take things as they are on stage without challenging them. In the transitional space of the theater, the boundaries between the real and the imaginary are so plastic that we are invited to cross and redraw them as a matter of course. Winnie herself oscillates between her imagined lifeworld where she is buried on a hill and exposed to a merciless sun and her life as an actress, happily playing her role day after day in endless repetitions. While in her lifeworld she constantly pulls herself from the edge of despair and her fear of being left alone as the last human in the wilderness, as an actress she imagines a timeless space of eternal repetitions, a "world without end"[5] and a life without death.

Winnie's almost seamless oscillation between the play's two levels suggests that for her there is no longer any difference between being in the world and being on stage. For those acting as Winnie in Beckett's play, however, the dynamic plays out differently. In 2013, I played the role of Winnie at the Studiobühne in Constance, Germany. We did an experimental trilingual staging of the play with three actresses who weaved Beckett's three languages together: English, French, and German. Often the days of rehearsal were anything but happy days. Each of the actresses emphasized a different aspect of Winnie's personality and we composed our trilingual collage of the play accordingly. The Irish Winnie was the humorous one, alluding to or inventing an entire range of funny lines. The French Winnie was the seductive one, always preoccupied with her appearance and her cosmetic objects. But she was also the one clinging to the consoling objects in her bag that help her to get through the day. I played the German Winnie, who was the philosophical and literary one, and the one most bent to the dark side of her existence.

What we all shared, regardless of these differences, was the pain and suffering that came with acting this excruciatingly difficult role. We had to get through the hours of sitting buried to the waist, and in the second act completely immobile, except for the motion of our eyes and facial expressions. We had to learn to do the entire acting with modulations of our facial expressions and with the movement of our eyes. By the time I had to cry out, "My neck is hurting me!" on most nights my neck *did* really hurt. For me, the hardest part was to keep my hands still under the canvas used to simulate the mound of sand since I tend to use my hands for emphasis while speaking. During the rehearsals, the stage director kept calling: "Your hands are moving the hill!" Yet, whenever I concentrated on keeping my hands from moving, it became extremely difficult to focus simultaneously on remembering the lines.

Embodying Winnie in her tortured position made us merge with her discomfort at a corporeal level. The more intense our physical strains and tensions grew, the more we gained a sense of "becoming Winnie." Beckett's "theater of cruelty" thus doubles the cruelty of language with the cruelty of the body. Actors have no choice but to embody Winnie's condition of being trapped in an impossible world and a language that is always already doomed to distort it. Inhabiting language under these conditions generates an intimate link of language to the body, a somatic form of language, a *biolingua*.

As actors we also shared Winnie's terror of no longer remembering "those wonderful lines." As many of the actresses who played Winnie had complained, this is a harrowingly hard role to memorize, especially because of the many repetitions and concomitant lack of a continuously evolving linear narrative. Moreover, affected by Winnie's mental state, we sensed the terrors of aging, of losing mobility, of losing one's mind. And yet, after many weeks of rehearsals, we also began to feel the comfort of knowing that the next day we would be there again on our hill, with our objects and with Willie behind us in his hole. The more we attuned ourselves to Beckett's unique poetic language and Winnie's mode of being in a catastrophic world, the more we felt a sense of comfort, and indeed bouts of happiness.

By the end we had internalized the rhythms and moods of Beckett's play and with it came a rare form of hitherto unknown paradoxical happiness. It was the happiness of merging with a theatrical experience both utterly alien and utterly familiar. It was the paradox where inhabiting failure becomes the only possible success. Or, to put it differently, adaptability under these conditions implies adaption to catachresis or, more precisely, a mobilization of catachresis that becomes transformational within a new ecology of mind. From this perspective, the only viable, if always already inadequate, answer to the crisis of representation provoked by the major catastrophes of human destructiveness that mark our time—the Holocaust, Hiroshima, and climate change—unfolds along Beckett's "wonderful lines" reiterated throughout much of his work, such as for example, "There is nothing to say; we'll say it," or "We can't go on; we'll go on."

This is also the sentiment we shared during the often very painful rehearsals of *Happy Days*. The persistent anxiety of drawing a blank and not remembering the lines that simply could not be securely embedded in a chronological narrative was accompanied and indeed aggravated by the physical discomfort that kept demanding attention and threatened to distract us from the rehearsed sequence of monologues. How often did we think we couldn't go on, and yet we kept going, day after day? As much as we suffered through times of pain, frustration, fear, and doubt, when I look back at our rehearsals and performances, I feel like affirming, yes, they were happy days . . . if this notion can be maintained. Perhaps we finally learned to inhabit the notion of "happy days" in the mode of a catachresis.

The oscillation between two levels of theatricality also affects the audience, albeit in less visceral corporeal affectations. Initially, the strongest pull comes from the intense atmosphere of Beckett's setting that is suggestive of disaster: a merciless light shining on an arid desert world and a lone woman buried to her waste in the sand. There is no way to escape this pull that is existential and aesthetic in one. Moreover, the first publication of *Happy Days* in 1961 by Grove Press inevitably engaged a cultural imaginary deeply informed by the nuclear age and the threat of a nuclear apocalypse. Many directors have staged the play with allusions to a postnuclear world. In an earlier version, Beckett himself had made references to a nuclear holocaust to explain Winnie's condition. He later took them out to remove the concreteness of a particular historical event and thus increase the play's horizon of possible references and thereby its timelessness in confronting always proliferating unpredictable catastrophes in the end times. In other words, if the play is timeless, it is so in the radical sense that it operates—like the nuclear—outside the scale of human time or outside chronology. To put it differently, it operates at a scale of radical unpredictability or, more specifically, the unpredictability of the final catastrophe. The latter, as Derrida reminds us, can only be apprehended as a rhetorical (or theatrical) condition, and, as Beckett compels us to add, in a mode of catachresis.

At the time when *Happy Days* first appeared on stage, images of Hiroshima, Nagasaki, and their aftermath were at the very core of the cultural imaginary. So were stories of humans exposed to the hellish light of the atomic bomb that melted skin and eyeballs and damaged genetic material for generations to come. In this context, Beckett's "hellish sun" recalls the "radiance of a thousand suns" Robert Oppenheimer quoted from the Hindu Bhagavad-Gita after the Trinity explosion.[6] Given the prominence of global warming in the cultural imaginary of the past decades, one might further read Beckett's vision of a dying world as the performative figuration not only of a nuclear wasteland but also of a world destroyed by climate change.

More generally, *Happy Days* could stand for any world in the aftermath of catastrophe. It is a deathworld where human beings linger in the end times in a state between life and death. Eventually, the play suggests, Winnie will be quite literally buried alive. For today's audience, her gradual sinking deeper and deeper into the ground may appear as an uncanny literal figuration of the "downward mobility" that comes with the environmental, political, social, and psychic precarity caused by late capitalism's catastrophic fall-out. Winnie's burial in the sand is further suggestive of a form of "existential immobility," as Ghassan Hage describes it in *Alter-Politics*.[7] Hage analyzes how what he calls "existential stuckedness" undermines any sense of a viable life. In today's neoliberal state of permanent crises, he argues, this existential immobility does not provoke resistance but is rather "transformed into an endurance test."[8]

In this vein, Winnie can be read as a literal figuration of existential immobility. Moreover, her attitude is beyond endurance as she mobilizes psychic defenses to define her state of being as a happy one that protects her from the "curse of mobility." Almost paradoxically, Winnie's corporeal confinement and immobility mobilizes psychic space. She becomes a master of emotional inversion, performing a generative balancing act on the tightrope that spans above the transitional space between happiness and despair. In fact, Winnie's habitual emotional inversion is reminiscent of Robert J. Lifton's reflections on "moral inversion."[9] Lifton describes how, in the aftermath of nuclear catastrophe, survivors tend to take recourse to moral inversion in order to avoid the abyss of unfathomable moral outrage. In a world like Winnie's that is beyond good and evil, generative defenses are mobilized less against moral outrage than against the abyss of unlivable despair. In today's world of living through a pandemic, we are all too familiar with the defenses mobilized collectively against acknowledging the daily threat.

Yet, as we witness between the first and the second act, Winnie is slowly moving further down into the ground. Her downward mobility forms an entropic system of sorts that includes her material, social and mental being. Buried before her time, Winnie does not seem to die but rather to go on endlessly, repeating the same routine day after day, except with a degree of entropy that makes her world, her life, and her body literally go downhill. Within the ruinous life of a dying planet, biological life or *bios* has become an anachronism, if not a threatening occurrence to be apprehended with disgust. "Yes, life," says Winnie, "I suppose there is no other word."[10] Any movement toward life always happens in recoil. One of the play's most salient moments is the emergence in front of Winnie's eyes of an ant, or as she calls it, an emmet. "Oh I say, what have we here? . . . Looks like life of some kind. . . . An emmet! *Recoils. Shrill.*" Just as Winnie recoils at the sight of animal life, she also balks at the idea that something could still be growing on earth. Her revulsion at the sight of the emmet recalls Clov's revulsion at the sight of a flee. And with her assertion "What a blessing nothing grows, imagine if all this stuff were to start growing. . . . Imagine. . . . Ah yes, great mercies,"[11] she echoes Clov's famous pained words in *Endgame*, "imagine if life would start all over again!" *Happy Days* is yet another one of Beckett's endgames in which the end of life on earth is performed in the mode of an inversion of expectable affect, an inversion that transforms the endgame into a consoling fantasy.

Winnie's relentlessly affirming iterations of "happy days" and "great mercies" amid all her woes begs the question of happiness. Given the play's dire setting in a merciless deathworld, how does Winnie manufacture happiness? How are we to read the fact that, seemingly unfazed by her miserable condition, Winnie holds on to what appears at the surface like an unreconstructed optimism, declaring every day another happy day? The fact that she manages to see even the dead earth and the absence of life as a blessing makes her, as one of the critics suggested, a veritable "comedian of misery."[12] From the perspective of such emotional inversion, every day can indeed be thankfully welcomed with her "happy expression" and perennial mantra, "This is going to be another happy day."

One might be tempted to see this as an instantiation of a particular form of optimism about adverse life-negating conditions, that is, yet another inversion of the type that Lauren Berlant calls "cruel optimism."[13] Or one might think of the findings in the brain sciences that humans are genetically hard-wired toward an "optimism bias" that makes them adjust their beliefs "more in response to information that was better than expected than to information that was worse."[14] Would this neurobiological bias predispose humans toward an incurable, if not cruel optimism, even at the cost of emotional inversion, if not an all-out denial of catastrophe? Placed at the cutting edge of a self-manufactured pursuit of happiness, Winnie not only seems to be endowed with a high level of the "optimism gene," but she is also a master of self-modulation and, as I stated earlier, of emotional inversion. She opens the play with the line, "Another heavenly day." Like a refrain she repeats with "happy expression" her ever slightly altered mantra: "This is going to be a happy day" or "This is a happy day! This will have been another happy day." Whenever her thoughts are drawn to darker matter, she instantly shrugs them off by mobilizing phrases such as "This is what I find so wonderful!" or "Oh the happy memories!" Could we then read Winnie as the embodiment of a human condition fully adapted to catastrophe and endowed with a psychic disposition of survival in the end times, a proclivity toward optimism that never settles for bare life? Could this be Winnie's secret appeal? Could it be why she continues to speak, even if no longer to us?

In "What Does Fiction Know?" Richard Powers asserts, "it won't be our capacity for despair that does the race in; we are damned by how easily we shrug the darkness off."[15] "Shrugging darkness off" is exactly Winnie's forte. And yet, in her self-modulation, darkness and happiness belong as inseparably together as the two sides of a Moebius strip. For her, any "happy," that is, accurate expression merges with the feedback loop of all expressions she borrows from the ruinous wonderful lines. Whatever disaster might have caused the dire conditions of her current situation—be it a nuclear holocaust, climate change, or simply the dying earth at the end of times—Winnie does not take it as the signature of a threatening future but as a given reality to which she has adapted with her particular manner of speaking, seemingly forever.

Reading Winnie as a biased, if not cruel optimist thus turns out to be just another Beckettian trap. From Winnie's perspective, the invocation of "happy days" and "old mercies" belongs, like all the other eternally reiterated "wonderful lines," to the "old style" of catachrestic remainders.[16] Adaptability can no longer be grounded in false hope or cruel optimism. Rather, if it were possible, it would reside in finding congruence between worlds and words. In this respect it could emerge from a specific adaptability, albeit not to a dying environment but to the simple persistence of objects and words within the cataclysms of environmental catastrophe. Whatever happens to them, Winnie's objects—the sunshade, the mirror, the bag full of stuff—will always be there for the next performance. And however inadequate, her words and wonderful lines will always be there, functioning against all odds as testimonies to the simple persistence of language. In Beckett's play, they too seem to be moved outside of chronological or historical human time.

The sense of timelessness and eternal recurrence is, of course, also related to the paradox of theatrical time. When Winnie's sunshade goes on fire, she muses: "Ah earth you old extinguisher... I presume this has occurred before though I cannot recall it," only to conclude: "The sunshade will be there again tomorrow, beside me on the mound, to help me through the day."[17] And, of course, so it will be on stage for the next performance. Winnie thus playfully uses the paradox of theatrical reality systematically to mitigate the existential conditions invoked by her role in the play. This paradoxical fusion of the play's two layers generates a figuration of affect that oscillates between the psyche of Winnie as protagonist and her psyche as actress. This explains why the prospect of an apocalyptic ending does not generate fear and trembling but a self-soothing state of waiting "for the day to come— . . .—happy day to come when flesh melts at so many degrees and the night of the moon has so many hundred hours."[18]

Here Winnie appropriates Hamlet's, "Oh that this too, too solid flesh would melt,"[19] as an apt metaphor for imagining the material effects of a burning planet on the human body. As if she were the last witch on earth who shares the fate of her medieval sisters, Winnie's sense of an ending is bound to the fantasy of being burned alive, igniting spontaneously like her sunshade, her flesh melting or being charred like a piece of coal: "With the sun blazing, so much fiercer down, and hourly fiercer, is it not natural things should go on fire never known to do so? . . . Shall I myself not melt perhaps in the end, or burn, oh I do not mean necessarily burst into flames, no, just little by little be charred to a black cinder, all this . . . visible flesh?"[20]. But before this fearful vision can congeal into an affective state, Winnie's mind rushes to Shakespeare's sonnet "Fear no more the heat o' the sun," which she cites for Willie with exalted bravado. And while she stops short of Shakespeare's next line, "Nor the furious winter's rages," she wonders later whether gravity is still what it used to be or whether the earth has lost its atmosphere. "It might be the eternal cold. . . . Everlasting perishing cold,"[21] she speculates.

It is the peculiar condensation of the play's dire life-world with its theatrical reality that generates a paradoxical space in between, a transitional space, that is, in which life is cast as theater and theater as life. Seen in this light, whatever is destroyed today will be there again tomorrow. The temperate times and torrid times Winnie speaks of are but empty words.[22] Winnie has an entire archive of "empty words" and "wonderful lines" that belong to the objects that help her through the day (or the play). She clearly has a literary education in a predominately Western classical canon—ranging from the bible and Dante, Shakespeare, Milton, Keats, and Yeats to a range of popular music and literature. Yet, within this archive, echoes and citations function as sources polluted by an endlessly distorting proliferation. Quoted in the end times of a dying earth, her archive—which is of course also Beckett's archive—exhibits the ruins of Western culture and is, to speak with Derrida, in the throes of an "archive fever" that puts the future into question.

As Derrida argues, traditional notions of the archive are turned toward the past, presupposing a closed heritage, and faithfulness to tradition.[23] A more dynamic notion of the archive should, according to Derrida, *call into question* the coming of the future."[24] It would, he concludes, have to attend to psychoanalysis and to "everything that can happen to the economy of memory and to its substrates, traces, documents, in their supposedly psychical or techno-prosthetic forms."[25] While Derrida certainly thought of very different uses of the archive than Beckett, Winnie performs a paradoxical use in which the archive puts the future into question: she hallucinates a ritualized endless reiteration of Western archives' "wonderful lines," a reiteration that moves the archive out of human time into a timelessness that is always out of sync. In this dislocated archive, the future is *now* and *never*; it is a future in which the dying earth already belongs to an entire archive of endlessly imagined extinctions.

Winnie's archive of "wonderful lines" from her classics,[26] however, just as her empty words and the objects in her bag, all become "consoling objects" that she shores up against the ruins of what she remembers of her former life. This I see as the true secret of Winnie's modulation of the self. Consoling objects facilitate her peculiar manufacture of happiness. They allow her with a supremely performative and mediated "cruel optimism" to continue and, in whatever minimal sense, to survive. Lauren Berlant links the term "cruel optimism" to optimistic attachments that hold on to "that moral-intimate-economic thing called 'the good life.'"[27] These attachments, she argues, are a fantasy that covers up the "dramas of adjustment" in the increasingly precarious conditions of life and life-building.[28] For Berlant, cruel optimism is an affective response to the crises and impasses of precarious lives. In Beckett, by contrast, cruel optimism—if the notion can be maintained—is an affective response to catastrophe and immobility in a state between life and nonlife. Optimistic attachments emerge from desperate attempts to stay attached to life, even if life is barely livable. If Berlant calls such optimism cruel, it is because under certain conditions optimistic attachments seem no longer to make sense even as they remain powerful. If life is cruel and we nonetheless sustain an optimistic attachment to it, Berlant seems to say, then the very optimism that sustains this life becomes cruel. "Even those whom you would think of as defeated are living beings figuring out how to stay attached to life from within it, and to protect what optimism they have for that, at least."[29]

Cruel optimism, in other words, appears as nothing but a defense against seeing the world in its brutal and cruel state. We might call it—with Christopher Bollas and Ackbar Abbas—a "negative hallucination,"[30] that is, the ability not to see what is in front of our very eyes or the refusal to see the existence of an object or an Other. Winnie is a master of negative hallucination, using even language as hallucination. She invokes Shakespeare's Ophelia to allude to the dangers of seeing what you rather would not want to see. "woe woe is me . . . to see what I see. Her immediate transition to the "blaze of hellish light" suggests that the problem is one of overexposure.[31] Ophelia utters her "woe is me to see what I see" when she realizes that Hamlet has gone mad.

One of Winnie's recurrent fears is that she might lose her mind. Yet, instead of letting these "woes" emerge, Winnie begins in slapstick fashion to polish her spectacles. To the extent that her optimism might seem cruel in relation to the cruelty and madness of her surrounding world, it is also life-affirming and self-sustaining in her use of language as a form of bio-lingual hallucination. And if optimism has always been first and foremost a psychic technology supposed to enable happiness and the "feeling good" that belongs to a good life, then consoling objects function to protect and facilitate such optimism.

In this context, Winnie's manufactured shifts in mood deserve closer attention. There is method in her madness. Her last remaining routine preoccupation is the handling of the defunct objects from her bag, mostly of a cosmetic nature: a mirror, a nailfile, a comb and a hairbrush, her spectacles and a magnifying glass, a toothbrush, the last bit of toothpaste, and, above all, Brownie, the revolver and a prized fetish object that reminds her of a time when it would still have been possible to end life voluntarily. Facilitating a futile routine, these consoling objects prevent Winnie from sinking into despair. They are the material tools of her ritualized "manufacture of happiness."

My concept of "consoling objects" draws on Donald W. Winnicott's theory of transitional objects. The latter, Winnicott holds, are the first objects an infant uses to create a sense of self and world. They are paradoxical objects, located in a transitional space in which the distinction between I and not I is not yet established. According to Winnicott, the cultural objects of later life are derivatives of these early transitional objects. In the transitional space of cultural objects, the boundaries between discourse, self and world are temporarily suspended. Consoling objects, I argue, are objects generated when a subject's environment has become a "landscape of risk," if not of devastation, personal or communal. It can be a nuclear landscape or a planet in the throes of climate change as suggested in *Happy Days*, but it can also be a war zone or a camp. Beckett's characters are masters at using consoling objects ranging from Molloy's sucking stones and Malone's last remaining objects in his room to Winnie's objects in her bag.

In a contemporary setting, discursive figurations of environment can also evoke the proliferating sites of waste, disposable lives, and global deathworlds. Its theatrical doubling as a comedy of misery notwithstanding, Beckett's *Happy Days*, I argue, can be read as a multiply mediated metaphor of the struggle for psychic survival in such landscapes of devastation, catastrophe, and death, albeit a metaphor that operates within Beckett's (psycho)logics of an always already failing arsenal of imposed rhetorical tools and figurations. In fact, the comic and absurd elements of Beckett's staging of a minimalist deathworld make its impact even more intense. "That is what I find so wonderful . . . The way man adapts himself . . . To changing conditions," says Winnie about her body's adaptation to the "hellish heat."

Exploring ways humans use to survive catastrophe, Beckett exhibits Winnie's psychic "splitting," that is, her strategy to ward off what Melanie Klein calls the "depressive position" by holding on to the fantasy of the "good life." Winnie uses her consoling objects to populate the space of her "good-enough life," to fill the unbearable void and to hold despair at bay. Her self-consoling techniques have become a psychic automatism, always at hand, yet always brittle and short-lived. She supplements her consoling material objects with consoling mental objects, composed of the literary remains and remainders of Western culture. These consoling objects are quotations, that is, linguistic objects, mediated by philosophical, poetic, and theatrical discourse. Borrowed from Thomas Gray's "Ode on a Distant Prospect of Eton

College," for example, one of her consoling "wonderful lines" is "laughing wild amid severest woe" (25). In his ode, Gray calls this condition a "moody Madness."[32] Moody madness is indeed an apt depiction of Winnie's persistent flight from moods of despair into a happiness that she has learned to manufacture with her arsenal of consoling objects.

Winnie's "woes" of course also echo Milton's "Oh fleeting joys / Of Paradise, dear bought with lasting woes" from *Paradise Lost*. But whenever a nostalgic sense of "paradise lost" enters Winnie's mind, she instantly transforms it into "paradise regained." Or she creatively counters allusions to *Paradise Lost* with the romantic hedonistic ideal "Paradise enow" remembered from Fitzgerald's translation of *The Rubaiyat of Omar Khayyam*.[33] Winnie's "moody madness" has the consistency of a psychic automatism. Removed from their function within a lived culture, her consoling mental objects—the "wonderful lines" from cherished classics to sentimental poems and songs—have become frozen bits of memory—reminiscent of Dali's frozen liquid clock—that she can nonetheless mobilize to modulate and transform moods of despair.

Consoling objects thus function primarily as "transformational objects."[34] As they modulate Winnie's sense of self, they also change her sense of being. Far beyond their initial use value as consumer objects, they assume the form of "vibrant matter."[35] As if the detritus of capitalist consumer culture has lost its functionality in the imagined far-distant postconsumer culture, it assumes a life of its own. "Things have their life, that is what I always say, *things* have a life" (40), says Winnie, as she handles the miscellaneous objects in her bag. And yet, for Winnie, things do not have a life in the sense of vibrant matter, a sense she would abhor as much as she abhors the sense of life itself. Things have a life for her because she animates them as hallucinatory stand-ins or props for a life that no longer is. Winnie is, in other words, not a speculative realist or a proponent of object-oriented ontology. Rather, she invokes the sense of vibrant matter as a performative ruse, a comic enactment, such as when the sunshade, for example, assumes a life of its own and spontaneously ignites. One of the ironies of this scene, of course, is that the very object that is supposed to give shade and protection from the searing heat is itself going up in flames.

I have focused my reading on the peculiar doubling of the play's imagined life-world and its theatrical self-reflection. In this context, I have highlighted how the quasi-referential linkages to a setting that features the diminished life of two humans in the aftermath of catastrophe is systematically disrupted by references to the play's theatrical reality. Beckett's removal of the explicit references to a nuclear holocaust from an earlier version of the play is symptomatic for his overall strategy to unsettle referentiality. We are once more returned to a question insistently raised in response to earlier texts and plays. How are we to take his warning "no symbols where none intended," given the fact that it constitutes a kind of double bind? Mustn't we realize that we are caught in this unavoidable double bind because it is not up to Beckett, the author, to resolve it? Rather, he posits it as foundational for the available (theatrical) modes of being and relating.

Highly suggestive of a world at the brink of extinction, Beckett's play is thus replete with what we could call symbolic traps. Its very setting virtually begs for allegorical readings. More precisely, these traps call for allegories in the Benjaminian sense. For Beckett as for Benjamin, allegories are reliant both on symbols or metaphors and the distortions they produce. I also see the ways in which Beckett draws the audience into a double bind as a particular form of what his analyst Bion calls "attacks on linking."[36] Bion defines the latter as "destructive attacks on anything which is felt to have the function of linking one object to another."³⁷ A veritable signature of Beckett's entire work, his attacks on linking are directed against language itself as the primary human tool of linking. In his theater, Beckett attacks possible referential linkages because he mistrusts the easy equivalence of language and world. Yet language is all we have as a link to the world. We must inhabit catachresis or remain silent. And remaining silent is, for Beckett as well as his characters, an always elusive and ultimately unattainable goal.³⁸

Happy Days, I have argued, performs this unsettling of referential horizons by doubling its quasi-material apocalyptic scenario with the self-reflexively staged theatrical reality. While Beckett evokes an entire range of possible extratheatrical references as hooks to solicit an existential engagement of the audience, he mocks these references by insisting on confinement to the theatrical frame. This is what creates the double bind for an audience forced constantly to oscillate between shifting perspectives and moods. According to Bion, attacks on linking are directed against too powerful emotions and by extension the external reality that stimulates them.³⁹ Beckett's attack on the linking function of referential realism as well as of language as "the medium of symbolic and cognitive linking" entails a paradoxical process of disidentification with the existential, cultural, and political implications of his theatrical world.⁴⁰ Commonly, the referential horizon of a play helps the audience in grasping its specific interventions that complicate or unsettle familiar conventions of either life worlds or theatrical worlds. Beckett, by contrast, lures the audience into a game of projections, only to have them undermined, rejected as inadequate, or mocked by his characters. Thus, questioning familiar expectations, habitus itself appears as a toxic residue from a bygone world. It can no longer provide a reliable orientation or sense of adequacy, let alone belonging. By helping the audience to viscerally experience these residues as a waste of old cultural baggage, it is as if Beckett's work itself turns into a screen or detoxifying repository of the terrors and horrors that are expelled from the world and the self in a creative act of self-preservation.[41]

Once the linkage between the world on stage and the world outside is challenged, this creative disidentification leaves the audience with an experimental poetic abstraction of psychic worlds and affects. This abstraction, however, has a rare affective intensity. Rather than represent the terrors of world and self, it absorbs and transforms them into a poetic alchemy according to the conditions of theatrical spacetime. Pushed beyond its referential function, language emerges in its very materiality as vibrant matter, as a biolingua that becomes itself the locus of an ecology with the power to affect through its formal and theatrical quality. The theatrical, in this context, is always entangled with a process of de-aestheticization that pushes language itself to the liminal space of failure. While the attacks on language as a medium of symbolic and cognitive linking modulate intolerable emotions, Beckett's dreamlike images and theatrical spaces release affects that were formerly encapsulated in ordinary language as well as conventional literary language. Together with other theatrical elements—light, sound, spatial organization, imagery, pace—language itself becomes a transformational biolingual object that generates a secondary aesthetic effect at the very threshold of its failure.

Seen in this light, *Happy Days* is also about intolerable, if not unsustainable emotions and affects mobilized by envisioning or living in the end times. Casting Winnie as a character who modulates intolerable emotions to manufacture happiness, Beckett attacks the manufacture of conventional emotions through theatrical realism as well as manufactured emotions encapsulated in the prison house of ordinary language. In breaking familiar referential ties to catastrophic worlds, he seems to suggest that habitual references have themselves become complicit with the vast expanse of negative hallucinations. Or, to put it even more radically, for Beckett ordinary language itself is complicit in helping us not to see what we do not want to see.

With his strategy of unsettling theatrical realism and its quasi-referential techniques, Beckett performs a unique intervention in the cultural imaginary that focuses on apocalyptic writings of disaster, including the proliferating environmental imaginary of destroyed ecologies in the end times, such as, for example, globally spread toxicity, environmental devastation, depletion of resources, climate change, the dying of species, and the threat of a nuclear holocaust. Beckett's tragicomic minimalist experimentalism undermines the lures of an apocalyptic imaginary as well as the trauma fatigue that creates a protective shield against realist depictions of zones of disaster and deathworlds. By defamiliarizing the audience's gaze on the dying (stage) world in *Happy Days*, Beckett reaches toward a deeper level of affect, lodged in an apocalyptic unconscious. Rather than allowing us to "shrug darkness off" like Winnie, Beckett's strategy makes us laugh from within the heart of darkness. It is a guilty laughter, reminiscent of the carnivalesque laughter at death that holds grief at arm's length. If we find ourselves "laughing wildly amidst severest woe," it is the scary laughter of a human on the verge of a cataclysmic breakdown of self and word. It is a laughter that returns us to the most fundamental questions of life and death.

If Winnie would give up her negative hallucinations and truly "see what she sees," would she be able to bear witness to the madness of her world or would she, like Ophelia, end her life in order not to see? If this is the alternative, is her optimism really so cruel? Is it cruel because it is an optimism of post-politics? Or does Beckett give us Winnie to show that we are, as Richard Powers asserts, damned because of how easily we shrug off darkness? But even these questions do not reach far enough. We need to remember that, in Beckett's theatrical world, they are no longer formulating viable alternatives: darkness and perishing cold belong together with hellish light and merciless sun and cruel optimism is but the mirror image of despair. In this world, happiness is but a more bearable form of suffering. The choice is only between different forms of suffering. As we have seen, in this theater of cruelty where choice is always, as Conrad puts in in *Heart of Darkness*, a choice between nightmares, "nothing is funnier than unhappiness" as Nell said in *Endgame*. Perhaps Winnie's clinging to a fake happiness explains why this might well be the darkest of Beckett's plays. Ultimately, we (the audience) don't "laugh wildly inmidst severest woe." We laugh the "stifled laughter" of those witnessing an ingenious performance of an ecology of mind spiraled out of control among the remainders and ruins of the "wonderful lines" left behind by an entirely disinherited language.[42]

5

COSMOGRAPHICAL MEDITATIONS ON THE IN/HUMAN

The Lost Ones

The effect of this climate on the soul is not to be underestimated.
—Samuel Beckett, *The Lost Ones*

In a short piece titled "Scapeland," included in *The Inhuman*, Jean-François Lyotard philosophizes on imaginary land- and soulscapes: uninhabitable spaces envisioned along the lines of a Western philosophy of space ranging from Aristotle to Kant and beyond.[1] In this context, he quotes Kant's reflection upon the transference of the soul to a standpoint of difference: "The soul is transferred to a quite different standpoint, so to speak, and from it sees all objects differently."[2] Lyotard calls this condition of the soul *vesania* or "systematic" madness.[3] Such "madness" emerges from a radical encounter with otherness in which one loses all familiar ground, categorical frameworks, or modes of perception and experiences a profound ontological and epistemological insecurity. This fundamental disorientation is not unlike the social death one suffers during the initial encounters of radical otherness in certain fieldwork experiences.[4] It is such a condition, one might argue, that Samuel Beckett's *The Lost*

Ones induces in its readers, albeit in a form far more radical that the one envisioned by Kant and Lyotard.

The Lost Ones opens like a play with stage directions for an eerie scene, evoking an abstract notion of space resonating with Dante's *Purgatorio*: "ABODE WHERE LOST bodies roam each searching for its lost one. Vast enough for search to be in vain. Narrow enough for flight to be in vain. Inside a flattened cylinder fifty metres round and sixteen high for the sake of harmony. The light. Its dimness. Its yellowness."[5]

Minutely constructed according to geometrical shapes and measurements, this cylindrical space is populated with an abject group of two hundred languishing and vanquished humans whose culture seems to be organized according to an elusive order, if not an unfamiliar harmony the principles of which have yet to be discovered. Dejection, futility, and a sense of loss pervade the mood in the cylinder. Did Beckett have the old Christian definition of the human as "a village of 200 souls" in mind when he populated his abode with the remnants of two hundred humans at their vanishing point?[6] Their naked bodies—only "flesh and bone subsist"—roam in futile search, some in perpetual motion, some climbing a ladder, others sedentary and immobile. The cylinder measures "some twelve million [centimetres] of total surface, contains niches and alcoves, sunk as cavities in the wall above "an imaginary line running midway between floor and ceiling." The abode is described by an anonymous disembodied voice bent on scientific observation, recording spaces and movements, harmony, and its disruptions. The flattened cylinder, we read, is "fifty meters round and sixteen high for the sake of harmony. (What harmony, we wonder?) The ladders, sole remaining objects in the abode, "are propped against the wall without regard to harmony." Harmony seems to be generated by irregularity rather than symmetry. The niches and alcoves, we are told, "are disposed in irregular quincunxes roughly ten meters in diameter and cunningly out of line. Such harmony only he can relish whose long experience and detailed knowledge of the niches are such as to permit a perfect mental image of the entire system. But it is doubtful that such a one exists."[7]

Who speaks about this distant abode and its mysterious location in an unknown space? The ominous, virtually untranslatable French title of Beckett's piece is *Le depeupleur*. Who is this *depeupleur* who, by virtue of his appearance in the title, marks a central perspective in Beckett's text? Alain Badiou describes him as a *singularizer*, someone who functions as a defining other, arguing that each searcher is on a quest to find his or her *depeupleur*: "It is everyone's proper other, one who singularizes and rips one out of anonymity."[8] If Badiou is right, the title would refer to an anonymous Other, one who never receives an incorporation as a character in Beckett's imaginary world. But one could also see the *depeupleur* as one who "de-peoples," who orphans a place—as the equally ominous German translation *Der Verwaiser* suggests. Finally, we could see him as the anonymous narrator who functions not as a character, but as a virtual organizer of this posthuman space, suggesting perhaps that the space and its population have a particular virtuality of their own, imagined into existence as it were by the organizer's computing eye. Necessary to conceive the harmony of the cylinder's construction, the computing eye is attuned to a virtual order invisible to the *eye of flesh*. Beckett, in fact, plays with distinct layers of virtuality. As the author, the one who authorizes the piece, he projects the abode as the virtual artifice of a closed cylinder, suspended in a "vast space of time impossible to measure."[9] In addition, he chooses a disembodied narrative voice that is figured as a computing eye able to perceive and record an order that is invisible to material eyes.

In the vein of current philosophical thought, one could therefore see Beckett's abode as a virtualization of posthuman characters living in the end times. In contrast, for example, to narratives of science fiction that figure the posthuman in the mode of a presumed reality of the future, Beckett insists on a future that is merely virtual in the sense that it is presented as the effect of a thought experiment. To the extent that one could perceive the lost ones as the last humans and the narrative agency as already posthuman, the thought experiment posits itself within a transitional space between the human and the posthuman. Many markers in the text evoke the sense of an ending, if not a future that announces the end of the human, as we know it. "It is perhaps the end of their abode."[10] "It is perhaps the end of all."[11] "But enough will always subsist to spell for this little people the extinction soon or late of its remaining fires."[12] Moreover, the piece ends with a glimpse on the last state of the cylinder and the end of the "little people:" "Hushed in the same breadth the faint stridulence mentioned above whence suddenly such silence as to drown all the faint breathings together. So much roughly speaking for the last state of the cylinder and of this little people of searchers one first of whom if a man in some unthinkable past for the first time bowed his head if this notion is maintained."[13]

What, then, does this apocalyptic vision convey of a posthuman people whose unthinkable past might have been that of mankind? Are they virtual remnants of humans who already languish beyond the end times in the confinement of a cylinder hovering above earth? Describing this utterly foreign lifeworld in a tone oscillating between quasi-objective observation and philosophical reflection, the narrative agency is figured as that of a cultural outsider, an ethnographer of sorts, albeit one who, while recording an alien culture, entirely depends upon his own perceptions and inferences. The "little people" seem neither to use a spoken or written language nor to be aware of or affected by an observer's presence. They either languish in supreme indifference or implode in rare outbursts of sudden violence. The narrative agency presumes a total vision of the cylinder that escapes its inhabitants. David Porush identifies the narrative voice as an "omniscient intelligence" that has imagined the cylinder into being, and Hugh Kenner speaks of "the voice from universal space."[14] To be perceived, the harmony of the cylinder's construction would, as we read, require an observer capable of projecting a perfect mental image of the entire system. The narrator thus projects the cylinder as a voluminous, yet virtually closed system whose "perception" depends upon a faculty of holistic vision requiring a virtual (posthuman?) eye rather than a corporeal eye pertaining to an embodied agency. Moreover, perception is not facilitated by solid objects but by virtual frontiers: "The bed of the cylinder comprises three distinct zones separated by clear-cut mental or imaginary frontiers invisible to the eye of flesh."[15] Space is thus "de-composed" into a virtual space with virtual boundaries, yet as rigorously conceived as any material space with solid frontiers. (I am playing with Beckett's sense of composition to create the space of "the lost ones." Beckett goes at great length to describe the abode's composition, but then he de-composes the space into a virtual space.) Composition and de-composition work together like yin and yang.

A disembodied narrative voice displays the vision attuned to this space, recording the scene in sequential aperçus. Rather than developing a quasi-realistic ethnography of the lost ones' alien culture, this voice presents us with a sequence of serial aperçus that view the cylinder from alternating perspectives. These aperçus cast brief spotlights onto different levels of abstraction such as spatial organization and cultural code, as well as different temporal frames culminating in an aperçu of the cylinder's last state. Instead of supplementing each other to form an integrated account of the lost ones' spatiotemporal and cultural organization, these aperçus convey the tentative mode of an observing voice that not only underscores its dependence on speculation but also doubts the very viability of the words and notions at its disposition. The narrative thus retains the lost ones' irreducible otherness, exhibiting but a series of hypothetical concretizations of a culture that is already cast in a mode of virtuality in the first place. In this vein, the narrative proceeds from a "first aperçu of the abode" to a "first aperçu of the climbers' code" and ends with an aperçu of "the last state of the cylinder."[16]

At the beginning of the text, the recording voice is attuned to vision, describing the consequences of the dim, yellow light for the "searching eye." Next, the voice attunes itself to touch and sound, describing the consequences of the cylinder's climate for the skin. Exposed to a temperature that oscillates between extremes of hot and cold in a rhythm of about four seconds, the skin shrivels, causing bodies to "brush together with a rustle of dry leaves." As the skin is reduced to sensations caused by involuntary contact or the impact of temperature, the ear is reduced to diminished sounds, numbed by a floor and walls of solid rubber. The tactile and the auditory converge in the "thud of bodies striking against one another," accompanied by the "silence of the steps, the "rustling of nettles," and the "indescribable sound of a kiss."[17] The last state of the cylinder and the end times of its languishing inhabitants is thus marked by extreme climate conditions that may recall visions of the earth and its extreme weather conditions due to climate change. We wonder if the lost ones might even be climate refuges now confined in the dire sanctuary offered by the cylinder.

Later the "soul" is introduced by "the effect of the climate on the soul." The soul suffers less than the skin, we hear, but then the voice immediately displaces its attention onto the skin that continues "none the less feebly to resist," more efficiently so than the eye that succumbs to "nothing short of blindness." This displacement, however, follows the logic of a gaze that perceives the soul in its inscriptions on the body. The "feeble resistance of the skin" is matched by a "feeble resistance of the soul," in which we detect a "slight taint of pathos" in the remainder of the human ("stirrings still").[18] It is this feeble resistance that inserts a vibration of difference into the cylinder's order of things and into the narrator's order of words and phrases. And it is in relation to this vibration of difference that the narrative voice becomes less secure, and more tentative in speculation, tone, and choice of words. Simply recording the certitudes of the cylinder, observation seems virtually infallible, but interpretation and language are prone to human error and to the erosion or obsolescence of familiar notions. Yet even the cylinder's certitudes are imbued with mystery: "For in the cylinder alone are certitudes to be found and without nothing but mystery."[19]

The text's holistic vision or "central computing eye" also becomes the organizing principle for a syncretistic reading that follows the textual and figural movements through space and language, even probing the mystery of its certitudes.[20] After all, even as it is organized as a central computing eye, the narrative voice in *The Lost Ones* is not the voice of a cyborg or an artificial intelligence that generates the data in the cylinder. Beckett seems rather to use this voice to tease out the paradox of an ineradicable enmeshment between body and soul, albeit without reducing the radical difference between the compilation of data and the recording of the soul's stirrings. In "Can Thought Go on Without a Body?" Lyotard notes: "If you think you're describing thought when you describe a selecting and tabulating of data, you're silencing truth. Because data aren't given, but givable, and selection isn't choice. Thinking, like writing or painting, is almost no more than letting a givable come towards you."[21]

For Beckett's narrator, however, the division between a cold tabulation of data and an artistic hospitality to animated truth no longer holds. This narrator is first and foremost a poet of the unknowable, of a presence that can be grasped viscerally and witnessed but not yet, if ever, understood. A poetics of minute recording seems to be the only mode to speak about this alien world. Cold data become animated by a vision that traces alien life where it seems most inconceivable. In this respect the abode can be seen as an experimental system *par excellence* in which the narrator records life like an ethnographer who at every step resists the temptation to reduce the alien to the familiar. As an imaginary ethnography that displays a vision of the future, *The Lost Ones* exhibits an ethics of generative epistemological doubt that opens itself to irreducible otherness by approaching it through approximation, attunement, and mindful speculation. This ethics requires a methodology and voice in which the discursive accumulation and recording of data is translated into animated figuration. Poetry alone seems adequate to witness an alien form of life that bears enough traces of the familiar to solicit human response and compassion, yet ultimately escapes familiar categories of comprehension.

In *Discours, Figure,* Lyotard insists that in literary language the relationship between discourse and figure cannot be reduced to purely linguistic operations because it is also generated under the impact of the primary process.[22] Primary process is driven by the force of affect and desire, inscribing the stirrings of the soul into the very forms of discourse and figuration. In *The Lost Ones*, the operations of the primary process seem to infiltrate those very descriptions of the cylinder that seem to be, on the surface, "coldly intent on all these data and evidences."[23] Beckett even teases his readers by mocking the cold distance of objective observation through insertions of barely perceptible errors and contradictions into the data, recognizable only to those readers who enter the narrator's game of mathematics, geometry, and computation. These mathematical *errors* are the equivalent of the narrator's many ungrammatical sentences, signaling not only the bold use of poetic license from linguistic or scientific codification but also the operation of a primary process sensibility that dedifferentiates language and its rules for purposes of poetic recomposition.

Relying on the traces of affect and desire, this technique prepares the ground for the intense affective cathexis elicited by Beckett's text. Mediated by the poetic voice, the subliminal inscription of affect onto the body of language exerts an intense appeal to the senses, evoking visualizations of bodies moving through or frozen in space, tactile sensations of heat and cold, sounds of clashing bodies and rustling dried skin. The choice of a narrative voice that operates as a computing eye creates a particular compression of discourse and figuration in which the figurative force of words and the rhythmical force of syntax convene to generate an appeal that transcends the visual sense, encompassing sound, touch, and smell. This intricate interplay between discourse and figure can be grasped only if one is attentive to the condensations, displacements, repetitions, ruptures, and folds that organize the computing eye, signaling both the operation and the scrupulous artistic recrafting of the primary process in Beckett's poetic language. In this process, the recording of cold data of the end time turns into a true poetics of the end.

This also affects the attunement of the poetic voice to the world it describes. Far from being reduced to the distance of a cold recording of data, the narrative voice becomes, on the contrary, highly sensitive to, if not intensely invested in, the culture of the "little people" it bespeaks in its discourse. Accordingly, the migration of the searchers and climbers is embedded in a rudimentary narrative, reflecting upon existential conditions such as the passion to search, endurance of privation, abandonment beyond recall, and horror of contact. At the same time, the narrative also records primordial manifestations of affect and instinctual behavior such as sudden surges of violence or occasional impulses to copulate. The most remarkable remainder of human life in the cylinder, however, is an unfathomable resilience that fuels the lost ones' persistent attachment to minimal forms of being. It is the visual and sensual order of the cylinder that conveys its emotional attunement to existential human remainders, establishing a distinctly compassionate mood even within the poetic abstractions of a detached tone of voice that records, in a mode of measured objectivity, this cosmic universe of lost souls. At times, it even seems as if the narrative voice, fearful of an all-too human pathos, needs to guard itself against an excess of attunement: "And the thinking being coldly intent on all these data and evidences could scarcely escape at the close of his analysis the mistaken conclusion that instead of speaking of the vanquished with the slight taint of pathos attaching to the term it would be more correct to speak of the blind and leave it at that."[24]

Objectivity, then, is posited in the text as a necessary yet ultimately unattainable goal. It's necessary to remain mindful of the pitfalls of anthropocentric reductions, but unattainable because the remainder of the human is all too pervasive and ever prone to attaching a "slight taint of pathos" to words and images. Reading *The Lost Ones* therefore requires a careful attunement to the nuances of voice and timbre created by the minute vibrations of difference. To return to Kant's statement, it is as if the act of reading transfers the soul to the narrator's alien vision, displacing the reader into an utterly foreign space that radically decomposes, transforms, and then reconfigures familiar modes of perception. This transmission of *vesania*, in turn, generates as a paradoxical effect the emergence of singular intensities, if not the sudden eruption of affect.

The resistance of the soul as the remainder of the human thus displays an obstinate resilience in a discourse bent on recording a vanishing and vanquished world in its end times. Remainders of human pathos cling to vision as much as to words. Periodically, the rhythms and movements of bodies and words are transformed into a verbal still life of sorts, fixing the imaginary eye on a "picturesque detail," thus causing the emergence of a scene of eerie beauty and terror. Imagine sedentary searchers flattening themselves with their backs to the wall while a young woman with white hair, eyes closed in abandonment, mechanically clasps to her breast "a mite" who strains away. Imagine "the woman vanquished," squatting against the wall with her head between her knees, her legs in her arms and her red hair, tarnished by the light, hanging to the ground.[25] Imagination dead imagine.[26] If a "slight taint of pathos" attaches to the voice that records these visions, it is because without it the text would be empty, inhuman. Bizarre, if not exotic, these scenes bespeak, as the narrator suggests, the condition of the human at its ultimate vanishing point.

It is the eerie beauty of prose and images in *The Lost Ones* that determines its unique mood and the transference the text elicits. In *On Beckett*, Alain Badiou argues that Beckett attempts to "seize in beauty the non-prescriptible fragments of existence."[27] Badiou is most attuned to Beckett's work when he chooses beauty as an entryway. "It is this beauty that tells us what it is that Beckett wishes to save. This is because the destiny of beauty, and in particular the beauty that Beckett aims at, is to separate. To separate appearance . . . from the universal core of experience."[28] And we may add that in Beckett's work it is the multifarious visions of the ultimate separation, the end, yet also the impossibility ever to grasp the end that forms the core of experience, be it the mortality of the species that inhabit the earth or the mortality of the planet. "The enduring patience of life and prose only exists for the immortal arousal of what fixes in beauty the possibility of an end, both as the interruption of the half-light and as the conjoined finalities of existence and saying," Badiou writes.[29] Considering the finalities of saying, however, everything can only be ill seen, ill said. What happens to thought and saying after the body ceases to exist? This is a question Beckett's characters keep reiterating obsessively, albeit indirectly, in the recursive loops of their discourse.

In "Can Thought Go on Without a Body?" Lyotard generates a different, albeit related, vision of the human from the vantage point of postmodernism's cultural imaginary with its survival myths and related efforts to create an artificial intelligence able to operate without a body. Lyotard argues that to survive the extinction of the planet—perhaps in the wake of a nuclear if not solar explosion—such a human intelligence will have to carry the force of desire within it on its interstellar voyage. But then he adds, "it isn't any human desire to know or transform reality that propels this techno-science, but a cosmic circumstance."[30] Does cosmic circumstance propel the emergence of the posthuman? Critics have already imagined the narrative agency in *The*

Lost Ones to figure as a disembodied artificial intelligence. One could indeed envision the narrator as inhabiting a posthuman space, looking back at the last vanquished humans secluded in a cylinder that is, like the nautilus Roland Barthes envisions in *Mythologies*, organized according to a "self-sufficient cosmogony, which has its own categories, its own time, space, fulfillment and even existential principle."[31] Yet somehow all these attempts at allegorizing this alien Beckettian world seem too referential and literalist, reducing both its mystery and unparalleled poetic depth. Beckett creates a virtual world emerging from a uniquely human imagination, albeit one incommensurable with anything we know.

No wonder, then, that *The Lost Ones* commands such an intense hold on a cultural imaginary haunted by the viable end of the human species and a related philosophical thought bent on conceptualizing the conditions of living in the end times. As always, Beckett draws on a rich arsenal of philosophical histories, transforming their distilled core elements into an alchemy of poetic abstraction. In one of *The Lost One*'s most extensive intertextual plays, Beckett constructs the transitional space between the human and the posthuman according to Dante's *Purgatorio*, that is, one of the most familiar cosmogonies in Western literature. The miniature cosmos of the cylinder with its caverns, for example, forms a distant echo of the cornices of Dante's Purgatory. Plunged in an intense gloom, the cylinder exudes a sensation of yellow, "not to say of sulfur,"[32] invoking the threat of hell to be faced by lost ones who are but remainders of human bodies and soul. In this context, Beckett's insistence on the soul resonates with the hope of a beyond—an afterlife that succeeds the purgatory—yet the narrative agency relegates such hope to the "amateurs of myth."[33] At the center in Dante's *Purgatorio* is the fourth cornice where the "lost ones" are punished for gloominess and indifference—the "defects" of love. As in *Purgatorio*, in the cylinder "gloominess and indifference" periodically lead to "zeal and fervent affection." Every so often, some of Beckett's vanquished resurrect to perform vain attempts at copulation, almost as if their bodies continued involuntarily to perform the action of a memory or instinctual impulse encoded from time immemorial. As we recall from Dante, love can be of two sorts: natural or of the soul. While natural love, for Dante, is unerring, love of the soul may err in respect to object or degree. Beckett's lovers are caught in desiccated bodies whose "hampering effect on the work of love" condemns them to perform a grotesque spectacle of "making unmakable love."[34] This is the spectacle in which the body and the skin converge with the soul: "This desiccation [effect of the climate on the skin] of the envelope robs nudity of much of its charm as pink turns grey and transforms into a rustling of nettles the natural succulence of flesh against flesh. . . . The spectacle then is one to be remembered of frenzies prolonged in pain and hopelessness long beyond what even the most gifted lovers can achieve in camera."[35]

Beckett's lovers err in both object and degree. The meetings between objects become indeterminate, contingent upon movements through space. Lovers are coming together without their knowledge, only "in virtue of the law of probabilities. The chance encounters between futile lovers who "search again neither glad nor even sorry" produce the "same vivacity of reaction as to the end of the world."[36]

The temporal ambiguity of this phrase is crucial because it leaves in suspense whether the end has already happened or is pending. Presupposing the end of the world—past or future— the searchers are on a quest, "darkward bound."[37] Prone to myth, they cling to the hope, sustained from "time immemorial by rumor of a way out beyond which "the sun and other stars would still be shining."[38] "So much for the inviolable zenith where for amateurs of myth lies hidden a way out to earth and sky."[39] This phrase, too, insists on ambiguity. Does the "way out to earth" suggest that the "little people" were suspended in space, somewhere above the earth as if in a futuristic artificial satellite world, an interstellar nautilus that may once have functioned as a galactic version of Noah's ark? The privation in the cylinder would then not only be the tangible material dearth of floor space but, at a more subliminal level, nothing less than the deprivation of a cosmos—an inhabitable universe bound by constellations and nourished by a sun.[40] In this sense, the quest of these "amateurs of myth" is cosmological—a residue of an "old craving" that disrupts in irregular fits their blind crawling in search of nothing, or, *if this notion were maintained*, the "all of nothing."[41]

Beyond the end of the world as we know it, the lost ones populate this "all of nothing" in futile quest or abandonment. We find these "little people of searchers" left in an "abandonment beyond recall," gravitating motionless toward an unthinkable future when "dark descends and at the same instant the temperature comes to rest not far from the freezing point."[42] This apocalyptic vision keeps readers suspended in this "all of nothing," attuning them to the condition of the vanquished who await the cylinder's eventual depopulation as suggested by the *depeupleur*. Abandonment beyond recall then refers not only to the cylinder that hovers somewhere in outer space, forever disconnected from the distant earth; it also refers to the lost ones themselves, each of which is encased in the catastrophic loneliness of a futile search for their lost one.

In 1965, one year before the composition of *The Lost Ones*, Beckett wrote *Imagination Dead Imagine*, a three-page piece he insisted was a novel. "No trace anywhere of life," this piece begins, and there too the narrator designs a highly artificial space, a vault, three feet in diameter and three in depth. Lying on the ground are two white bodies, each in a semicircle. The light, without any visible source, is of a glaring white, casting no shadows, exuding a strong heat until it changes in pauses of varying length to complete darkness with temperatures approaching the freezing point. Countless rhythms mark these passages from white and heat to black and cold, enclosing the two bodies in absolute stillness. "Hold a mirror to their lips, it mists," we read. And then: "they might well pass for inanimate but for the left eyes which at incalculable intervals suddenly open wide and gaze in unblinking exposure long beyond what is humanly possible."[43]

Once again, we are returned to the question: What do these Beckettian human worlds in the end times, if not beyond the end times, tell us? Are they alien worlds bespeaking a condition beyond what is humanly possible, yet resonant of an order of the human remembered from time immemorial? Does Beckett write some unfathomable history of the future, some imaginary ethnography of the posthuman? "Leave them there, sweating and icy, there is better elsewhere,"[44] the narrator says of the two bodies in the vault. Then he continues: "No, life ends and no, there is nothing elsewhere, and no question now or ever finding again that white speck lost in whiteness, to see if they still lie still in the stress of that storm, or of a worse storm, or in the black dark for good, or the great whiteness unchanging, and if not what they are doing."[45]

What are the philosophical and epistemological implications of such visions of an ending, and what do they contribute to a contemporary archaeology of thought on the human and posthuman? Beckett's scene recalls the solar storm raging before the solar explosion invoked in Lyotard's vision of the posthuman. It also recalls Foucault's copiously cited conclusion at the end of *The Order of Things*, published in 1966, the same year as *The Lost Ones*:

> As the archeology of our thought easily shows, man is an invention of recent date. And one perhaps nearing its end. If those arrangements were to disappear as they appeared, if some event of which we can at the moment do no more than sense the possibility—without knowing either what its form will be or what it promises—were to cause them to crumble . . . then one can certainly wager that man would be erased, like a face drawn in sand at the edge of the sea.[46]

The recent invention and possibly pending erasure of man in the vast expanse of the universe's history introduces a notion of scale that resonates with Beckett's archeology of thought. Beckett's scale extends from microscopic to planetary scale, from the "white speck lost in whiteness" to the space beyond the cave where "the sun and other stars would still be shining."[47] We are confronted with a poetic vision suggestive of miniature thought and minimal thought. Yet it is a minimalism that enfolds magnitude, a "white speck lost in whiteness" that enfolds the implicate order of planetary thought, a posthuman compression of cosmic vision. It is miniature in its scrupulous attention to detail—the white speck lost in whiteness—an attention so scrupulous that it perceives more than meets the "eye of flesh." It is minimal in its faithfulness to an ever-increasing scarcity of parameters, its movement toward reduction and compression: the "all of nothing." It is planetary thought in the emergence of a vast expanse from minute detail, cosmic in this thought's investment in a universe *in which the sun and other stars would still be shining*. Thus, combining microscopic and planetary vision, Beckett attunes his readers to expand the scale of their imagination beyond the familiar human range. It is an indispensable attunement needed to comprehend the threat of extinction propelled by events that exceed the scale of human imagination or "hyperobjects" such as nuclear catastrophes or climate change, as Timothy Morton calls them in his philosophical reflections on "ecology after the end of the world."[48]

If a "slight taint of pathos" attaches to this reading—as it does to Beckett's (and, for that matter, Lyotard's and Foucault's) vision of the posthuman—it is because the affects inscribed in Beckett's voices are contagious, soliciting a transference that must first absorb and then move through them. Beckett engineers the emergence of soulscapes out of the void of his virtual *scapelands*: imaginary, alien and vanishing spaces that are evoked through words that grasp the effects of unearthly light, inconceivably foreign sounds, and unbearably extreme temperatures on body and soul. Beckett's language generates textual vision with the craft of a theatrical lighting engineer. Understanding light's function in transcoding body and soul and in producing minute vibrations of difference, he generates light effects from within language. The narrator's eye, whose power of perception surpasses that of "the eye of flesh," seems able to sustain a vision of the lost ones in the dark, almost as if they were endowed with bioluminescence or an imaginable psychic equivalent of it. This may be an effect of the poetic force of Beckett's language that generates a sense of the paradoxical resilience of light, as if the trace of a memory of luminescence will forever remain inscribed in the final dark as the last memory trace of past human life.

These vibrations of difference that produce the light effects in Beckett's visual universe also register in the depth and scale of poetic language. Understanding the function of timbre,

Beckett generates a voice that pulverizes language until its particles aggregate in unforeseeable ways. It is a pulverization, we could argue in a Deleuzian vein, which dissolves the molar organization of language in order to generate molecular language effects that resonate with the dissolution of molar forms in the cylinder and the simultaneous persistence of life at a molecular register.[49] These pulverizing operations of difference also recall the Kantian experimental displacement of the soul from the *sensorium communi*, alluded to in the epigraph, which Lyotard calls *vesania*. The effects of this induction of *vesania* are subtle and transformative. It is not that we are made to see what the text evokes visually, to hear the sounds it describes, or to feel the temperatures. Rather, Beckett's language breaks through the familiar registers of vision, sound, and touch, allowing us to see or hear something we have never seen or heard before. In Deleuzian fashion, we could almost say that we are made to hear with the eye and see with the ear of a schizo.

This induction of a systematic madness—to return to Lyotard's phrase—requires a subliminal transference between text and reader. It involves a process that resembles Paul Klee's notion of artistic vision Lyotard refers to in *Discours, Figure*: "to see with one eye, to feel with the other."[50] At the level of sound, it also resembles what Lyotard says about the "internal ear," namely that it registers the "unthought of the ear."[51] The fact that Beckett induces the emergence of an internal ear and eye not through the art forms primarily attuned to these sense organs but through language is crucial. Literature as the sole artistic medium that participates in all senses allows for a transference that transforms their very relationship, thus inscribing itself simultaneously into body and soul. The sensual effects of vision and sound that

Beckett evokes might be invisible and inaudible, but they are imaginable, and the very act of imagining them transforms the available registers. The immateriality of textual vision, sound, and touch has material corporeal effects. Lyotard, however, is also right in asserting: "reading is understanding/hearing (*entendre*) and not seeing."[52] We do not see what the text describes, but its visions and sounds decompose and retune our modes of perception, while the timbre of voice assumes nearly a tactile quality, touching us at the level of something that seems utterly familiar but has never been thought—an "unthought known."[53]

While Beckett's technique presupposes the dedefinition and dedifferentiation of the familiar orders of the *sensorium communi*, it also depends upon the minute vibrations of difference that introduce negentropy into an otherwise entropic universe.[54] While "amateurs of myth" may simply remain caught up in the phantasm of a vanishing world or the myth of a way out, Beckett's text induces a larger vision, attuned to the emergence of difference and negentropy. Vanishing in Beckett is tied to and inseparable from emergence. The decomposition of a familiar world releases the unthought, however painful its emergence. The failing vision of "the eye of flesh" becomes the precondition for the emergence of an immaterial, not to say inward, gaze able to perceive invisible harmonies and dissonances. Dedifferentiation of familiar boundaries, categories, words, and worlds generates the emergence of differentiation at another scale, as if the human is perceived from a macroscopic or microscopic distance that dissolves the units of body and mind. We witness a compression of dedifferentiation and differentiation in a vision highly sensitized to minute detail and minimal difference, or the production of molecular language effects, that defines the signature of Beckett's work. It is this compression that generates the emergence of what Lyotard calls an *event*. An event, for

Lyotard, presupposes an indeterminacy that facilitates the emergence of an unthought. What he says in "Scapeland" about the freeing of landscape from definition—note "*depaysant*" and "*depeupleur*"—is true for Beckett's freeing of human abodes as well: "Indeterminacy exercises a gentle violence over the determinate, so as to make it give up its QUOD. And it is not I, nor anyone, who begets this non-place."[55]

Such "gentle violence over the determinate" marks Beckett's texts throughout. Form, grammar, and semantics no longer domesticate the matter of language; they prevent it from becoming consumable by subjecting it to the prerogatives of understanding. Lyotard says the desire simply to wander through a landscape authorizes "a transfer of material powers to scents, to the tactile quality of the ground, of walls, of plants. Beckett performs such a transfer of material powers to language, rendering its very materiality tactile, sonorous, and visual, thus producing effects in language that touch those able to receive it at a molecular level of sensation. Literary form itself is no longer instrumental but material in Beckett's texts, and its materialization causes an estrangement resembling the one Lyotard calls an "intimist exoticism." The uncanny quality of Beckett's texts results from the paradoxical use of such estrangement to evoke the most intimately familiar abyss of the human. As a result, these texts generate a mood that is at once utterly strange and utterly familiar—"intimist exoticism." "States of mind are states of spiritual matter,"[56] says Lyotard. Beckett's skill in generating abstraction out of utmost concretion and vice versa always aspires—like his characters—to transcend the outmoded binary division of mind and matter that was often so abused to demarcate the boundaries of the human.

Beckett's explorations of human liminality may well have been the true inspiration of Lyotard's vision of the *in/human* in

"Scapeland." Lyotard seems to credit Beckett when he describes the face in a photograph of Beckett at eighty as a landscape "parched with drought, the flesh defied. And in the wrinkles, in the creases where the pupils flash with anger, a cheerful incredulity. So the mummy is still alive. Just." Referring to the "MELANCHOLIA of all landscapes," Lyotard says they leave the mind desolate, exposing the "wretchedness of the soul rubbed raw by the tiderace of matter."[57] Like Lyotard, Beckett invokes philosophical discourses of the soul to explore the condition of the end times. However, while Beckett invokes the soul throughout *The Lost Ones*, it is not without also recalling the "slight taint of pathos" that inevitably attaches to the use of the term. Drawing on posthumanist French philosophers and writers ranging from Deleuze and Derrida to Lyotard that invoke the soul in their mapping of the posthuman, Beckett constructs the soul of the lost ones as a site of a transference between the human and its Other. One can hardly avoid recalling the infamous history of Western discourses that constructed the soul as the site of the most unabashed ethno- and anthropocentrism, used to expel indigenous people, along with animals, from the community of humans. Mindful of this history, Lyotard defines the making of humans—their "soul-making"—as a process of violent domestication.

The bodies of Beckett's lost ones seem to bear the traces of such violence. However, Beckett also invokes the soul of the vanquished as a last site of resilience. The soul with its resilience seems to be a testing ground for the last remainders of humane reflexes under the experimental conditions of a closed cylinder: the abode of vanquished humans. Lyotard coins the word "*l'immonde*" to speak of a place that causes the *in/human* condition of "little sensations" (a term Lyotard borrows from Cézanne) to which affect is reduced in states of "inner desolation."[58] The lost ones' "abandonment beyond recall" is reminiscent of such inner desolation.[59] However, the insistence on minute "vibrations of difference"[60] in Beckett signals that "little sensations" may also emerge from the resilience of life under the conditions of an "*l'immonde*." "Unworlding" might be another term to invoke the vanishing and vanquishing of the lost ones, including the contraction of their inner spaces to little sensations that manifest as the last but most resilient stirrings of the soul. As a metaphor to describe the end times, unworlding also refers to the gradual vanishing of worlds before the end.

The remaining inner spaces of psychic life with their little sensations and vibrations of difference that reach beyond conscious perception, involving the undoing of the boundaries of self, make Beckett's "little people" seem as if they emerged from an "unthought known," creating a mood utterly strange yet strangely familiar. To inhabit these spaces, one needs to traverse the boundaries of consciousness and thought, opening them toward the unthought. "The unthought hurts because we're comfortable in what's already thought,"[61] Lyotard affirms. Pain is endemic to Beckett's world. It is endemic to his vanquished characters languishing in their abandonment beyond recall, or in the disembodied narrative voices obsessively trying to think the unthought. Pain afflicts his actors when they are forced to inhabit bodies pushed beyond known postures,[62] and even his readers when they try to attune themselves to his alien imaginary worlds.

Encountering the unthought requires either a loss of self or an expansion of self to a different scale that enfolds the inscriptions of sensations into our bodies—sensations that have never been registered at the level of conscious thought, and that are therefore operative as an "unthought known." "The self is left behind," Lyotard writes, "sloughed off, definitely too conventional, too sure of itself and over-arrogant in the way it puts things into scale."[63] As the self vanishes, emotions devolve into sensations and intensities. Relationality shrinks to minimal reflex. Fraternity, the narrator notes for example, is an outlived sentiment as foreign to the lost ones "as to butterflies."[64] In this sense, Beckett's text is about scale, too. The microscopic perception and planetary vision used to create an experimental imaginary world is matched by a micropsychology that explores the "soul" in its raw states, its intensities, without the support of a scaffold or armor for the self. Raw souls appear off-scale and thrust into cosmic abandonment.

Lyotard links these states with a new understanding of poetry or the poetic, one marked by an "implosion of forms themselves."[65] Rather than generating alternative "ways of worldmaking,"[66] Beckett's poetry engages in unmaking the world, or, as I called it earlier, in "unworlding." In this very process, he generates not an alternative world, but a new way of being in the world and in language. Beckett's language implodes the mind along with the forms it harbors to organize its perceptions according to codes and laws. "*L'immonde*," "*l'informe*," and the "*in/human*" are terms Lyotard uses to refer to these states of dedifferentiation, dis-*inform*-ation, or dissolution of the self. But with Beckett we must be careful to avoid confusing the "*informe*" with the undifferentiated or the unformed. Beckett's "*informe*" is an implosion of form generated from within the symbolic order of language, in fact, unthinkable from without.

At the same time, *The Lost Ones* projects an imaginary world made of words that creates the effects of an implosion of the self and the very forms of self-organization. Nobody reveals with more clarity than Beckett that such implosion of forms is possible only through a most rigorous and refined shaping and crafting of what one could call, with Lyotard, the "matter in thought."⁶⁷ But it is a highly artificial and artistic shaping that reaches beyond both the descriptive and the categorical. Undoing the very conventions through which we organize our perception of the world, this "poetry" exposes us to an ontological abyss, generating the vertiginous mental spirals, the delirious void so familiar to Beckett's readers. Far from being presymbolic or prelinguistic, this artistic practice or poetics continues to rely entirely on craft, even while undoing the history of its conventional uses. Beckett's poetics of the end times renews the texture of the written word, the architecture of space, and the intricacies of coloration and timbre. "How could we capture the breath of wind that sweeps the mind into the void . . . if not in the texture of the written word?" asks Lyotard.⁶⁸ How could we capture that "white speck lost in whiteness" invoked at the end of *Imagination Dead Imagine*, if not in the texture of Beckett's writing or the architecture of his theater? Poetry, Lyotard insists, must emerge from the superplenitude of the void, "otherwise it is merely a staging [*mise en scene*] and a mobilization [*mise en oeuvre*] of the powers of language."⁶⁹

Lyotard links this poetic state with infancy and its modes of exchange with the world: "A baby must see its MOTHER's face as a landscape. Not because its mouth, fingers and gaze move over it as it blindly grasps and sucks, smiles, cries and whimpers. Not because it is 'in symbiosis' with her. . . . We should assume, rather, that the face is indescribable for the baby. It will have forgotten it, because it will not have been inscribed. . . . This mother is a mother who is a timbre 'before' it sounds, who is there 'before' the coordinates of sound, before destiny."⁷⁰ At the end of Beckett's "Fizzle 6" we read: "For an instant I see the sky, the different skies, then they turn to faces, agonies, loves, the different loves, happiness too, yes, there was that, too, unhappily. . . . No but now, now simply stay still, standing before a window, one hand on the wall, the other clutching your shirt, and see the sky, a long gaze, but no, gasps and spasms, a childhood sea, other skies, another body."[71] The "childhood sea" that emerges in many of Beckett's texts when their narrators' strive for the end is one of those soulscapes that create the "unworld" (*l'immonde*). The coordinates of "the real" dissolve into a resonance of something that may only be recalled in the vagueness of a timbre, or a mood.

The figure of the child occupies a central place in both Beckett's and Lyotard's thinking about the human. The very terms *human* and *inhuman*, Lyotard argues, must oscillate between native indetermination and instituted or self-instituting reason. The notions of the *immonde*, the *informe*, and the *inhuman* are, for Lyotard, intimately tied to the notion of the *infant*. He aligns *immonde*, *informe*, *inhuman*, and *infant* metonymically on a chain that facilitates the transcoding of the political, the cultural, the psychological, and the aesthetic. "Native indetermination," by contrast, seems constrained, "forced" into a development "where it is not mankind which is at issue, but differentiation."[72] This stance against determination, differentiation, and development is the core of Lyotard's politics and poetics. "'Development' is the ideology of the present time," he writes, "development is the very thing which takes away the hope of an alternative to the system from both analysis and practice."[73] Tapping into the resources of native indetermination is, for Lyotard, accordingly, the only form of resistance we have left. "What else remains as 'politics' except resistance to this inhuman? And what else is left to resist with but the debt which each soul has contracted with the miserable and admirable indetermination from which it was born and does not cease to be born?—which is to say, with the other inhuman? "It is the task of writing, thinking, literature, arts to venture to bear witness to it [this debt to childhood]," writes Lyotard at the conclusion of his introduction to *The Inhuman*.[74] What he propagates, then, is a poetics and politics of indeterminacy that draws on the unformulated, the undifferentiation, nonconceptuality, and indetermination of the earliest modes of a child's exchange with the world as a resource that allows one to resist the ideologies, constraints, and impositions of the symbolic order.

Conceiving his model of the "inhuman" as a form of radical antihumanism, Lyotard proclaims our very need to interrogate the "value of man."[75] His notion of the human coincides with philosophical notions of the subject in which an infant is not yet a subject until she or he enters the symbolic order. If humans were born human, Lyotard argues, it would not be possible to educate them. It is then the institutions of culture that make humans human. In this sense, literature, as Lyotard conceives it, would be a *writing against culture* rather than a form of *writing culture*.[76]

Beckett's work, however, would seem to render such a clearcut opposition obsolete. Doesn't Lyotard, despite his deep suspicion against the ideologies of conventional categorization, import here a deeply Western categorization of the subject into his model—a categorization that posits infancy as a prehuman phase? In such a model, the human proper presupposes acculturation and the entry into the symbolic order. A broader notion of the subject (and the human), however, would include infants more productively, allowing one to rethink the dynamic between the presymbolic and the symbolic in less exclusive or antagonistic terms. Beckett systematically collapses and reorganizes the boundaries between the presymbolic and the symbolic, primary and secondary process, differentiation and dedifferentiation or, for that matter, between *discours* and *figure*. Aren't the boundaries between the two spheres so malleable that maintaining a rigidly antagonistic distinction between them feeds precisely into the notion of linear development that Lyotard wants to resist? And finally, doesn't the notion that infants are not yet human repeat the fallacy of a dated historical model that relegates infants as well as indigenous people to "prehistory"?

To do justice to Lyotard, we need to view his concept of the "inhuman" in light of the ambiguous status he accords to the child in relation to culture. He distinguishes the inhumanity of the system (or the symbolic order, in Lévi-Strauss's term) from the inhumanity of infants that results from what he calls a "native lack." It is in this latter sense that he can say that what is proper to humankind is inhabited by the inhuman. Because of his use of two diametrically opposite notions of the inhuman, the boundary between the human and the inhuman oscillates for Lyotard. Precisely because the infant is not yet granted the status of human, it is "eminently the human" in a different sense. "Hostage of the adult community," the child calls on that community to become more human. If the designations of human and inhuman oscillate between "native indetermination" and "instituted reason," one may indeed conclude that all education is inhuman because it does not happen without constraint or terror.[77] Yet such a perspective requires one to view the processes that induce differentiation in the child's development exclusively under the perspective of constraint. Considering development to be the true ideology of the time, regardless of whether it applies to capitalist economy or child development, Lyotard aims his critique of postmodernism at a "metaphysics of development," that is, at development without finality or a value system attached to it.[78] In a similar vein, Lyotard rejects, at the theoretical level, conceptualization and the construction of theoretical systems (grand narratives) because of the constraints they impose, which, in turn, he once again views in terms of totalization.

This is where Beckett's work assumes a more radical dimension. Moved beyond good and evil or beyond familiar polarities more generally, differentiation and dedifferentiation emerge in Beckett's imaginary worlds from within a process of continual semiosis in which they are distinct yet inseparable. Without differentiation, infants would remain in a desolate state of native lack. Without differentiation, the "little people" in the cylinder would be frozen in the monotonous indifference of mere entropy. Vibrations of difference and picturesque details such as, for example, the two vanquished women (one with white, the other with red hair), or the mite that strains away from his mother's dried breast would become unthinkable. Without differentiation, infants would never be completely born, hovering like so many of Beckett's characters in a psychic limbo beyond life and death. Finally, without dedifferentiation they would, like other Beckett characters, approach a state of soulless automata, deprived of the pleasures and pains of drives and desires. A perspective that highlights the ambivalence of both constructive and destructive potentials of early differentiation does not ignore the power relations involved in, nor the constraints and terrors of, education. Rather, such a perspective resists the temptation to ontologize domination as a human condition. In the same vein, it also resists the temptation to reduce the structural ambivalence of differentiation to a mere ideology of development.

Politics is, for Lyotard, the resistance to the *inhuman* of a systemic development that follows the internal logic and dynamic of the system alone. He considers such resistance a "debt to childhood" and calls upon literature and philosophy to provide a thinking *from the outside* able to bear witness to this debt.[79] One would hope that, in fulfilling this function, literature and philosophy also take part in a process of differentiation not entirely bound up with power, constraint, and terror. Just as the *human* and the *inhuman* in Lyotard's sense, *differentiation* thus has a double side as well. It is not only a tool of adults for "holding the child's soul hostage," as Lyotard says, but also a tool for freeing the infant from the bondage of his/her early dependency. The infant's gradual attunement to differentiation would, for Lyotard, already be overly bound up in constraints because it would impose determination upon the indeterminate. But where would we be without the "form-giving" experience that differentiates perception and the "word-forming experience" that induces differentiation into the infant's use of sounds?[80] Wouldn't we resemble the lost ones in their wordless search?

Beckett's work bears witness to the ambivalence of indetermination, the ontological abyss, and the emergence of productivity that are linked to the indeterminate. His texts and plays expose the constraints and traps of conceptualization as well as the hegemony of a "spirit of system."[81] They also expose the wretchedness of the undifferentiation that comes with an "incomplete birth."[82] Without acculturation, differentiation and the impositions of form we would be suspended, like the Unnamable and all his imaginary clones, in an abysmal void free from the constraints of manifestation perhaps, but also deprived of an inhabitable world. In contrast to Lyotard, Beckett exposes the irresolution between the two modes of being as a curse that threatens any viable ontology. "Decomposed" and suspended in virtual space seems, in fact, to be a condition that Beckett envisions as a symptom of our impending end times.

Lyotard invokes Kant's notion of the *sensus communis* not only in his notion of the inhuman but also in his notion of aesthetics. He opposes an unmediated "community of feeling" to theories of aesthetic communication, arguing that the *sensus communis* is anterior to and can therefore not be reduced to communication and pragmatics.[83] As Lyotard reminds us, Kant attributes aesthetic feeling to the inscription of artistic/literary form on the subject. Drawing on this Kantian notion in his theory of the sublime, Lyotard argues that the feeling of the sublime resists immediate communicability and is therefore compatible with the formless, the *informe*. But we recall that, for Lyotard, the *informe* is modeled on the indifferentiation of the *infant*. There are, in other words, multiple resonances that link Lyotard's theory of the *in/human* with his aesthetics of the sublime.

A text such as Beckett's *The Lost Ones* requires a notion of aesthetic experience much broader than conscious communication and aesthetic judgement. The most subliminal forms of aesthetic experience are, as Christopher Bollas has shown, intimately related to the "unthought known," that is, the mnemonic traces of undifferentiation in infancy.[84] This is precisely why literature and the arts are capable, through subliminal processes of transference, of bearing witness to the early cultural imprints on the subject. At the same time, they are also capable of helping one to overcome some of the constraints imposed at the time. Seen in this way, we could even say that literature contributes to loosening the bonds that would otherwise keep humans hostage to their early cultural formation.

In the act of reading *The Lost Ones*, literary transference operates by experimenting with new effects, never seen, never heard, nor understood before. The alien textual world of the cylinder creates its own reference; its object is not identifiable. It also creates its own addressee: a reader's disconcerted body, invited to stretch its sensory capacities beyond measure.[85] At the same time, however, this world would not be able to touch or move us if it did not appeal to an "unthought known." We attune ourselves to Beckett's worlds because of a faint recognition of undifferentiated visual, sonorous, and tactile spaces that have left their imprint on our bodies before they encountered words and meaning, order and form, sound and sense, touch and smell. The transformation of written signifiers into sensations and moods operates via a transference that engages what Lyotard defines as the boundaries of the human, stretching them into the area of the *informe*, the *infant*, and the *inhuman*.

If this reading has highlighted the resonance between Beckett's posthuman world of "little people" and Lyotard prehuman world of infants—a resonance that supersedes their ideological difference concerning the status of differentiation—it is because both Beckett and Lyotard draw on a "polyaesthetics" that engages the body's primordial inscriptions.[86] Both are interested in the processes of transference that engage these inscriptions and transform their immaterial effects on the soul. Beckett returns to the primordial as the last remainder of the human, as that which subsists throughout space and time immemorial and continues to imprint the soul. Lyotard writes: "The 'soul' has at its disposal the only language. The body is a confused speaker: it says 'soft,' 'warm,' 'blue,' 'heavy,' instead of talking straight lines, curves, collisions and relations."[87] Perhaps this vision of a body language may suggest why the inseparable linkage between the concrete and the abstract in Beckett's work exerts such a strong appeal. "Abstraction is not a negation of form: it posits it as folded, existing only as a 'mental landscape' in the soul or in the mind, in upper altitudes," writes Deleuze in *The Fold*.[88] Beckett uses his imaginary geographies of straight lines, curves, collisions, and relations less as a geometrical discourse to map out an alien space, than as a language of the soul to map out a soulscape hitherto unknown to humans. The alien space of the cylinder with its virtual boundaries, its ruptures and folds, its passages, niches and alcoves, its vaults, caves and crypts, becomes a space of transference in which the immateriality of the soul is affected by the immateriality of the lines, curves, collisions, and relations generated by Beckett's words.

David Porush perceives the cylinder as an enormous cybernetic machine controlled from some outside source. There is, however, a ghost (or a soul) in the machine, because, as Porush asserts, "In order to understand some of the quirks and paradoxes in style and expression in Beckett's prose, *the machines of the cylinder and the text itself must be understood as ones that do not work.*"[89] While they do not work as machines, they work at a different level—that of the literary or aesthetic—as spaces that facilitate the emergence of hitherto unimagined visions and sensations that exert a unique appeal to the senses and generate an intense cathexis. Like the cylinder, Beckett's language contains niches and alcoves, and like the skin of the lost ones, it contains recesses and folds from within which we witness vibrations of difference in words and images. These vibrations open a space for the emergence of the unthought (the *impense*) in the form of an imaginary posthuman from which we may finally intuit the vast expanse of the human to come *if that notion were maintained*. This is perhaps the most subliminal transformational use of literature—a form of "soul-making" that continually reconfigures the boundaries of the human and its primordial imprints. It is also a form of soul-making supremely attuned to the ontological and epistemological insecurities that haunt those living in the end times.

CODA

Breath and the Vicissitudes of Animation

Decidedly it will never have been given to me to finish anything, except perhaps breathing. One must not be greedy.
—Samuel Beckett

The first chapter of Antonin Artaud's *The Theater and Its Double* is titled "The Theater and the Plague." Selecting the plague as his first elemental double of the theater, Artaud, like the many books on the plague he studied, is much less interested in its "morbid symptoms" than in "the demoralizing and prodigious effect produced on the victims' minds" as well as the "profound political upheavals" it generates.[1] He observes that "the only two organs really affected and injured by the plague, the brain and the lungs, are both directly dependent on the consciousness and the will."[2] This is why, focusing on what he calls "the spiritual image of the plague," Artaud links the plague to its double, the theater: "The action of theater, like that of the plague, causes the mask to fall, reveals the lie, the slackness, baseness and hypocrisy of our world; it shakes off the asphyxiating inertia of matter which invades even the clearest testimony of the senses."[3] While the COVID-19 pandemic sweeps vulnerabilities and contradictions to the surface, it also confronts us with the essentials of life and death. Teaching us how to let go, pandemics offer a lesson in the art of dying. And who, in the theater, but Samuel Beckett provides a better double for this hardest of all life lessons?

In the late 1950s, my first encounter with Samuel Beckett when *Waiting for Godot* was aired on German television transformed my life in subliminal ways that I understood only much later. As I mentioned in the introduction, Beckett became my lifelong obsession. Now, in the Beckettian world of pandemic surrealism, he became my spiritual companion. I am not the only one who takes refuge in Beckett's alien, yet all too uncannily familiar worlds. His characters mirror us with the artifices and consoling objects we have created to help us live in the end times. On May 26, the *Los Angeles Times* published an article that suggests that we are all confined "to a narrow loop of existence."[4]

Confinement is a familiar Beckettian theme. Beckett's characters are trapped in wheelchairs, urns, or trashcans. Winnie in *Happy Days* is buried in a heap of sand under the blazing desert sun. While all explore the existential conditions of confinement, the latter can assume many forms. In Beckett's work these include, first and foremost, the confinement in one's own mind as well as, differently, in one's own body. In *How It Is*, Beckett pushes this confinement even further with a male character who is creeping through mud, struggling for breath. Like Malone, the narrator is preoccupied with breath and breathing. It is the rhythm of breath that organizes the composition of *How It Is*. The lines in the text, which was originally written without punctuation marks, are eventually broken up according to the protagonist's rhythm of breath. Paul Sheehan writes: "The unpunctuated bursts of text . . . are like prosodic 'breaths,' framing the narrator's gasps as he periodically emerges from the 'familiar slime' into the mephitic air."[5] Moreover, the original French *Comment C'est*, a homophonic pun on "commencer," invokes the beginning, that is, the first breath. In the same vein, the crawling through the mud resonates with Beckett's lifelong preoccupation with prenatal memories and phantasms of incomplete birth. The journey through the mud of the birth canal is, however, already transcoded with a journey toward decomposition and death. At the same time, the text also refers to the primal mud that, almost four billion years ago, formed the ground for the emergence of the origin of life and the first breath, and that will after the last breath form the final mud of decomposition in the end times. Finally, this planetary vision that links breath to the creation of life on earth is transcoded with a vision of the creative process. The protagonist's excruciating journey through the mud is also an allusion to the creative process, that is, the striving toward form and its emergence from formlessness. In this context, the struggle for breath is also a struggle for inspiration with *spirare* serving as the link that denotes both breath and inspiration.

In his endeavor to pull himself through the mud, the protagonist of *How It Is* struggles to hear through his exhausted panting the voices that tell him what to say. Voice, too, is then linked to breath because breathing is the physical precondition of speaking. Witnessing his own decomposition, the narrator envisions himself without a head, imagination dead, and at the end, without breath. Beckett's composition follows a relentless trajectory of depletion, aiming toward characters without bodies or even without heads or toward a theater that moves in the direction of acts without words or plays without texts. The last thing that remains in the end is breath, at least until there will be, as the character in *How It Is* anticipates, the end without breath.

One of the most excruciating Beckett pieces in which breath and its link to voice and speech plays a major role is *Not-I*. Remembering Billie Whitelaw's famous performance, I am struck by how, chased by a flood of words and the "buzzing in her skull," she is literally out of breath as she tells bits and pieces of a story about childhood trauma, and possibly abuse. We can hear her gasp for air during the breathtaking speed of her monologue and those involuntary gasps are the only seconds of break during the cascade of words. Linked to trauma, breath in *Not-I* is haunted breath, like the exasperated breath and first cry of the newborn invoked in so many of Beckett's plays, including *Endgame*. Breath in Beckett is also linked to silence and stillness. At the heart of silence, breath is the remaining audible trace that marks the absence of voice. S. E. Gontarski writes that by the mid-1960s Beckett "essentially abandoned stories featuring the compulsion to (and so solace in) movement, in favor of stories featuring stillness or some barely perceptible movement, at times just the breathing of a body or the trembling of a hand."[6]

Finally, as Gontarski reminds us in "A Sense of Unending: Fictions for the End of Time," "in Beckett's world, birth, creation, and breath itself are punishments."[7] Gontarski links the Beckettian notion of punishment to Nietzsche's *The Birth of Tragedy out of the Spirit of Music* and specifically to the Dionysian vision that the best of all would be "not to be born, not to be, to be nothing" and the second best "quickly to die."[8] Gontarski points to a resonance of this Nietzschean vision with Beckett's invocation of "the sin of having been born" in his early essay on *Proust*: "Tragedy is the statement of an expiation.... The tragic figure represents the expiation of original sin, of the original and eternal sin of him and all his 'soci malorum,' the sin of having been born."[9]

If we follow Gontarski's argument that, in the Beckettian world, birth, creation and breath are punishments, we may see a transcoding between expiation and expi(r)ation. Expiation, that is atonement, then appears as embedded in expi(r)ation referring both to the exhalation of breath and the ending or expiration of a lifetime. This transcoding, in turn, provides a compelling framework for reading Beckett's *Breath* from a perspective of the end times. In 1969, with the student revolution in Paris still ongoing, Beckett performed one of his most minimalist and elusive plays, *Breath*.[10] As Llewellyn Brown writes in *Beckett, Lacan and the Voice*: "The most extreme diminution of any spatial reality is without doubt found in the play *Breath*, where no human figure appears, but which unfolds in a total duration of thirty-five seconds, between the scansion marked by the poles inspiration/expiration."[11]

At first glance, this radical condensation of theater and the life it invokes seems to challenge the most basic theatrical conventions and philosophical notions of subjectivity and being. According to Alain Badiou's reflections on Beckett's "ascetic method," the minimal conditions of theater and fundamental theatrical operations, *Breath* would even no longer qualify as theater. In *On Beckett*, Alain Badiou emphatically states: "there is theater only as long as there is dialogue, discourse and discussion between two characters."[12] Yet, *Breath* retains if not enhances the "physical immediacy" that Badiou sees as a characteristic feature of Beckett's theater. Moreover, the play retains and even crystallizes what Badiou identifies as Beckett's temptation by mime. One could say that this shortest of all plays illustrates that breathing as the most essential operation of living is also the most essential theatrical operation. *Breath*, then, condenses the two in a mime that invokes life in mimetic identification.

Beckett's artistic meditation on breathing emerges after his own existential confrontation with the vicissitudes of breath and its essential role in the precarity of human existence. In April 1968, a year before the first performance of *Breath*, Beckett suffered from severe shortness of breath and chest pains and was diagnosed with a cyst in his lung. Confined for several weeks to his room, he was forced to watch the historical student uprising on television. In October of that year, he wrote *Breath*.

Breath is a meditative reflection on the most essential condition of life, breathing. In 2020, the pandemic year in which I wrote this short piece, we endured what I called the year of breath. Victims of COVID-19 died because they could not breathe. George Floyd's dying words "I can't breathe" ignited the 2020 revolution. People were feeling and felt longer after that they were being suffocated by the lockdown and its heightened states of anxiety that took their breath away. But people also can't breathe because in the age of climate change the air fills with toxic smog. During the California fires in 2020, people were asked to stay indoors to prevent them from breathing the highly toxic air outside that had reached a critically dangerous level. Some meditated, using breath to ground themselves in this new alien world.

Breathing is the most elemental form of life. It is, as Luce Irigaray writes, "the first autonomous gesture of the human being. To come into the world supposes inhaling and exhaling by oneself."[13] It is also the last autonomous gesture of the human being. The last exhalation marks the end of life. In light of the transcoding between expiration and expiation, we may argue that Beckett's *Breath* contains his vision of a punishment for having been born in the most condensed form possible. If the second-best thing after not being born, according to Nietzsche, is to die quickly, the short span of a lifetime between the first and the last breath envisioned in *Breath* is a concrete manifestation of this second-best thing. Moreover, the expiration that ends this brief lifetime already contains the atonement (expiation) for the sin of having been born.

Breathing also connects the human being to the environment. It is the mode of a continual exchange between inside and outside, organism and environment. Like our minds, our breaths extend into the environment. Beckett's *Breath* entails a figuration of the living organism and its dependence on an environment that filters air in and out of cells. Breath needs oxygen but oxygen also needs breath. Living organisms and breath form a relationship of mutual dependence. Because of its high chemical reactivity, oxygen needs to be continually replenished by the photosynthetic action of living organisms to remain a free element in air. We can almost think of this relationship as an elemental symbiosis without which there would be no life. To put it differently, oxygen is the fundamental element in the ecology of survival. When we breathe, we exhale the carbons in the carbon dioxide molecules. The oxygen we breathe in is used by cells in the disposal of sugary carbohydrates during the metabolization of food and its transformation into chemical energy. Establishing the most fundamental connection between organism and environment, oxygen is the elixir of life. Since, next to hydrogen and helium, oxygen is the universe's third most abundant element by mass, we could even say that its connection to the environment also extends to the universe.

To make energy molecules, oxygen removes electrons and hydrogen ions. The inspiration of air is thus an essential element of composing and decomposing, the processes that underlie the rhythms of life. Like breath, decomposition plays one of the most central roles in Beckett's work. In short, oxygen constitutes the most vital element in an organism's engagement with its narrower and larger environments. In the continual processes of exchange between organism and environment the energies and constraints are created that enable living and being in the world and having a place in the universe. Breath is an essential element in Beckett's composition of his theater plays, but it is always haunted by its opposite, decomposition. Breath and composition or inspiration are shadowed by the end of breath: expiration and decomposition.

Beckett's *Breath* has four performative agents: rubbish, cry, breath, and light. Beckett thus follows through with his dream of staging a play without actors. As Deirde Bair recounts in her biography, Beckett stated that the best possible play would be one without actors, consisting only of text.[14] Fascinated and indeed driven by the logic of subtraction, Beckett had already composed *Acts Without Words*. With *Breath*, he pushes this subtraction even further, offering us a play without actors and text. Yet it is precisely through this subtraction that he aims at approximating his theater to the essence of living. In *The Theater and Its Double*, Artaud writes: "And through the hieroglyph of a breath I am able to recover an idea of the sacred theater."[15] It is as if Beckett has literalized Artaud's vision in the shortest play ever put on stage. In his reflections on Artaud, Derrida argues that the theater of cruelty needs to substitute hieroglyphics for purely phonic signs.[16] Beckett's *Breath* is a play without any phonic signs, purely composed with the hieroglyph of one breath. As perhaps the most radical figuration possible of the brevity of life, Beckett's play resonates with Artaud's notion of a sacred theater inspired by divine cruelty. But like in all of Beckett's plays, there cannot be any approximation to the sacred without the profane.

In the first act of *Breath*, the curtain opens on a faintly lit stage littered with rubbish, the detritus of a polluted world. From the outset, Beckett thus links the elemental force of breathing to environmental forces. More precisely, with rubbish as the agent that is named first, Beckett invokes a polluted environment that contributes to the inhalation of toxic air. Imagine for a moment Beckett's *Breath* without the agent of rubbish. The central rhythm of birth, life and death could be retained, yet it would be an entirely different play. The agent rubbish alludes to processes of decomposition that cannot be absorbed and metabolized by the environment. Alluding to industrialization, it locates the play historically in the age of environmental pollution.

At the same time, however, in using "rubbish" as a central agent, Beckett also performs one of the subtle metaphorical transcoding operations that are characteristic of his plays. Rubbish also invokes the Beckettian idea, revealed in letters to his actors, that a writer picks from the detritus of memory, the odds and ends, or even from the discarded scraps of his own archive. Manuscripts, writes Friedhelm Rathjen in his biography, are picked out of rubbish.[17] This resonates incidentally with an intriguing staging of *Happy Days* in a small avant-garde theater in Santa Ana, California. In this performance Winnie was buried not in sand but in a heap of shredded manuscripts, thus visually emphasizing Beckett's focus on catachresis in his endgame with citation.

At the opening of *Breath*, we thus gaze at a faintly lit stage littered with rubbish. Then the second agent, "breath," appears on stage. But how does one represent breath without the breathing actor? In Beckett's play we hear breath for exactly twenty-five seconds, ten seconds inhale, five seconds hold, and ten seconds exhale. Given that breath is invisible, we thus receive it theatrically as a mere sound effect. The third agent, equally rendered as mere sound, is "cry." The breath we hear is followed by a faint brief cry that precedes "inspiration and slow increase of light."[18] Inspiration, from Late Latin *spirare*—to breathe—invokes the double meaning of inhalation or breathing and a flash of inspiration (light). It also resonates with the biblical invocation of divine influence. Beckett thus doubles the material plane of existence with a spiritual one. Light, the fourth agent in *Breath*, is figured as an element that is necessary to support the organism's capacity to perceive the world with sensory organs. It is also figured as the source of inspiration, a flash of inner vision. With this condensed double figuration of light as a source of perception and inspiration, Beckett thus links the material and the spiritual world.

Inspiration is followed by "expiration and slow decrease of light."[19] As always, Beckett's choice of words is meticulous. It is crucial that he uses inspiration and expiration instead of inhalation and exhalation. If the emphasis were on the organic alone, it would again be an entirely different play. Inspiration and expiration, breathing in and breathing out, life and death, light and darkness, the fundamental conditions of living and being. In the spiritual world, they are also the fundamental conditions of meditation and transcendence.

The second act features the same four agencies: rubbish, cry, breath, and light. Once again, the curtain opens on scattered rubbish, this time followed by an "instant of recorded vagitus."[20] With *vagitus* as the Latin word for the cry of a newborn, Beckett introduces the second agent, "cry," alluding to the theme of birth and the infant's cry at the exact moment when it takes its first breath. Intimately linked to the ability to breathe, cry marks the infant's entry into the world of breath and air. For Beckett, cry, however, also marks, as his biographer Knowlson reminds us, the beginning of the long journey toward the last cry that leaves life behind.[21]

Soon after, two identical cries switch on and off with "strictly synchronized light and breath."[22] The cry of the newborn, identical with the cry of the dying. Birth and death, inspiration and expiration, light and darkness, the synchronies of being or the lack thereof, the flash of existence in the transitional space between, marked by the amplified recording of breath and the faintly fluctuating movement of light. Llewellyn Brown writes: "The entirety of *existence* is contained here, in the absence of anything that could be called *being*."[23] Beckett's meditation on breath confronts the audience with mortality and the brevity of life between our first and last breaths and our first and last cries. Inspiration and expiration, breathing in and breathing out, life and death, light and darkness, the fundamental conditions under which being is but a faint cry in between.

Uniquely attuned to our pandemic confinement, this short play strips living in the end times of everything but the essentials of being, that is, breath, life, and death. But the essentials of being also include rubbish and light. Revisiting Beckett's work, including *Breath*, during the times of pandemic surrealism, we become painfully aware that he has anticipated many of the environmental catastrophes we are facing today. Scientists, for example, have linked the onset of the COVID-19 pandemic, if not the pandemic age, with the global effects of environmental destruction that include, among other things, rampant deforestation, the production of industrial waste ("rubbish"), and the displacement and extinction of species.[24] These developments that lead toward pending catastrophes call for new narratives able to grasp the staggering scale of environmental threats and their impact on humans and other species. Ahead of his time, Beckett has presented us with the algorithms of life under conditions of catastrophe. Drawing on age-old traditions, including classical antiquity, that link breath and spirit, *Breath* portrays living reduced to its essentials among which Beckett includes, the spiritual dimensions of light and inspiration.

The ancient Greek word *pneuma*, for example, means both breath and spirit or soul. Pneuma, the element from which not only thought and movement but also life itself originated, refers to air in motion and soul is considered to consist of air. In Stoic philosophy, pneuma, the "breath of life" links the individual and the cosmos and organizes both. Encapsulating breath, life, and light in its foundational elements and entanglements, Beckett's *Breath* resonates not only with ancient philosophies of life but also with the current wave of environmental artistic works and projects that are centered around the increasing fragility and precarity of breath, air, light, and life. Among those, I want to single out Tomás Saraceno, whose art resonated for me with Beckett's *Breath* in the sense that Saraceno revisits the ancient philosophical connections between breath, light and the cosmos from the perspective of current environmental threats.[25] While Beckett invokes the pollution of air with the trash that litters his stage, Saraceno zooms in on particulate matter in the air caused by pollution and toxicity. In the ongoing piece *We do not all breathe the same air,* he visualizes the air quality of cities around the word. In a sequence of prints, Saraceno shows measurements of the particulate matter in the air over time. In another piece, *Particular Matter(s)*, Saraceno projects a single beam of light into the darkness. The result is a stunning visualization of earthly and cosmic dust particles that resemble galaxies and stars in the Milky Way. When viewers come close to the beam of light, they realize that their own breath or hand movements become part of the exhibition, animating the particles, and changing their rhythms. I was reminded of Beckett's characters, like the narrator in "The Calmative," or Molloy, or Malone, who watch the stars or feel the sky fall on them. And I was reminded of the linkage in *Breath* between pollution, air, light, and breath.

Finally, Beckett's *Breath* also resonated for me with Laurent Testot's *Cataclysms: An Environmental History of Humanity*. Pointing to the fact that in evolutionary history our nose was designed to improve aspiration and our larynx to optimize airflow in the lungs and that we can use our muscles to control our breath, Testot concludes that "in our respiratory system, evolution encouraged the development of the essential characteristics for endurance."[26] As Beckett's characters struggle with the cataclysms of life, they betray an astounding endurance, albeit often against their own will. Feeling that they can't go on, they go on and on and on. For many of them, including most prominently Molloy and Malone, it is the process of writing that keeps them going. And writing itself is entangled with breath through inspiration.

As we know, Beckett also linked breath to the process of writing. He told his biographers of an epiphany he had on a visit to Ireland immediately after World War II that generated what we could call an affective turn in his writing. From that moment on, he says, he wrote what he felt and "recognized the world he had to create in order to be able to breathe."[27] And in 1973, during the years he still struggled with difficulties being published, Beckett stated: "It's not that bad not being published. After all, one writes in order to be able to breathe."[28] This is, after all, the most elemental form of writing in order not to die. Writers, for Beckett, are creatures of air.

This is also true for his characters who are writers. As Paul Sheehan points out, "for Malone, who returns again and again to the notions of 'air,' 'oxygen' and 'breath,' the written word does not destroy memory, it enhances or even replaces it."[29] As oxygen and breath are the basic operations that support the life of the body, writing and memory are the operations that support the life of the mind.

I kept writing bits and pieces of this piece on *Breath* in Berlin, first under the lockdown during the second wave of the pandemic in December 2020, and now almost a year later in 2021. On December 24, 2020, *Der Spiegel* published thoughts on the pandemic collected from one hundred people whom a group of reporters had followed for an entire year and interviewed monthly. In November, they registered a state of widespread pandemic fatigue. Nanette, a bookkeeper, stated: "Depressions are in my circles a growing topic of conversation. People who had hoped that Corona would give them a 'pause to breathe' (*eine Atempause*), had certainly not been aware of the impact the pandemic would have on them. If a 'pause to breathe' lasts too long, one will eventually suffocate from it."[30] This statement resonates with the difference between "pause" and "silence" that Beckett marked as a crucial distinction for the actors in his stage directions for *Endgame*. Pause is in many ways an antidote of silence. The pandemic may offer a pause to many people, but it rarely gives them the gift of silence. Filled with the fears of the time, the "pause to breathe" offered by the pandemic generates a paradoxical state of high anxiety, if not a breathlessness that is suffocating. Returning to Beckett's *Breath* during this time conveys the crucial difference between pause and silence. The pandemic undermines precisely that element of *spirare* or flash of insight that Beckett evokes with "inspiration and slow increase of light." The "pause to breathe" gives way to a depression that we can feel weighing heavily on the chest. This is another way in which COVID-19 is linked to breath and suffocation.

During the pandemic lockdown in Berlin everything was closed except stores considered to provide the essentials of life.

These included supermarkets, pharmacies, and bookstores. Providing spiritual nourishment, bookstores in my country of origin are held to be essential for survival in the ruins of the pandemic. They help people breathe by filling the suffocating pandemic state of siege with imaginary life. I recently found a bookstore in a small street in Kreuzberg that prominently displayed Beckett's complete works in the Suhrkamp translation by Elmar Tophoven. Beckett taught us the difference between pause, life on hold, and silence. In contrast to pause and life on hold, silence is a meditative state of mind or, as Beckett says, "my mind at peace, that is to say empty."[31] Meditation is linked to breath because it is through deep breathing that we strive to an empty mind at peace. During the first seven months of the lockdown in California, I joined a walking meditation group. We met at a small knoll in the neighborhood and walked silently with our masks on in circles on the path surrounding the hill, one and a half feet apart. One day I suddenly saw us as if I were an outside observer and almost burst into laughter. We resembled Beckett figures, doing their endless rounds just like the hooded figures in *Quad I* and *Quad II*.

Life on hold is, of course, also linked to another of Beckett's central themes: waiting. As I write this, we have been waiting for more than a year and a half for the pandemic lockdown to end. We are sitting in seemingly endless Zoom meetings, waiting for them to end. Even cartoonists are comparing the tedium of waiting during the pandemic to *Waiting for Godot*.

I have come to think about our quotidian pandemic world in terms of pandemic surrealism. This perspective, of course, only holds for those lucky enough not to catch the virus or have a mild case due to vaccines or medical interventions. Pandemic surrealism resonates deeply and in so many ways with Beckettian worlds. "Real life" often no longer feels natural. Even on their

FIGURE 6.1. "Waiting for Godot to Join the Zoom Meeting." From "Revenge of the Librarians" by Tom Gauld, *Drawn & Quarterly* (Montreal), 2022.

walks in the neighborhood, people have turned into ghost walkers, ambling around with their masks. Some of them shoot across the street as soon as they see another lonely walker on their sidewalk. We are turning into Beckett figures doing our endless rounds, walking without a sound, masks shielding us from each other and the hostile world, words spinning in our heads. We become prisoners of mind, walking in a circle, day in, day out. Not to speak of the real prisons in the United States, a criminally carceral nation, where inmates have no protection and are dying at shocking rates. The lockdown also feels surreal because even in the most beautiful surroundings every encounter is a potential threat. We have become afraid of each other. Beckett taught us the algorithms of life reduced to its essentials, and now, more than ever, he belongs to this life and its essentials.

Seen from this perspective, we could also say that *Breath*, like Beckett's other theatrical works, becomes a testimony to the irrefutable tenacity of life to hold on to the last breath, no matter what. As Alain Badiou puts it, there is a relentlessness in Beckett's characters "in persevering in their being, in maintaining—come hell or high water—a principle of desire, a vital power that circumstances seem to render illegitimate or impossible at each and every instant."[32] Or, as Beckett suggests through the voice in *Malone Dies*, "a little breath of fulfillment revives the dead longings and a murmur is born in the silent world, reproaching you affectionately with having despaired too late."[33]

Perhaps *Breath* ultimately suggests that, having despaired too late, a little breath of fulfillment returns us to what Badiou calls "a powerful love for human obstinacy, for tireless desire, for humanity reduced to its stubbornness and malice."[34] But Badiou's emphatically optimistic reading can hold only if notions such as love, desire and humanity were maintained in a Beckettian world in which, as Jean-Michel Rabaté puts it, "man can only be man by catachresis, that is to say, by an abuse of language."

NOTES

INTRODUCTION

1. This poem of mine is freely composed from quotes and memories of Jacques Derrida and Samuel Beckett. See also Gabriele Schwab, "Derrida, the Parched Woman, and the Son of Man," *Discourse* 30, nos. 1–2 (2008): 226–41.
2. Ihab Hassan, *Paracriticisms: Seven Speculations of the Times* (Urbana: University of Illinois Press, 1975), 63–73.
3. Patti Smith, *M Train* (New York: Vintage, 2015), 257.
4. See Gabriele Schwab, "Pandemic Surrealism," *Foundry*, VIRUSHUMANS (special issue), October 2020, https://uchri.org/foundry/pandemic-surrealism/.
5. Theodor W. Adorno, "Trying to Understand Endgame," trans. Michael T. Jones, *New German Critique* 26 (1982): 123.
6. Charles McNulty, "Beckett Wrote It Out for You: Life Tends to Stall, Yet We Persevere. Here's a Playwright in Sync with COVID Times," *Los Angeles Times*, May 26, 2020.
7. See Dietmar Kamper, "Zeit Gewinnen: Eine Erinnerung an die Zukunft," in *Vor der Jahrtausendwende: Berichte zur Lage der Zukunft*, ed. Peter Sloterdijk (Frankfurt: Suhrkamp, 1990), 2:679. Kamper bases this argument on his reading of Derrida's "No Apocalypse, Not Now."
8. Adorno, "Trying to Understand Endgame," 148.
9. Samuel Beckett, *Endgame* (London: Faber & Faber, 1958), 20.

10. Frank Kermode, *The Sense of an Ending: Studies in the Theory of Fiction* (Oxford: Oxford University Press, 1967).
11. Beckett, *Endgame*, 15, 45.
12. Beckett, *Endgame*, 35.
13. Beckett, *Endgame*, 51.
14. Earlier sections of chapter 2 appeared in "The Intermediate Area Between Life and Death: Fantasies in Samuel Beckett's *Malone Dies*," in *Memory and Desire: Aging, Literature and Psychoanalysis*, ed. Kathleen Woodward and Murray Schwartz (Bloomington: Indiana University Press, 1985), 205–18. I added an opening reading of "The Calmative" and revised the chapter in light of the focus on poetics of the end times.
15. Samuel Beckett, "The Calmative," in *First Love and Other Novellas*, ed. Gerry Dukes (London: Penguin, 2000), 47.
16. Beckett, "The Calmative," 47.
17. Samuel Beckett, *Molloy*, in *Three Novels: Molloy, Malone Dies, The Unnamable* (New York: Grove, 2009), 21.
18. Beckett, "Molloy," 27.
19. An earlier version of the chapter on *The Unnamable* was published as "Not-I Fiction of a First Person Narrator: *The Unnamable*, in Gabriele Schwab, *Subjects Without Selves: Transitional Texts in Modern Fiction* (Cambridge, MA: Harvard University Press, 1994), 132–71.
20. Samuel Beckett, *The Unnamable* (New York: Grove, 1958), 94, 10.
21. Ruby Cohn, *Back to Beckett* (Princeton, NJ: Princeton University Press, 1973), 101.
22. Chapter 4 is a republication with minor revisions of "Coda: Postnuclear Ecologies—Language, Body, and Affect in Beckett's *Happy Days*," in Gabriele Schwab, *Radioactive Ghosts* (Minneapolis: University of Minnesota Press, 2020), 267–84. I am grateful to the University of Minnesota Press for granting me the copyright.
23. Achille Mbembe defines deathworlds as "new and unique forms of social existence in which vast populations are subjected to conditions of life conferring upon them the status of living dead." "Necropolitics," *Public Culture* 15, no. 1 (Winter 2003): 11–40, at 40.
24. An early version of chapter 5 appeared as "Cosmographical Meditations on the In/Human: Beckett's *The Lost Ones* and Lyotard's

'Scapeland,'" *Parallax* 6, no. 4 (2000): 58–75. A revised version titled "Cosmographical Meditations on the Inhuman: Samuel Beckett's *The Lost Ones*" is included in my book *Imaginary Ethnographies: Literature, Culture & Subjectivity* (New York: Columbia University Press, 2012). I am grateful to the press for granting me permission to reprint the chapter with minor revisions.

25. Samuel Beckett, *The Lost Ones* (New York: Grove, 1972), 52.
26. Antonin Artaud, *The Theater and Its Double*, trans. Mary Caroline Richards (New York: Grove, 1958), 21.
27. Artaud, *The Theater and Its Double*, 31–32.
28. Samuel Beckett, *Breath*, in *The Collected Shorter Plays of Samuel Beckett* (New York: Grove, 1984), 209–11.

1. MOMENTS FOR NOTHING

An earlier and shorter version of this chapter, with a different focus, previously appeared as Gabriele Schwab, "On the Dialectic of Closing and Opening in Samuel Beckett's End-Game," trans. D. L. Selden, *Yale French Studies* 67 (1984): 191–202. See also Gabriele Schwab, *Samuel Becketts Endspiel mit der Subjektivität* (Stuttgart: Metzler, 1981).

1. Samuel Beckett, *Endgame* (London: Faber & Faber, 1958), 24.
2. Beckett, *Endgame*, 12.
3. Beckett, *Endgame*, 12. In U.S. editions of *Endgame*, the word "Shelter" is used here rather than "Refuge."
4. Beckett, *Endgame*, 16.
5. Beckett, *Endgame*, 17.
6. The quotations in this paragraph are from Beckett, *Endgame*, 27–28.
7. Beckett, *Endgame*, 27.
8. See Alan Weisman, *The World Without Us* (London: Random House, 2008).
9. Beckett, *Endgame*, 25, 23.
10. Beckett, *Endgame*, 25.
11. Beckett, *Endgame*, 33.
12. Alain Badiou, *On Beckett*, ed. Alberto Toscano and Nina Power (Manchester: Clinamen, 2003), 44.
13. Adorno, "Trying to Understand Endgame," 119.

14. Adorno, "Trying to Understand Endgame," 122.
15. Stanley Cavell, "Ending the Waiting Game: A Reading of Beckett's *Endgame*," in *Must We Mean What We Say: Modern Philosophical Essays in Morality, Religion, Drama, Music and Criticism* (New York: Scribner's, 1969), 133.
16. Cavell, "Ending the Waiting Game," 135.
17. Cavell, "Ending the Waiting Game," 133.
18. Cavell, "Ending the Waiting Game," 134.
19. Cavell, "Ending the Waiting Game," 137.
20. Cavell, "Ending the Waiting Game," 143.
21. Beckett, *Endgame*, 12.
22. Beckett, *Endgame*, 32.
23. Beckett, *Endgame*, 20.
24. Frank Kermode, *The Sense of an Ending: Studies in the Theory of Fiction* (Oxford: Oxford University Press, 1967).
25. Steven Connor, *Samuel Beckett: Repetition, Theory, and Text* (Aurora, CO: Davies Group, 2007), 12.
26. Rhys Tranter, *Beckett's Late Stage: Trauma, Language, and Subjectivity* (Stuttgart: ibidem-Verlag, 2018), 34.
27. Cavell, "Ending the Waiting Game," 119, 120.
28. Cavell, "Ending the Waiting Game," 131.
29. Herbert Blau, *Reality Principles: From the Absurd to the Virtual* (Ann Arbor: University of Michigan Press, 2011), 148.
30. Beckett, *Endgame*, 25.
31. Martin Esslin, *Theatre of the Absurd* (New York: Anchor, 1961).
32. "Moment upon moment, pattering down, like the millet grains of . . . [*he hesitates*] . . . that old Greek, and all life long you wait for that to mount up to a life." Beckett, *Endgame*, 70.
33. Jacques Derrida, "Structure, Sign and Play in the Discourse of the Human Sciences," in *Writing and Difference*, trans. Alan Bass (London: Routledge & Kegan Paul, 1978), 278–79.
34. David Lapoujade, "To Act at the Limit," in *Aesthetics of Standstill*, ed. Reinhold Görling, Barbara Gronau, and Ludger Schwarte (Berlin: Sternberg, 201), 285.
35. Lapoujade "To Act at the Limit," 296, 298.
36. Lapoujade "To Act at the Limit," 296.

37. Beckett, *Endgame*, 32, 14; 11, 29.
38. See Derrida, "Structure, Sign, and Play in the Discourse of the Human Sciences": "The one seeks to decipher, dreams of deciphering, a truth or an origin . . ." (292).
39. Beckett, *Endgame*, 32.
40. Claude Lévi-Strauss quoted by Derrida, in "Structure, Sign, and Play in the Discourse of the Human Sciences," 289. The term "double meaning" is used here in the way Paul Ricoeur uses "La structure du double sens" ("The structure of double meaning") in his book on Freud, *De l'interprétation: Essai sur Freud* (Paris: Seuil, 1965), 13–63.
41. See Samuel Beckett, *Watt* (London: John Calder, 1963), 79.
42. Peter Brook, "Mit Beckett leben," in *Materialen zu Becketts "Endspiel,"* ed. Michael Haerdter (Frankfurt: Suhrkamp, 1968), 32 (my translation).
43. The complexity of this double strategy has to be somewhat simplified here. For a more detailed analysis, see Schwab, *Samuel Becketts Endspiel mit der Subjektivität*, 105–25.
44. This is not to be understood metaphorically, but rather in the sense of concrete, irreconcilable directives that force the audience into a paradoxical situation: (1) You must construe meaning. (2) This is possible only by means of projection. (3) You must not project. Compare *Double-Bind: The Foundation of the Communicational Approach to the Family*, ed. C. E. Sluzki and D. C. Ransom (New York: Psychological Corp, 1976).
45. Wolfgang Iser, "The Reading Process: A Phenomenological Approach," *New Literary History* 3, no. 2 (1972): 279–99.
46. See Helmuth Plessner, *Laughing and Crying: A Study of the Limits of Human Behavior*, trans. James Spencer Churchill and Marjorie Grene (Evanston, IL: Northwestern University Press, 2020).
47. Beckett, *Endgame*, 28.
48. Beckett, *Endgame*, 45.
49. Beckett, *Endgame*, 28.
50. S. E. Gontarski, "Fictions for the End of Time," in *Revisioning Beckett: Samuel Beckett's Decadent Turn* (New York: Bloomsbury Academic, 2018), 245.
51. For a detailed analysis of the concept of transformational objects, see Christopher Bollas, *The Shadow of the Object: Psychoanalysis of the*

Unthought Known (New York: Columbia University Press, 1987), 13–96; Gabriele Schwab, "Words and Moods: The Transference of Literary Knowledge," *SubStance* 26, no. 3 (1997): 107–27; and Gabriele Schwab, "Cultural Texts and Endopsychic Scripts," *SubStance* 30, nos. 1–2 (2001): 160–76.
52. Bollas, *The Shadow of the Object*, 13–96.
53. Beckett, *Endgame & Act Without Words I*, 93.

2. THE TRANSITIONAL SPACE BETWEEN LIFE AND DEATH

1. I have chosen the term "speech performance" because I think it is more adequate to express the performative qualities of Beckett's prose than the terms "language game" (Wittgenstein) or "speech act" (Austin/Searle). I even think that a detailed analysis of these performative qualities might provide an interesting contribution to the contemporary debate in analytical language philosophy. For the importance of the performative dimension in postmodern literature and theory (and for the postmodern sensitivity to performance), see also Herbert Blau, *Blooded Thought: Occasions of Theatre* (New York: Performing Arts Journal Publications, 1982).
2. This is an argument I have developed at length in my book *Samuel Beckett's Endspiel mit der Subjektivität: Entwurf einer Psychoaesthetik des modernen Theaters* (Stuttgart: Metzler, 1981). A summary of the book in English appears in *English and American Studies in German: Summaries of Theses and Monographs* (Tübingen: Max Niemeyer, 1981), 106–8. See also my "The Dialectic of Opening and Closure in Samuel Beckett's *Endgame*," *Yale French Studies* 67 (1984): 191–202.
3. Samuel Beckett, "The Calmative," in *First Love and Other Novellas*, ed. Gerry Dukes (London: Penguin, 2000), 47.
4. Beckett, "The Calmative," 47.
5. *Whole Earth Catalog* (Menlo Park, CA: Portola Institute, 1968).
6. This and preceding quotations in this paragraph are from Beckett, "The Calmative," 47.
7. Beckett, "The Calmative," 48–49.
8. Quotations in this paragraph are from Beckett, "The Calmative," 48.
9. Beckett, "The Calmative," 49.

2. THE TRANSITIONAL SPACE ༀ 231

10. Beckett, "The Calmative," 52.
11. This and the preceding quotations in this paragraph are from Beckett, "The Calmative," 56–63.
12. For a detailed discussion of transformational literary objects, see Gabriele Schwab, "Words and Moods: The Transference of Literary Knowledge," *SubStance* 26, no. 3 (1997): 107–27, and "Cultural Texts and Endopsychic Scripts," *SubStance* 30, nos. 1–2 (2001): 160–76.
13. Samuel Beckett, *Molloy*, in *Three Novels: Molloy, Malone Dies, The Unnamable* (New York: Grove, 2009), 3.
14. Beckett, *Molloy*, 3.
15. Beckett, *Molloy*, 15.
16. This and preceding quotations in this paragraph are from Beckett, *Molloy*, 13–14.
17. Beckett, *Molloy*, 10.
18. Beckett, *Molloy*, 5.
19. This and preceding quotations in this paragraph are from Beckett, *Molloy*, 5–7.
20. Beckett, *Molloy*, 11.
21. Samuel Beckett, *Malone Dies*, in *Three Novels: Molloy, Malone Dies, The Unnamable* (New York: Grove, 2009), 178.
22. Beckett, *Molloy*, 9.
23. This and the preceding quotation are from Beckett, *Molloy*, 21.
24. Beckett, *Molloy*, 23.
25. This and the two preceding quotations are from Beckett, *Molloy*, 27.
26. Beckett, *Molloy*, 170.
27. Beckett, *Molloy*, 170.
28. Beckett, *Malone Dies*, 173.
29. Beckett, *Malone Dies*, 213.
30. This and the preceding quotation are from Beckett, *Malone Dies*, 177.
31. Beckett, *Malone Dies*, 180.
32. Jean-François Lyotard, "Can Thought Go on Without a Body?," trans. Bruce Boone and Lee Hildreth, *Discourse* 11, no. 1 (1988): 74–87. I will develop the implication of this question in more detail in chapter 5.
33. Beckett, *Malone Dies*, 174.
34. Beckett, *Malone Dies*, 174.
35. Beckett, *Malone Dies*, 227, 174.

36. Beckett, *Malone Dies*, 178.
37. See Kathleen Woodward, "Transitional Objects and the Isolate: Samuel Beckett's 'Malone Dies,'" *Contemporary Literature* 26, no. 2 (1985): 140–54.
38. Woodward, "Transitional Objects," 145.
39. See especially Freud's analysis of "Fort-Da" in his *Beyond the Pleasure Principle*, trans. and ed. James Strachey (New York: Norton, 1961).
40. Samuel Beckett, *The Unnamable* (New York: Grove, 1958), 3.
41. Jean-Michel Rabaté, *Think, Pig! Beckett at the Limit of the Human* (New York: Fordham University Press, 2016), 198.
42. Woodward, "Transitional Objects," 145.
43. See Blau, *Blooded Thought*, where he analyzes "presence with no illusion" (154) as one of the most prominent latent desires in postmodern thought.
44. Beckett, *The Unnamable*, 81.
45. Beckett, *Malone Dies*, 173.
46. Rabaté, *Think, Pig!*, 198–99.
47. See Donald W. Winnicott, *Playing and Reality* (London: Tavistock, 1971).
48. For an elaboration of this, see Gabriele Schwab, "Genesis of the Subject, Imaginary Functions, and Poetic Language," *New Literary History* 15, no. 3 (Spring 1984), 453–93.
49. Franco Basaglia, *L'istituzione negata* (Turin: G. Einaudi, 1968).
50. I have borrowed the term "creative paranoia" from Thomas Pynchon's *Gravity's Rainbow* (New York: Viking, 1973).
51. See James Joyce's poem "Bahnhofstrasse" (1918), in *The Norton Anthology of Modern Poetry*, ed. Richard Ellmann and Robert O'Clair (New York: Norton, 1973), 275.

3. END TIMES OF SUBJECTIVITY

1. Israel Shenker, "An Interview with Beckett," in *Samuel Beckett: The Critical Heritage*, ed. Lawrence Graver and Raymond Federman (London: Routledge & Kegan Paul, 1979), 148; Samuel Beckett, *The Unnamable* (New York: Grove, 1958), 179.
2. Beckett, *The Unnamable*, 4.

3. Gilles Deleuze and Felix Guattari, *What Is Philosophy?*, trans. Hugh Tomlinson and Graham Burchell (New York: Columbia University Press, 1994), 2.
4. Beckett, *The Unnamable*, 4.
5. Beckett, *The Unnamable*, 53.
6. Beckett, *The Unnamable*, 92.
7. Beckett is especially interested in philosophies that work with the notion of a transcendental subject precisely because this allows him to endow his literary characters with features that differ radically from those of empirical subjects.
8. Beckett, *The Unnamable*, 10.
9. See Søren Kierkegaard, *Die Krankheit zum Tode* (Düsseldorf: Eugen Diederichs, 1971), 396 (my translation).
10. Regarding ontological insecurity see Ronald D. Laing, *The Divided Self* (Harmondsworth: Penguin, 1970), esp. 39–45.
11. The allusions in *The Unnamable* are to such diverse philosophies as those of Plato, Plotinus, Descartes, Berkeley, Leibniz, Spinoza, Kant, Schopenhauer, Kierkegaard, Heidegger, Merleau-Ponty, Sartre, Wittgenstein, Lacan, and Derrida, as well as Western and Eastern mysticism.
12. Allen Thiher, *Words in Reflection: Modern Language Theory and Postmodern Fiction* (Chicago: University of Chicago Press, 1984), 131.
13. Thiher, *Words in Reflection*, 133.
14. See Plato, *The Republic*, trans. H. D. P. Lee (Baltimore, MD: Penguin, 1961), Part 7, The Philosopher Ruler, no. 7: "The Simile of the Cave," 278–86.
15. Beckett, *The Unnamable*, 22.
16. Beckett, *The Unnamable*, 23.
17. See Peter Erhard, *Anatomie de Samuel Beckett* (Stuttgart: Birkhauser, 1976).
18. On the notion of the organless body, see Gilles Deleuze's and Felix Guattari's *Anti-Oedipus*, trans. Robert Hurley, Mark Seem, and Helen R. Lane (New York: Viking, 1977).
19. Beckett, *The Unnamable*, 128. See Margaret Mahler, Fred Pine, and Annie Bergman, *The Psychological Birth of the Human Infant* (New York: Basic Books, 1975). Mahler analyzes the necessary conditions for

a psychological birth (a psychological birth requires much more than a biological birth), and the psychological problems of living without being born. There is a striking similarity in the metaphors Beckett uses in *The Unnamable*.

20. This and the preceding quotation are from Beckett, *The Unnamable*, 134.
21. The use of the word "schizo" here is not intended to be pejorative. Instead, it is in keeping with the work of Gilles Deleuze and Félix Guattari and their set of theories and techniques called "schizoanalysis." Schizoanalysis was first described in their book *Anti-Oedipus* (1972) and furthered in their follow-up book, *A Thousand Plateaus* (1980). See Deleuze and Guattari, *Anti-Oedipus*, esp. ch. 1.
22. I deliberately use the masculine gender here, since I have the impression that Deleuze's and Guattari's schizosphere is decidedly masculine, despite its ambition to transcend the boundaries of gender. I would even read their economy of production in light of Michael Carrouges's concept of the bachelor's birth in his work *Les machines célibataires* (Paris: Arcanes, 1954). See also Alice Jardine's reading of Deleuze and Guattari in *Gynesis* (Ithaca, NY: Cornell University Press, 1985).
23. Beckett, *The Unnamable*, 306.
24. Beckett, *The Unnamable*, 134.
25. See Sigmund Freud's definition of the "I" as the "projection of a surface" in *The Ego and the Id* (1923), trans. Joan Riviere, rev. and ed. James Strachey (New York: Norton, 1962), 16.
26. See Leo Navratil, *Schizophrenie und Kunst* (Munich: Deutscher Taschenbuch Verlag, 1965), 69–80.
27. See Sigmund Freud, "The Ego and the Id," in *The Standard Edition of the Complete Psychological Works of Sigmund Freud*, vol. 19, trans. James Strachey (London: Hogarth, 1950). See also Gilles Deleuze, *Logique du sens* (Paris: Minuit, 1969), 11–20.
28. Beckett, *The Unnamable*, 134.
29. Beckett, *The Unnamable*, 149.
30. Ruby Cohn, *Back to Beckett* (Princeton, NJ: Princeton University Press, 1973), 101.
31. Beckett, *The Unnamable*, 82.

3. END TIMES OF SUBJECTIVITY ❧ 235

32. Beckett, *The Unnamable*, 83–84.
33. Beckett, *The Unnamable*, 3.
34. See Dieter Henrich, "Identität," in *Identität*, ed. Odo Marquard and Karlheinz Stierle (Munich: W. Fink, 1979), 177–78. See also Ernst Tugendhat, *Self-Consciousness and Self-Determination*, trans. Paul Stern (Cambridge, MA: MIT Press, 1986), 59.
35. Beckett, *The Unnamable*, 161.
36. Ernst Tugendhat, *Selbstbewusstsein und Selbstbestimmung* (Frankfurt: Suhrkamp, 1979), 75. See also Tugendhat, *Self-Consciousness and Self-Determination*, 62, 66.
37. Of course, at one level, the presupposition that a literary text has to be meaningful at all is challenged in *The Unnamable*. By repeatedly calling for a willful suspension of disbelief, *The Unnamable* inverts one of the most basic literary conventions. Nevertheless, the presupposition remains valid, since that very inversion establishes a metalevel of discourse. The problem of meaning is accordingly shifted to a different level of abstraction. In addition, Beckett's strategy of withholding meaning on an immediate level engages the reader in a very different process of meaning constitution. For a detailed analysis of the dynamic, see Gabriel Schwab, *Samuel Becketts Endspiel mit der Subjektivität: Zur Psychoästhetik des Modernen Theaters* (Stuttgart: Metzler, 1981). Regarding the same problem from the perspective of a theory of language, see Michel Foucault, *Archéologie du savoir* (Paris: Gallimard, 1969), 116–17. See also Michel Foucault, *The Archeology of Knowledge*, trans. A. M. Sheridan Smith (New York: Pantheon, 1972).
38. Beckett, *The Unnamable*, 164.
39. This paradox also necessarily affects the critic, since it is impossible to immediately situate oneself outside the textual perspective on a metalevel.
40. Tugendhat, *Self-Consciousness and Self-Determination*, 273.
41. Beckett, *The Unnamable*, 3, 16, 94.
42. Beckett, *The Unnamable*, 159.
43. Beckett, *The Unnamable*, 163.
44. Regarding Beckett's metalanguage and textual self-reflexivity see Manfred Smuda, *Becketts Pros als Metasprache* (Munich: Fink, 1970).
45. Beckett, *The Unnamable*, 13.

46. Regarding a critical reading of Derrida from the perspective of Beckett's texts, see Floyd Merrell, *Deconstruction Reframed* (West Lafayette, IN: Purdue University Press, 1985), ch. 7, "Beckett's Dilemma: or, Pecking Away at the Ineffable," 165–95.
47. See Manfred Frank, "Das Individuum in der Rolle des Idioten: Die hermeneutische Konzeption des Flaubert," in *Sartres Flaubert lessen: Essays zu Der Idiot in der Familie*, ed. Traugott König (Reinbek bei Hamburg: Rowohlt, 1980), 90.
48. Ulrich Pothast, *Die eigentlich metaphysische Tätigkeit: Über Schopenhauers Ästhetik und ihre Anwendung durch Samuel Beckett* (Frankfurt: Suhrkamp, 1982), 355 (my translation).
49. Søren Kierkegaard, *Fear and Trembling and The Sickness Unto Death*, trans. Walter Lowrie (Garden City, NY: Doubleday Anchor, 1954), 146.
50. The Kierkegaard quotations are from *Fear and Trembling*, 163–66.
51. Beckett, *The Unnamable*, 31.
52. Regarding Beckett's affiliations with mysticism, see Waltraud Gölter, *Entfremdung als Konstituens bürgerlicher Literatur, dargestellt am Beispiel Samuel Becketts: Versuch einer Vermittlung von Soziologie und Psychoanalyse als Interpretationsmodell* (Heidelberg: Carl Winter, 1976), 209–26.
53. See Bruce Kavin, "On Not Having the Last Word: Beckett, Wittgenstein, and the Limits of Language," in *Ineffability: Naming the Unnamable from Dante to Beckett*, ed. Peter S. Hawkins and Anne H. Schotter (New York: AMS, 1984), 195.
54. See Sigmund Freud, "On Negation," *Standard Edition*, vol. 19; and René Spitz, *No and Yes: On the Genesis of Human Communication* (New York: International Universities Press, 1957).
55. Beckett, *The Unnamable*, 161.
56. Beckett, *The Unnamable*, 4.
57. Manfred Smuda has pointed out that with increasing complexity in Beckett's texts, the possibilities of writing have proportionally decreased. In this development, *The Unnamable* marks a turning point in Beckett's development toward the later, minimalist texts. See Manfred Smuda, "Kunst im Kopf—Becketts spätere Prosa und das Imaginäre," in *Samuel Beckett*, ed. Hartmut Engelhardt (Frankfurt: Suhrkamp, 1984), 212.
58. Merrell, *Deconstruction Reframed*, 191.

59. J. E. Dearlove, *Accommodating the Chaos: Samuel Beckett's Nonrelational Art* (Durham, NC: Duke University Press, 1982), 61.
60. Beckett, *The Unnamable*, 170.
61. See Sigmund Freud, "Formulations on the Two Principles of Mental Functioning," *Standard Edition*, vol. 12.
62. Beckett, *The Unnamable*, 170.
63. See Sigmund Freud, "Jokes and Their Relation to the Unconscious," *Standard Edition*, vol. 8.
64. Beckett, *The Unnamable*, 170.
65. Beckett, *The Unnamable*, 4.
66. Kavin, "On Not Having the Last Word," 201.
67. Beckett, *The Unnamable*, 170–71.
68. Beckett, *The Unnamable*, 179.
69. For a detailed discussion of this effect of Beckett's texts, see Gabriele Schwab, *Samuel Becketts Endspiel mit der Subjektivität*, esp. ch. 4.
70. Merrell, *Deconstruction Reframed*, 193–94. Herbert Blau, whose own work is deeply influenced by Beckett, describes a similar paradox of subjectivity in his staging of *The Donner Party*. His description precisely fits the Unnamable's self-performances: "There is, then, an exploration of the dissolution of ego and the release of consciousness into structure, becoming an image of the ultimate subtraction, the death of self, which—as it materializes—is refused. In that respect, the works are emblematic arousals of residual will fighting off the loss of the self in the striations of thought." Herbert Blau, *Take up the Bodies: Theater at the Vanishing Point* (Urbana: University of Illinois Press, 1982), 163.
71. See Pierre Miranda, "The Dialectic of Metaphor: An Anthropological Essay on Hermeneutics," in *The Reader in the Text*, ed. Susan R. Suleiman and Inge Crosman (Princeton, NJ: Princeton University Press, 1980), 183–204. See also Gabriele Schwab, "Reader Response and the Aesthetic Experience of Otherness," *Stanford Literary Review* 3, no. 1 (1986): 107–36.
72. See also the following readings of Beckett, which use Donald W. Winnicott's theory of the intermediate area: Kathleen Woodward, "Transitional Objects and the Isolate: Samuel Beckett's *Malone Dies*," in *Contemporary Literature* 26, no. 2 (1985): 140–54; and Gabriele

Schwab, "The Intermediate Area Between Life and Death: On Samuel Beckett's *The Unnamable*," in *Memory and Desire: Aging—Literature—Psychoanalysis*, ed. Kathleen Woodward and Murray Schwartz (Bloomington: Indiana University Press, 1986), 205–17.

73. Dieter Henrich, "Kunst und Kunstphilosophie der Gegenwart—Überlegungen mit Rücksicht auf Hegel," in *Immanente Ästhetik—Ästhetische Reflexion*, ed. Wolfgang Iser (Munich: Fink, 1966), 27–28.
74. Henrich, "Kunst und Kunstphilosophie," 30.
75. I think here not only of the Unnamable's multiple phantasmatic bodies but also of Jameson's imperative that postmodern culture help us grow new organs.

4. "LAUGHING WILDLY INMIDST SEVEREST WOE"

1. Sigmund Freud, "Civilization and Its Discontents," in *The Standard Edition of the Complete Psychological Works of Sigmund Freud, Volume XXI (1927–1931): The Future of an Illusion, Civilization and Its Discontents, and Other Works*, ed. Jim Strachey, trans. Joan Riviere (London: Hogarth and Institute of Psycho-Analysis, 1930), 76.
2. Freud writes, "This principle dominates the operation of the mental apparatus from the start. There can be no doubt about its efficacy, and yet its programme is at loggerheads with the whole world. . . . There is no possibility at all of its being carried through; all the regulations of the universe run counter to it. One feels inclined to say that the intention that man should be 'happy' is not included in the plan of 'Creation.'" Freud, *Civilization and Its Discontents*, 76.
3. See William S. Burroughs, *Naked Lunch* (New York: Grove Weidenfeld, 1992).
4. See Beckett's remarks on failure in Samuel Beckett and Georges Duthuit, *Three Dialogues: Tal Coat—Masson—Bram Van Velde* (London: Transition, 1949).
5. Samuel Beckett, *Happy Days: A Play in Two Acts* (New York: Grove, 1989), 10.
6. Quoted in Peter Goin, *Nuclear Landscapes* (Baltimore, MD: Johns Hopkins University Press, 1951), 7.
7. Ghassan Hage, *Alter-Politics: Critical Anthropology and the Radical Imagination* (Melbourne: Melbourne University Press, 2015), 3.

4. "LAUGHING WILDLY INMIDST SEVEREST WOE"   239

8. Goin, *Nuclear Landscapes*, 3.
9. Robert J. Lifton, *Death in Life: Survivors of Hiroshima* (Chapel Hill: University of North Carolina Press, 1991).
10. Beckett, *Happy Days*, 23.
11. This and the preceding quotation are from Beckett, *Happy Days*, 27.
12. See Louis Menand, "Now What I Wonder Do I Mean By That," *Slate*, August 21, 1996, https://slate.com/news-and-politics/1996/08/now-what-i-wonder-do-i-mean-by-that.html.
13. Lauren Berlant, *Cruel Optimism* (Durham, NC: Duke University Press, 2011).
14. See Tali Sharot, Christoph W. Korn, and Raymond J. Dolan, "How Unrealistic Optimism Is Maintained in the Face of Reality," *Nature* 14, no. 11 (November 2011): 1475–79.
15. Richard Powers, "What Does Fiction Know?," *Places Journal*, August 2, 2011, https://placesjournal.org/article/what-does-fiction-know/.
16. Within the traditions that formed this "old style," happiness used to be tied to understanding, predicting and ultimately controlling the events and workings of nature. In Winnie's stage-world in which the destruction of natural ecologies and resources as well as a sustainable planetary future seems to be a given, any belief in the control of nature is irrevocably shattered. Moreover, at least since the advent of the nuclear age, the power to control the workings of nature has succumbed to a necro- or thanatopolitical desire not only to create death-worlds but also to become, as Oppenheimer imagined himself, the God of destruction and apocalypse. How then may *Happy Days* challenge our notion of happiness in the face of disaster, catastrophe, and necropolitical desire?
17. Beckett, *Happy Days*, 28, 30.
18. Beckett, *Happy Days*, 16.
19. E. E. Gontarski, "Literary Allusions in 'Happy Days,'" in *On Beckett, Essays and Criticism*, ed. E. E. Gontarski (New York: Grove, 1986), 314.
20. Beckett, *Happy Days*, 29.
21. Beckett, *Happy Days*, 39.
22. Beckett, *Happy Days*, 29.
23. Jacques Derrida, *Archive Fever: A Freudian Impression*, trans. Eric Prenowitz (Chicago: University of Chicago Press, 1996), 33.

24. Derrida, *Archive Fever*, 33.
25. Derrida, *Archive Fever*, 34.
26. Beckett, *Archive Fever*, 13.
27. Berlant, *Cruel Optimism*, 2.
28. Berlant, *Cruel Optimism*, 3.
29. Berlant, *Cruel Optimism*, 10.
30. See Chris Bollas's introduction to Edward Said, *Freud and the Non-European* (London: Verso, 2014), as well as M. Ackbar Abbas, *Hong Kong: Culture and the Politics of Disappearance* (Minneapolis: University of Minnesota Press, 1997).
31. Beckett, *Happy Days*, 11.
32. Gontarski, "Literary Allusions in 'Happy Days,'" 316.
33. Beckett, *Happy Days*, 25. I credit Gontarski with pointing out this reference in "Literary Allusions in 'Happy Days,'" 312.
34. See Gabriele Schwab, *Subjects Without Selves: Transitional Texts in Modern Fiction* (Cambridge, MA: Harvard University Press, 1994).
35. See Jane Bennett, *Vibrant Matter: A Political Ecology of Things* (Durham, NC: Duke University Press, 2010).
36. W. R. Bion, "Attacks on Linking," *Psychoanalytic Quarterly* 82, no. 3 (2013): 285.
37. Bion, "Attacks on Linking," 285.
38. For a detailed discussion of this Beckettian philosophy of language, see Schwab, *Subjects Without Selves*, ch. 6.
39. W. R. Bion, *Second Thoughts: Selected Papers on Psychoanalysis* (London: Maresfield Reprints, 1984), 107.
40. See Steven Connor, 1998, "Beckett and Bion," paper presented at the Beckett and London conference, Goldsmiths College, 1998, http://www.stevenconnor.com/beckbion/.
41. This idea was inspired by Steven Connor's overview of Bion's concept of "attacks on linking," especially his notion that the mother acts for the infant as a "screen or detoxifying repository of the terrors and horrors expelled from the self." Connor, "Beckett and Bion."
42. See Wolfgang Iser, *Prospecting: From Reader Response to Literary Anthropology* (Baltimore, MD: Johns Hopkins University Press, 1993), ch. 8.

5. COSMOGRAPHICAL MEDITATIONS ON THE IN/HUMAN

1. Jean-François Lyotard, "Scapeland, " in *The Inhuman: Reflections on Time* (Stanford, CA: Stanford University Press, 1988), 182–90.
2. Immanuel Kant, *Anthropology from a Pragmatic Point of View*, trans. and ed. Robert B. Louden (Cambridge: Cambridge University Press, 2006), 110.
3. Kant, *Anthropology from a Pragmatic Point of View*, 182.
4. See Orlando Patterson, *Slavery and Social Death: A Comparative Study* (Cambridge: Cambridge University Press, 1985). See also Mario Erdheim and Maya Nadig, "Gössenphantasien und sozialer Tod," *Kursbuch* 58 (1979): 115–26.
5. Samuel Beckett, *The Lost Ones* (New York: Grove, 1972), 7.
6. *The Tormont Webster's Illustrated Dictionary* (Boston: Houghton Mifflin, 1987), 1586.
7. The quotations in this paragraph are from Beckett, *The Lost Ones*, 7–12.
8. Alain Badiou, *Beckett: L'increvable désir* (Paris: Hachette, 1995), 49: "C'est l'autre propre de chacun, celui qui le singularise, qui l'arrache à l'anonymat." My translation.
9. Beckett, *The Lost Ones*, 35.
10. Beckett, *The Lost Ones*, 7.
11. Beckett, *The Lost Ones*, 8.
12. Beckett, *The Lost Ones*, 15.
13. Beckett, *The Lost Ones*, 62–63.
14. David Porush, *The Soft Machine: Cybernetic Fiction* (New York: Methuen, 1985), 158. Porush, however, overlooks the fact that the voice posits itself in many instances as unknowing, hesitant, and reduced to speculation when it comes to interpreting as opposed to merely observing the culture of the little people, even when it comes to the appropriate use of language and categorical attributions. See also Hugh Kenner, *Samuel Beckett* (Berkeley: University of California Press, 1968), 17.
15. Beckett, *The Lost Ones*, 43.
16. Beckett, *The Lost Ones*, 13, 27, 62.
17. The quotations in this paragraph are from Beckett, *The Lost Ones*, 8–9 and 53.

18. This and the two preceding quotations are from Beckett, *The Lost Ones*, 52–53.
19. Beckett, *The Lost Ones*, 42.
20. Gilles Deleuze and Félix Guattari, *A Thousand Plateaus: Capitalism and Schizophrenia*, trans. Brian Massumi (London: Continuum, 2004), 233.
21. Lyotard, *The Inhuman*, 18.
22. Jean-François Lyotard, *Discours, Figure* (Paris: Editions Klincksieck, 1978), 311.
23. Beckett, *The Lost Ones*, 39.
24. Beckett, *The Lost Ones*, 39–40.
25. This and the two preceding quotations are from Beckett, *The Lost Ones*, 30 and 56.
26. I will later return to this resonance with Beckett's piece of the same title. See Samuel Beckett, *Imagination Dead Imagine*, in *The Complete Short Prose of Samuel Beckett, 1929–1989*, ed. S. E. Gontarski (New York: Grove, 1997), 182–85.
27. Alain Badiou, *On Beckett* (London: Clinamen, 2003), 41.
28. Badiou, *On Beckett*, 44.
29. Badiou, *On Beckett*, 76.
30. Lyotard, *The Inhuman*, 22.
31. See Roland Barthes, "The *Nautilus* and the Drunken Boat," in *Mythologies*, trans. Annette Lavers (New York: Hill and Wang, 1972), 65.
32. Beckett, *The Lost Ones*, 36.
33. Beckett, *The Lost Ones*, 21.
34. Beckett, *The Lost Ones*, 53, 37.
35. Beckett, *The Lost Ones*, 53.
36. The quotations in this paragraph are from Beckett, *The Lost Ones*, 53–55.
37. Beckett, *The Lost Ones*, 20.
38. Beckett, *The Lost Ones*, 17, 18.
39. Beckett, *The Lost Ones*, 21.
40. Beckett, *The Lost Ones*, 60.
41. Beckett, *The Lost Ones*, 21, 31, 32.
42. Beckett, *The Lost Ones*, 60–63.

43. The quotations in this paragraph are from Beckett, *Imagination Dead Imagine*, 182 and 184.
44. Beckett, *Imagination Dead Imagine*, 185.
45. Beckett, *Imagination Dead Imagine*, 185.
46. Michel Foucault, *The Order of Things: An Archeology of the Human Sciences* (New York: Random House, 1970), 387.
47. Beckett, *Imagination Dead Imagine*, 185; Beckett, *The Lost Ones*, 18.
48. I have developed this argument in more detail in *Radioactive Ghosts* (Minneapolis: University of Minnesota Press, 2020). See Timothy Morton, *Hyperobjects: Philosophy and Ecology After the End of the World* (Minneapolis: University of Minnesota Press, 2013).
49. See Gilles Deleuze and Félix Guattari, "The Social Field" and "The Molecular Unconscious," in *Anti-Oedipus: Capitalism and Schizophrenia*, trans. Robert Hurley, Mark Seem, and Helen R. Lane (Minneapolis: University of Minnesota Press, 1983), 273–96.
50. Lyotard, *Discours, Figure*, 228. My translation.
51. Lyotard, *The Inhuman*, 172.
52. Lyotard, *Discours, Figure*, 217.
53. I borrow this term and the concept from Christopher Bollas, *The Shadow of the Object: Psychoanalysis of the Unthought Known* (New York: Columbia University Press, 1987). See also my discussion of the relevance of this concept for literary studies in Gabriele Schwab, "Words and Moods: The Transference of Literary Knowledge," *SubStance: A Review of Theory and Literary Criticism* 26, no. 3 (1997): 107–27.
54. See also Porush's reading of the cylinder as an entropic space in *The Soft Machine*. My reading differs from Porush's in emphasizing the negentropic forces that render the space more complex and ultimately more interesting.
55. Lyotard, *The Inhuman*, 184.
56. The quotations from Lyotard are from *The Inhuman*, 186.
57. The quotations from Lyotard are from Lyotard, *The Inhuman*, 184–86.
58. Lyotard, *The Inhuman*, 187.
59. Beckett, *The Lost Ones*, 60.
60. Beckett, *The Lost Ones*, 38.

61. Lyotard, *The Inhuman*, 20.
62. See also the theatrical conception developed for Beckett's theater by Michael Fox as well as the arguments developed in his unpublished work on Beckett.
63. Lyotard, *The Inhuman*, 187.
64. Beckett, *The Lost Ones*, 21.
65. Lyotard, *The Inhuman*, 189.
66. Nelson Goodman, *Ways of Worldmaking* (Indianapolis: Hackett, 1978).
67. Lyotard, *The Inhuman*, 38.
68. Lyotard, *The Inhuman*, 188.
69. Lyotard, *The Inhuman*, 188.
70. Lyotard, *The Inhuman*, 189.
71. Samuel Beckett, "Fizzle 6," in *Samuel Beckett: The Complete Short Prose 1929–1989*, ed. S. E. Gontarski (New York: Grove, 1995), 238–39.
72. Lyotard, *The Inhuman*, 231–36.
73. Lyotard, *The Inhuman*, 231–36, 7.
74. Lyotard, *The Inhuman*, 7.
75. Lyotard, *The Inhuman*, 1.
76. I use this term in the sense of James Clifford and Georges Marcus, ed., *Writing Culture: The Poetics and Politics of Ethnography* (Berkeley: University of California Press, 1986). See also Gabriele Schwab, "Literary Transference and the Vicissitudes of Culture," in *The Anthropological Turn in Literary Studies*, ed. Jürgen Schlaeger (Tübingen: Gunter Narr, 1996), 115–39.
77. The quotations from Lyotard are from *The Inhuman*, 4.
78. Lyotard, *The Inhuman*, 6.
79. Lyotard, *The Inhuman*, 7.
80. Christopher Bollas uses these terms in *The Shadow of the Object*.
81. This is a core term in Samuel Beckett's *The Unnamable*.
82. See Margaret S. Mahler, Fred Pine, and Anni Bergman, eds., *The Psychological Birth of the Human Infant: Symbiosis and Individuation* (New York: Basic Books, 1975). See also the chapter on *The Unnamable* in Gabriele Schwab, *Subjects Without Selves: Transitional Texts in Modern Fiction* (Cambridge, MA: Harvard University Press, 1994), 132–71.
83. Lyotard, *The Inhuman*, 117.

84. See Bollas, *The Shadow of the Object*, and Schwab, "Words and Moods."
85. This final turn of my reading echoes Lyotard's reading of Michael Snow's *La region centrale*. See "The Unconscious as Mise-en-scene," in Michel Benamou and Charles Caramello, *Performance in Postmodern Culture* (Madison, WI: Coda, 1977), 96–98.
86. This is Lyotard's term.
87. Lyotard, *Discours/Figure*, 38.
88. Deleuze, *The Fold*, 35.
89. Porush, *The Soft Machine*, 161.

CODA

1. Antonin Artaud, *The Theater and Its Double*, trans. Mary Caroline Richards (New York: Grove, 1958), 17, 18.
2. Artaud, *The Theater and Its Double*, 21.
3. Artaud, *The Theater and Its Double*, 31–32.
4. Charles McNulty, "Beckett Wrote It Out for You: Life Tends to Stall, Yet We Persevere. Here's a Playwright in Sync with COVID Times," *Los Angeles Times*, May 26, 2020.
5. Paul Sheehan, "Scenes of Writing: Beckett and the Technology of Inscription," *Samuel Beckett Today/Aujourd'hui* 29 (2017): 138–49, at 145.
6. S. E. Gontarski, *Revisioning Beckett: Samuel Beckett's Decadent Turn* (New York: Bloomsbury Academic, 2018), 249.
7. Gontarski, *Revisioning Beckett*, 245.
8. Friedrich Nietzsche, *The Birth of Tragedy out of the Spirit of Music*, trans. Clifton Fadiman (New York: Dover, 1995), 42.
9. Samuel Beckett, *Proust* (New York: Grove, 1957), 49.
10. Samuel Beckett, *Breath*, in *The Collected Shorter Plays of Samuel Beckett* (New York: Grove, 1984), 209–11.
11. Llewellyn Brown, *Beckett, Lacan and the Voice* (Stuttgart: ibidem-Verlag, 2016), 112.
12. Alain Badiou, *On Beckett*, ed. and trans. Alberto Toscano and Nina Power (London: Clinamen, 2003), 74.
13. Luce Irigaray, *Between East and West: From Singularity to Community*, trans. Stephen Pluhácek (New York: Columbia University Press, 2002), 73.
14. Deirde Bair, *Samuel Beckett: Eine Biographie* (Hamburg: Rowohlt, 1994), 646.

15. Artaud, *The Theater and Its Double*, 141.
16. Jacques Derrida, "The Theater of Cruelty and the Closure of Representation," in *Writing and Difference*, trans. Alan Bass (Chicago: University of Chicago Press, 1978), 243.
17. Friedhelm Rathjen, *Samuel Beckett* (Reinbek bei Hamburg: Rowohlt Taschenbuchverlag, 2006), 123.
18. Beckett, *Breath*, 211.
19. Beckett, *Breath*, 211.
20. Beckett, *Breath*, 211.
21. James Knowlson, *Samuel Beckett: Eine Biographie*, trans. Wolfgang Held (Frankfurt: Suhrkamp, 2001), 784.
22. Beckett, *Breath*, 211.
23. Brown, *Beckett, Lacan and the Voice*, 112.
24. In an article responding to the pandemic, John Vidal, for example, writes: "A number of researchers today think that it is actually humanity's destruction of biodiversity that creates the conditions for new viruses and diseases such as Covid-19. . . . We disrupt ecosystems, and we shake viruses loose from their natural hosts. When that happens, they need a new host. Often, we are it." John Vidal, "'Tip of the Iceberg': Is Our Destruction of Nature Responsible for Covid-19?," *Guardian*, March 18, 2020, https://www.theguardian.com/environment/2020/mar/18/tip-of-the-iceberg-is-our-destruction-of-nature-responsible-for-covid-19-aoe.
25. Tomás Saraceno, *We Do Not All Breathe the Same Air*, gallery exhibition, Neugerriemschneider, Berlin, September 18–October 31, 2021.
26. Laurent Testot, *Cataclysms: An Environmental History of Humanity* (Chicago: University of Chicago Press, 2020), 18.
27. Beckett, quoted in Rathjen, *Samuel Beckett*, 79.
28. Beckett, quoted in Rathjen, *Samuel Beckett*, 80.
29. Sheehan, "Scenes of Writing," 143.
30. "Ein Jahr in hundert Leben," *Der Spiegel*, December 12, 2020 (trans. mine.)
31. Samuel Beckett, *Three Novels: Molloy, Malone Dies, The Unnamable*, trans. Patrick Bowles in collaboration with Samuel Beckett (New York: Grove, 1991), 311.

32. Badiou, *On Beckett*, 75.
33. Beckett, *Three Novels*, 277.
34. Badiou, *On Beckett*, 75.
35. Jean-Michel Rabaté, *Think, Pig! Beckett at the Limit of the Human* (New York: Fordham University Press, 2016), 113.

BIBLIOGRAPHY

Abbas, M. Ackbar. *Hong Kong: Culture and the Politics of Disappearance*. Minneapolis: University of Minnesota Press, 1997.
Adorno, Theodor W. "Trying to Understand *Endgame*." Trans. Michael T. Jones. *New German Critique* 26 (1982): 119–50.
Artaud, Antonin. *The Theater and Its Double*. Trans. Mary Caroline Richards. New York: Grove, 1958.
Badiou, Alain. *Beckett: L'increvable désir*. Paris: Hachette, 1995.
Badiou, Alain. *On Beckett*. Ed. Alberto Toscano and Nina Power. London: Clinamen, 2003.
Bair, Deidre. *Samuel Beckett: Eine Biographie*. Hamburg: Rowohlt, 1994.
Barthes, Roland. "The *Nautilus* and the Drunken Boat." In *Mythologies*, 65. Trans. Annette Lavers. New York: Hill and Wang, 1972.
Basaglia, Franco. *L'istituzione negata*. Turin: G. Einaudi, 1968.
Beckett, Samuel. *Breath*. In *The Collected Shorter Plays of Samuel Beckett*, 209–11. New York: Grove, 1984.
Beckett, Samuel. *Endgame*. London: Faber & Faber, 1958.
Beckett, Samuel. *First Love and Other Novellas*. Ed. Gerry Dukes. London: Penguin, 2000.
Beckett, Samuel. "Fizzle 6." In *Samuel Beckett: The Complete Short Prose 1929–1989*, ed. S. E. Gontarski, 238–39. New York: Grove, 1995.
Beckett, Samuel. *Happy Days: A Play in Two Acts*. New York: Grove, 1989.
Beckett, Samuel. *Imagination Dead Imagine*. In *The Complete Short Prose of Samuel Beckett, 1929–1989*, ed. S. E. Gontarski, 182–85. New York: Grove, 1997.

Beckett, Samuel. *The Lost Ones*. New York: Grove 1972.
Beckett, Samuel. *Proust*. New York: Grove, 1957.
Beckett, Samuel. *Three Novels: Molloy, Malone Dies, The Unnamable*. New York: Grove, 2009.
Beckett, Samuel. *The Unnamable*. New York: Grove, 1958.
Beckett, Samuel. *Watt*. London: John Calder, 1963.
Beckett, Samuel, and Georges Duthuit. *Three Dialogues: Tal Coat—Masson—Bram Van Velde*. London: Transition, 1949.
Bennett, Jane. *Vibrant Matter: A Political Ecology of Things*. Durham, NC: Duke University Press, 2010.
Berlant, Lauren. *Cruel Optimism*. Durham, NC: Duke University Press, 2011.
Bion, W. R. "Attacks on Linking." *Psychoanalytic Quarterly* 82, no. 2 (2013): 285–300.
Bion, W. R. *Second Thoughts: Selected Papers on Psychoanalysis*. London: Maresfield Reprints, 1984.
Blau, Herbert. *Blooded Thought: Occasions of Theatre*. New York: Performing Arts Journal, 1982.
Blau, Herbert. *Reality Principles: From the Absurd to the Virtual*. Ann Arbor: University of Michigan Press, 2011.
Blau, Herbert. *Take up the Bodies: Theater at the Vanishing Point*. Urbana: University of Illinois Press, 1982.
Bollas, Christopher. *The Shadow of the Object: Psychoanalysis of the Unthought Known*. New York: Columbia University Press, 1987.
Brook, Peter. *Materialen zu Becketts "Endspiel."* Ed. Michael Haerdter. Frankfurt: Suhrkamp, 1968.
Brown, Llewellyn. *Beckett, Lacan and the Voice*. Stuttgart: ibidem-Verlag, 2016.
Burroughs, William S. *Naked Lunch*. New York: Grove Weidenfeld, 1992.
Carrouges, Michael. *Les machines célibataires*. Paris: Arcanes, 1954.
Cavell, Stanley. "Ending the Waiting Game: A Reading of Beckett's *Endgame*." In *Must We Mean What We Say: Modern Philosophical Essays in Morality, Religion, Drama, Music and Criticism*, 107–50. New York: Scribner's, 1969.
Clifford, James, and Georges Marcus, eds. *Writing Culture: The Poetics and Politics of Ethnography*. Berkeley: University of California Press, 1986.
Cohn, Ruby. *Back to Beckett*. Princeton, NJ: Princeton University Press, 1973.

Connor, Steven. "Beckett and Bion." Paper presented at "Beckett and London," Goldsmiths College, 1998. http://www.stevenconnor.com/beckbion/.
Connor, Steven. *Samuel Beckett: Repetition, Theory, and Text*. Aurora, CO: The Davies Group, 2007.
Connor, Steven, ed. *Samuel Beckett's "Waiting for Godot" and "Endgame:" A New Casebook*. Basingstoke: Macmillan, 1992.
Dearlove, J. E. *Accommodating the Chaos: Samuel Beckett's Nonrelational Art*. Durham, NC: Duke University Press, 1982.
Deleuze, Gilles. *The Fold: Leibniz and the Baroque*. Minneapolis: University of Minnesota Press, 1992.
Deleuze, Gilles. *Logique du sens*. Paris: Minuit, 1969.
Deleuze, Gilles, and Felix Guattari. *Anti-Oedipus: Capitalism and Schizophrenia*. Trans. Robert Hurley, Mark Seem, and Helen R. Lane. Minneapolis: University of Minnesota Press, 1983.
Deleuze, Gilles, and Félix Guattari. *A Thousand Plateaus: Capitalism and Schizophrenia*. Trans. Brian Massumi. London: Continuum, 2004.
Deleuze, Gilles, and Felix Guattari. *What Is Philosophy?* Trans. Hugh Tomlinson and Graham Burchell. New York: Columbia University Press, 1994.
Derrida, Jacques. *Apokalypse*. Trans. Michael Wetzel. Vienna: Passagen, 1985.
Derrida, Jacques. *Archive Fever: A Freudian Impression*. Trans. Eric Prenowitz. Chicago: University of Chicago Press, 1996.
Derrida, Jacques. "Structure, Sign and Play in the Discourse of the Human Sciences." In *Writing and Difference*, trans. Alan Bass, 278–94. London: Routledge & Kegan Paul, 1978.
Derrida, Jacques. *Writing and Difference*. Trans. Alan Bass. Chicago: University of Chicago Press, 1978.
"Ein Jahr in hundert Leben." *Der Spiegel*, December 12, 2020.
Erdheim, Mario, and Maya Nadig. "Gössenphantasien und sozialer Tod." *Kursbuch* 58 (1979): 115–26.
Erhard, Peter. *Anatomie de Samuel Beckett*. Stuttgart: Birkhauser, 1976.
Esslin, Martin. *Theatre of the Absurd*. New York: Anchor, 1961.
Foucault, Michel. *Archéologie du savoir*. Paris: Gallimard, 1969.
Foucault, Michel. *The Archeology of Knowledge*. Trans. A. M. Sheridan Smith. New York: Pantheon, 1972.
Foucault, Michel. *The Order of Things: An Archeology of the Human Sciences*. New York: Random House, 1970.

Frank, Manfred. "Das Individuum in der Rolle des Idioten: Die hermeneutische Konzeption des Flaubert." In *Sartres Flaubert lessen: Essays zu Der Idiot in der Familie*, ed. Traugott König, 84–108. Reinbek bei Hamburg: Rowohlt, 1980.

Freud, Sigmund. *Beyond the Pleasure Principle*. Trans and ed. James Strachey. New York: Norton, 1961.

Freud, Sigmund. *Civilization and Its Discontents*. In *The Standard Edition of the Complete Psychological Works of Sigmund Freud*, vol. 2. Ed. James Strachey, trans. Joan Riviere. London: Hogarth and Institute of Psycho-Analysis, 1930.

Freud, Sigmund. *The Ego and the Id*. Trans. Joan Riviere, rev. and ed. James Strachey. New York: Norton, 1962.

Freud, Sigmund. "The Ego and the Id." In *The Standard Edition of the Complete Psychological Works of Sigmund Freud*, vol. 19. Trans. James Strachey. London: Hogarth, 1950.

Freud, Sigmund. "Formulations on the Two Principles of Mental Functioning." In *The Standard Edition of the Complete Psychological Works of Sigmund Freud*, vol. 12. Trans. James Strachey. London: Hogarth.

Freud, Sigmund. "Jokes and Their Relation to the Unconscious." In *The Standard Edition of the Complete Psychological Works of Sigmund Freud*, vol. 8. Trans. James Strachey. London: Hogarth.

Freud, Sigmund. "On Negation." In *The Standard Edition of the Complete Psychological Works of Sigmund Freud*, vol. 19. Trans. James Strachey. London: Hogarth.

Goin, Peter. *Nuclear Landscapes*. Baltimore, MD: Johns Hopkins University Press, 1951.

Gölter, Waltraud. *Entfremdung als Konstituens bürgerlicher Literatur, dargestellt am Beispiel Samuel Becketts: Versuch einer Vermittlung von Soziologie und Psychoanalyse als Imterpretationsmodell*. Heidelberg: Carl Winter, 1976.

Gontarski, S. E. "Literary Allusions in 'Happy Days.'" In *On Beckett: Essays and Criticism*, ed. S. E. Gontarski, 232–44. New York: Grove, 1986.

Gontarski, S. E. *Revisioning Beckett: Samuel Beckett's Decadent Turn*. New York: Bloomsbury Academic, 2018.

Goodman, Nelson. *Ways of Worldmaking*. Indianapolis: Hackett, 1978.

Hage, Ghassan. *Alter-Politics: Critical Anthropology and the Radical Imagination*. Melbourne: Melbourne University Press, 2015.

Hassan, Ihab. *Paracriticisms: Seven Speculations of the Times*. Urbana: University of Illinois Press, 1975.
Henrich, Dieter. "Identität." In *Identität*, ed. Odo Marquard and Karlheinz Stierle, 177–78. Munich: Fink, 1979.
Henrich, Dieter. "Kunst und Kunstphilosophie der Gegenwart—Überlegungen mit Rücksicht auf Hegel." In *Immanente Ästhetik—Ästhetische Reflexion*, ed. Wolfgang Iser, 27–28. Munich: Fink, 1966.
Irigaray, Luce. *Between East and West: From Singularity to Community*. Trans. Stephen Pluhácek. New York: Columbia University Press, 2002.
Iser, Wolfgang. *Prospecting: From Reader Response to Literary Anthropology*. Baltimore, MD: Johns Hopkins University Press, 1993.
Iser, Wolfgang. "The Reading Process: A Phenomenological Approach." *New Literary History* 3, no. 2 (1972): 279–99.
Jardine, Alice. *Gynesis*. Ithaca, NY: Cornell University Press, 1985.
Joyce, James. "Bahnhofstrasse." In *The Norton Anthology of Modern Poetry*, ed. Richard Ellmann and Robert O'Clair, 275. New York: Norton, 1973.
Kamper, Dietmar. "Zeit Gewinnen: Eine Erinnerung an die Zukunft." In *Vor der Jahrtausendwende: Berichte zur Lage der Zukunft*, ed. Peter Sloterdijk, 2:672–92. Frankfurt: Suhrkamp, 1990.
Kant, Immanuel. *Anthropology from a Pragmatic Point of View*. Trans. and ed. Robert B. Louden. Cambridge: Cambridge University Press, 2006.
Kavin, Bruce. "On Not Having the Last Word: Beckett, Wittgenstein, and the Limits of Language." In *Ineffability: Naming the Unnamable from Dante to Beckett*, ed. Peter S. Hawkins and Anne H. Schotter, 189–202. New York: AMS, 1984.
Kenner, Hugh. *Samuel Beckett*. Berkeley: University of California Press, 1968.
Kermode, Frank. *The Sense of an Ending: Studies in the Theory of Fiction*. Oxford: Oxford University Press, 1967.
Kierkegaard, Søren. *Die Krankheit zum Tode*. Düsseldorf: Eugen Diederichs, 1971.
Kierkegaard, Søren. *Fear and Trembling and The Sickness Unto Death*. Trans. Walter Lowrie. Garden City, NY: Doubleday Anchor, 1954.
Knowlson, James. *Samuel Beckett: Eine Biographie*. Trans. Wolfgang Held. Frankfurt: Suhrkamp, 2001.
Laing, Ronald D. *The Divided Self*. Harmondsworth: Penguin, 1970.

Lapoujade, David. "To Act at the Limit." In *Aesthetics of Standstill*, ed. Reinhold Görling, Barbara Gronau, and Ludger Schwarte, 284–89. Berlin: Sternberg, 2019.

Lifton, Robert J. *Death in Life: Survivors of Hiroshima*. Chapel Hill: University of North Carolina Press, 1991.

Lyotard, Jean-François. "Can Thought Go on Without a Body?" Trans. Bruce Boone and Lee Hildreth. *Discourse* 11, no. 1 (1988): 74–87.

Lyotard, Jean-François. *Discours, Figure*. Paris: Editions Klincksieck, 1978.

Lyotard, Jean-François. *The Inhuman: Reflections on Time*. Stanford, CA: Stanford University Press, 1988.

Lyotard, Jean-François. "The Unconscious as Mise-en-scene." In *Performance in Postmodern Culture*, ed. Michel Benamou and Charles Caramello, 96–98. Milwaukee: Center for Twentieth Century Studies, University of Wisconsin-Milwaukee, 1977.

Mahler, Margaret, Fred Pine, and Annie Bergman. *The Psychological Birth of the Human Infant: Symbiosis and Individuation*. New York: Basic Books, 1975.

Mbembe, Achille. "Necropolitics." *Public Culture* 15, no. 1 (Winter 2003): 11–40.

McNulty, Charles. "Beckett Wrote It Out for You: Life Tends to Stall, Yet We Persevere. Here's a Playwright in Sync with COVID Times." *Los Angeles Times*, May 26, 2020.

Menand, Louis. "Now What I Wonder Do I Mean By That." *Slate*, August 21, 1996. https://slate.com/news-and-politics/1996/08/now-what-i-wonder-do-i-mean-by-that.html.

Merrell, Floyd. *Deconstruction Reframed*. West Lafayette, IN: Purdue University Press, 1985.

Miranda, Pierre. "The Dialectic of Metaphor: An Anthropological Essay on Hermeneutics." In *The Reader in the Text*, ed. Susan R. Suleiman and Inge Crosman, 183–204. Princeton, NJ: Princeton University Press, 1980.

Morton, Timothy. *Hyperobjects: Philosophy and Ecology After the End of the World*. Minneapolis: University of Minnesota Press, 2013.

Navratil, Leo. *Schizophrenie und Kunst*. Munich: Deutscher Taschenbuch Verlag, 1965.

Neumann, Stella, ed. *English and American Studies in German 1981: Summaries of Theses and Monographs*. Tübingen: de Gruyter, 1981.

Nietzsche, Friedrich. *The Birth of Tragedy out of the Spirit of Music*. 1872. Trans. Clifton Fadiman. New York: Dover, 1995.
Patterson, Orlando. *Slavery and Social Death: A Comparative Study*. Cambridge: Cambridge University Press, 1985.
Plato. *The Republic*. Trans. H. D. P. Lee. Baltimore, MD: Penguin, 1961.
Plessner, Helmuth. *Laughing and Crying: A Study of the Limits of Human Behavior*. Trans. James Spencer Churchill and Marjorie Grene. Evanston, IL: Northwestern University Press, 2020.
Porush, David. *The Soft Machine: Cybernetic Fiction*. New York: Methuen, 1985.
Pothast, Ulrich. *Die eigentlich metaphysische Tätigkeit: Über Schopenhauers Ästhetik und ihre Anwendung durch Samuel Beckett*. Frankfurt: Suhrkamp, 1982.
Powers, Richard. "What Does Fiction Know?" *Places Journal*, August 2, 2011. https://placesjournal.org/article/what-does-fiction-know/.
Pynchon, Thomas. *Gravity's Rainbow*. New York: Viking, 1973.
Rabaté, Jean-Michel. *Think, Pig! Beckett at the Limit of the Human*. New York: Fordham University Press, 2016.
Rathjen, Friedhelm. *Samuel Beckett*. Reinbek bei Hamburg: Rowohlt Taschenbuchverlag, 2006.
Ricoeur, Paul. *De l'interprétation: Essai sur Freud*. Paris: Seuil, 1965.
Said, Edward. *Freud and the Non-European*. London: Verso, 2014.
Saraceno, Tomás. *We Do Not All Breathe the Same Air*. Gallery exhibition, Neugerriemschneider, Berlin, September 18–October 31, 2021.
Schwab, Gabriele. "Cosmographical Meditations on the In/Human: Beckett's *The Lost Ones* and Lyotard's 'Scapeland.'" *Parallax* 6, no. 4 (2000): 58–75.
Schwab, Gabriele. "Cultural Texts and Endopsychic Scripts." *SubStance* 30, nos. 1–2 (2001): 160–76.
Schwab, Gabriele. "Derrida, the Parched Woman, and the Son of Man." *Discourse* 30, nos. 1–2 (2008): 226–41.
Schwab, Gabriele. "Genesis of the Subject, Imaginary Functions, and Poetic Language." *New Literary History* 15, no. 3 (Spring 1984): 453–93.
Schwab, Gabriele. *Imaginary Ethnographies: Literature, Culture & Subjectivity*. New York: Columbia University Press, 2012
Schwab, Gabriele. "The Intermediate Area Between Life and Death: On Samuel Beckett's *The Unnamable*." In *Memory and Desire:*

Aging—Literature—Psychoanalysis, ed. Kathleen Woodward and Murray M. Schwartz, 205–17. Bloomington: Indiana University Press, 1986.

Schwab, Gabriele. "Literary Transference and the Vicissitudes of Culture." In *The Anthropological Turn in Literary Studies*, ed. Jürgen Schlaeger, 115–39. Tübingen: Gunter Narr, 1996.

Schwab, Gabriele. "On the Dialectic of Closing and Opening in Samuel Beckett's End-Game." Trans. D. L. Selden. *Yale French Studies* 67 (1984): 191–202.

Schwab, Gabriele. "Pandemic Surrealism." *Foundry*, VIRUSHUMANS special issue, October 2020. https://uchri.org/foundry/pandemic-surrealism/.

Schwab, Gabriele. *Radioactive Ghosts*. Minneapolis: University of Minnesota Press, 2020.

Schwab, Gabriele. "Reader Response and the Aesthetic Experience of Otherness." *Stanford Literary Review* 3, no. 1 (1986): 107–36.

Schwab, Gabriele. *Samuel Becketts Endspiel mit der Subjektivität: Entwurf einer Wirkungsästhetik des Modernen Theaters*. Stuttgart: J. B. Metzler, 1981.

Schwab, Gabriele. *Subjects Without Selves: Transitional Texts in Modern Fiction*. Cambridge, MA: Harvard University Press, 1994.

Schwab, Gabriele. "Words and Moods: The Transference of Literary Knowledge." *SubStance* 26, no. 3 (1997): 107–27.

Sharot, Tali, Christoph W. Korn, and Raymond J. Dolan. "How Unrealistic Optimism Is Maintained in the Face of Reality." *Nature* 14, no. 11 (November 2011): 1475–79.

Sheehan, Paul. "Scenes of Writing: Beckett and the Technology of Inscription." *Samuel Beckett Today/Aujourd'hui* 29 (2017): 138–49.

Shenker, Israel. "An Interview with Beckett." In *Samuel Beckett: The Critical Heritage*, ed. Lawrence Graver and Raymond Federman, 160–64. London: Routledge & Kegan Paul, 1979.

Sloterdijk, Peter, ed. *Vor der Jahrtausendwende: Berichte zur Lage der Zukunft*, vol. 2. Frankfurt: Suhrkamp, 1990.

Sluzki, C. E., and D. C. Ranson, eds. *Double-Bind: The Foundation of the Communicational Approach to the Family*. New York: The Psychological Corp, 1976.

Smith, Patti. *M Train*. New York: Vintage, 2015.

Smuda, Manfred. *Becketts Pros als Metasprache*. Munich: Fink, 1970.
Smuda, Manfred. "Kunst im Kopf—Becketts spätere Prosa und das Imaginäre." In *Samuel Beckett*, ed. Hartmut Engelhardt, 211–34. Frankfurt: Suhrkamp, 1984.
Spitz, René. *No and Yes: On the Genesis of Human Communication*. New York: International Universities Press, 1957.
Testot, Laurent. *Cataclysms: An Environmental History of Humanity*. Chicago: University of Chicago Press, 2020.
Thiher, Allen. *Words in Reflection: Modern Language Theory and Postmodern Fiction*. Chicago: University of Chicago Press, 1984.
The Tormont Webster's Illustrated Dictionary. Boston: Houghton Mifflin, 1987.
Tranter, Rhys. *Beckett's Late Stage: Trauma, Language, and Subjectivity*. Stuttgart: ibidem-Verlag, 2018.
Tugendhat, Ernst. *Selbstbewusstsein und Selbstbestimmung*. Frankfurt: Suhrkamp, 1979.
Tugendhat, Ernst. *Self-Consciousness and Self-Determination*. Trans. Paul Stern. Cambridge, MA: MIT Press, 1986.
Vidal, John. "'Tip of the Iceberg': Is Our Destruction of Nature Responsible for Covid-19?" *Guardian*, March 18, 2020.
Weisman, Alan. *The World Without Us*. London: Random House, 2008.
Whole Earth Catalog. Menlo Park, CA: Portola Institute, 1968.
Winnicott, Donald W. *Playing and Reality*. London: Tavistock, 1971.
Woodward, Kathleen. "Transitional Objects and the Isolate: Samuel Beckett's 'Malone Dies.'" *Contemporary Literature* 26, no. 2 (1985): 140–54.

INDEX

Abbas, Ackbar, 164
abstraction, 49–50, 98
absurd, 50
Acts Without Words I and II (Beckett), 14–15, 214
adaptability, 152–53, 160–61
Adorno, Theodor W., 28, 44
aesthetics: de-aestheticization of, 170; Lyotard on, 202–3; poly, 204; of standstill, 55; of *The Lost Ones*, 203–4; of *The Unnamable*, 138–44
"Aesthetics of Response in Beckett's *Endgame*" (Schwab, G.), 2–3
affective cathexis, 133–34, 136–37, 180
affirmation, double negation for, 130
aging, 34
Aligheri, Dante, 174, 185–86
all of nothing, 187
Alter-Politics (Hage), 157
Anthropocene, 29, 47

aperçus, 178
aphasia, 24–25
apocalypse, 35, 75; in "The Calmative," 38–39; depicting, 46–47; disaster, 149–50; in *Happy Days*, 156–57, 171; Judeo-Christian, 30; nuclear, 156–57; rhetorical construction of, 34
apocalyptic imaginaries: in *Endgame*, 42; language games undermining, 38; waiting linked to, 30
apocalyptic scenery, 149
aporias, 102
archive fever, 163
Arezzo (Italy), psychiatric hospital in, 5–6, 68
Aristotle, 105, 115
Artaud, Antonin, 39–40, 207, 214
artificial intelligence, 184–85
Asmus, Walter D., 17
atomic bomb (the Bomb), 37, 44, 45, 155, 157

audience, 62; Clov on, 52, 57–58; double binds engaging, 51, 58, 61; *Endgame* and, 50–51, 63; end times experienced by, 52; meaning depended on by, 63–64
autogenesis, 112

Badiou, Alain, 44, 175, 184, 211, 223
Barthes, Roland, 185
Basaglia, Franco, 93
Basil (character), 120
beauty, in *The Lost Ones*, 183–84
Beckett, Lacan and the Voice (Brown), 211
Beckett's Head (*Beckett's Kopf*) (bar), 26
Beckett's Waiting for Godot and Endgame (Connor), 33
being, 217
Benjamin, Walter, 49
Benveniste, Émile, 114
Berlant, Lauren, 159, 164
biolingua, 154, 170
Bion, Wilfred Ruprecht, 12, 29–30, 67, 87; on attacks of linking, 168–69, 240*n*41
birth (born): canal, 209; death linked with, 87–88; never, 111–13; sin of, 210–11; types of, 233*n*19
Birth of Tragedy out of the Spirit of Music, The (Nietzsche), 210
Blau, Herbert, 9, 19, 49, 88; paradox of subjectivity by, 237*n*70; *The Donner Party* by, 237*n*70; *Waiting for Godot* performed by, 18
body: as confused speaker, 204; fantasies of, 110–11; grotesque, 71, 108, 186; imaginary, 107–8; in literature, 106–9; organless, 107–9; phantasms of, 36–37; self-observation of, 106–7, 111–12; thought without, 38, 180, 184
Bollas, Christopher, 67, 164, 203
Bomb, the. *See* atomic bomb
bookstores, 221
Borrowings of Dante, Bruno, and Vico from Finnegans Wake, The (Unnamable, the), 19
breath: gasps of, 210; of life, 218; of Malone, 208–9, 219, 223; meditation and, 221; silence and, 210, 220; struggling for, 208–10, 212; suffocation and, 220; writing connected to, 219
Breath (Beckett), 55, 207–23; breath agent in, 215–17; COVID-19 pandemic compared with, 40, 212, 217, 222–23; cry agent in, 215–17; environment and, 213–15, 217–19; first act of, 214–16; four preformative agents of, 214; light agent in, 216–18; rubbish agent in, 215–16; second act of, 216–17
Brook, Peter, 60
Brown, Llewellyn, 211, 217
Brownie (revolver), 165
Burroughs, Edgar Rice, 151

"Calmative, The" ("Le calmant") (Beckett), 34, 35, 75–80; apocalypse in, 38–39; *Malone Dies* tangled with, 80; poetry in,

77; temporarily in, 74; transitional space in, 72, 90
"Can Thought Go on Without a Body?" (Lyotard), 180, 184
Capitalocene, 29
cartoon, 221, 222
catachresis, 34, 47, 156, 157, 223
Cataclysms: An Environmental History of Humanity (Testot), 219
catastrophe: setting in *Happy Days*, 149–50, 156–57, 161, 171; surviving, 166–67
cathexis, affective, 133–34, 136–37, 180
cave, Plato's, 104, 109–10
Cavell, Stanley, 49
characters, 28, 29, 35; creative paranoia of, 93; end times experienced by, 42; entanglement between, 80; infinite play of language performed by, 54; old age experienced by, 91; others mirroring, 78; posthuman, 176–77, 185, 188, 190; singular presentation of, 59–60; speech obscuring, 55–56; transitional, 89–90, 144–48. *See also specific characters*
children, 15, 200–1; abandoned, 90; poetics, politics and, 197–99
Civilization and Its Discontents (Freud), 150
climate, 157, 166, 178–79, 212, 246n24
closeness, 141

Clov (character), 41, 53–54; Hamm in relation to, 51–52; as overdetermined, 60; projections revealed by, 52, 57–58; revulsion of, 159
Cohn, Ruby, 112
composition, 177
concord fictions, 62; the end experienced through, 48; endings and, 31
confinement, 208
Connor, Steven, 33, 48, 240n41
Conrad, Joseph, 172
consciousness, 138–39, 147
consoling objects, 66, 68; as containing objects, 77; of Winnie, 165–68
containing objects, 77
contradiction, 129
Corona virus pandemic. *See* COVID-19 pandemic
cosmogony, 185
COVID-19 pandemic (Corona virus pandemic), 25, 39, 207–8; *Breath* compared with, 40, 212, 217, 222–23
creative act, 120–21
creative paranoia, 93
cruel optimism, 159–60, 163–65
cruelty, 152–53, 154, 214
cultural imaginary, 32, 157
cultural objects, 89
cultural schizophrenia, 103–4
culture, writing against, 199

Dante. *See* Aligheri, Dante
darkness, 48–49, 218–19

David, Betty, 19–20
Dearlove, J. E., 132
death (dead), 19, 48, 71–72; birth linked with, 87–88; in life, 76, 208; narrative voice of, 85; sickness unto, 125; social, 173; speech haunted by, 91; of subject, 144; undeath and, 111–12
deathworlds, 38, 150, 157, 166, 226n23
decomposition, 76, 87, 92, 96; breath, environment and, 213–15; Malone fascinated by, 85; Molloy seeking, 35; writing as, 83–84
deconstructionism, 122
dedifferentiation, 92, 146, 196; differentiation and, 117–18, 139, 192, 201
Deleuze, Gilles, 96, 108, 204, 234nn21–22
Denkbilder (thought images), 49
depeupleur, Le (Beckett), 175, 187
deprivation, sensual, 104
Derrida, Jacques, 53–54, 157; archive fever of, 163; contrast with, 15–17
Der Verwaiser (Beckett), 175
Descartes, René, 114
desire, queer, 79
desolation, 64–65
despair, 125–26
dialogue, feedback loops in, 53
differentiation, 56; dedifferentiation and, 117–18, 139, 192, 201; in *Endgame*, 60; human, inhuman and, 202; indifferentiation and,

201; in *The Unnamable*, 117–18; undifferentiation and, 140–41, 202
disbelief, 145, 235n37
Discours, Figure (Lyotard), 180–81, 191–92
disintegration, 99, 196; psychotic, 111; schizoid subject threatened by, 100–101
distant earth, 74–75
Donner Party, The (Blau), 237n70
double bind, 99; audience engaged through, 51, 58, 61; endings sublated by, 33, 47
double meaning, 58–59
dying planet, 150

earth, 73; as distant, 74–75; worlds beyond, 58
Eastern philosophy, 126, 137
Elrod, Norman, 3–4
emotional inversion, 159–60
emotional turmoil, 76
emotions, language and, 128–32
end, the: concord fictions experiencing, 48; silence, end point and, 125; waiting for, 42–43, 55
Endgame (Beckett), 8, 10, 13, 30, 41–69, 172; apocalyptic imaginaries in, 42; audience ensnared by, 50–51; the Bomb spotlit by, 45; differentiation in, 60; Elrod staging, 3–4; end times in, 4–49; eschatological imaginary debunked by, 57; laughter inspired by, 62–63;

Molloy echoing, 81–82; open-endedness within, 64; personal tragedy precipitating, 65; projections reflected on in, 61–62; responses to, 63; sensorial aspects of, 67; structure of, 58, 99, 152; World War II and, 43–44
Endgames (Wellmer), 12
endings: concord fictions and, 31; double binds sublating, 33, 47
end times, 71; audience experiencing, 52; the Bomb and, 45; characters experiencing, 42; cultural imaginary of, 32; darkness in, 48–49; describing, 31; in *Endgame*, 47–49; epistemological uncertainty required by, 46; in *Happy Days*, 170; living in, 34; meaning sought in, 54; negative hallucination in, 29–30; poetics of, 26–40, 181–82; silence in, 48–49, 220; in *The Lost Ones*, 176, 185–90, 194; in *The Unnamable*, 95–96; transitional imaginaries of, 72; in twenty-first century, 27–28
environment: adaptability, failure and, 152–53, 160–61; breath connected to, 213–15, 217–19
epistemological doubt, 38–39
epistemological insecurity, 64
epistemological paradox, 122
epistemological skepticism, 146–47
epistemological uncertainty, 46
eschatological imaginary, 57

Esslin, Martin, 18, 50
event, 192–93
existential stuckedness, 157–58
expiation, 216; of sin, 210–11
extinction, 168–69
extremes, 31–32, 129

failure, 153, 160–61; better, 105; worth pursuing, 152
feedback loops, 53
fiction: concord, 31, 48, 62; epistemological skepticism of, 146–47; fictionality of, 119–20, 121–22; philosophical subjects in, 97–98, 105–6; transitional space, reality and, 145–47
Film (Beckett), 13
first-person narrator, 118, 125, 140
"Fizzle 6" (Beckett), 197–98
Fletcher, John, 9
Floyd, George, 212
Fold, The (Deleuze), 204
Footfalls (Beckett), 24, 68
Foucault, Michel, 189
Frank, Manfred, 123
Freud, Sigmund, 110, 134, 150, 234*n*25, 238*n*2
future, archive and, 163

gender, 234*n*22
glossolalia, 134–35
God, 121, 126
Gontarski, S. E., 65, 210–11
Gray, Thomas, 166–67
grotesque bodies, 71, 108, 186
Guattari, Felix, 96, 108, 234*nn*21–22
guilty laughter, 171

Habilitationsschrift (Schwab, G.), 11–12
Hage, Ghassan, 157
hallucination: negative, 29–30, 164–65, 171–72; suggestions, 151, 167–68
Hamm (character), 33, 41, 53–54, 69; Clov in relation to, 51–52; desolation communicated by, 64–65; meaning stressing, 57–58; the Other unmasked by, 56; as overdetermined, 60
happiness, 238n2, 239n16; humans desiring, 150; paradoxical, 155; suffering as bearable, 172
Happy Days (Beckett), 17–18, 23–24, 68, 149–72; brink of extinction in, 168–69; catastrophe setting in, 149–50, 156–57, 161, 171; end times in, 170; Hiroshima influencing, 37, 44, 155, 157; not remembering lines in, 155–56; staging of, 153–56; theatrical realism and, 151–52. *See also* Winnie
Harry (former partner), 3, 6; aphasia impacting, 24–25
Hartman, Geoffrey, 22
Hassan, Ihab, 19
Heart of Darkness (Conrad), 172
Henrich, Dieter, 22–23, 146–47
"Her Absence Filled the World" (Kentridge), 65
Hiroshima (atomic bombing), 37, 44, 155, 157
horror vacui, 80, 100, 125
Howe, Fanny, 21

Howe, Susan, 20–21
How It Is (Beckett), 81–82, 208–9
humanity, 117–18
human liminality, 193–94
humans: happiness desired by, 150; last, 26, 37, 150, 153, 176; obstinacy, 223; posthuman characters and, 176–77, 185, 188, 190. *See also* inhuman
Husserl, Edmund, 110
hyperconscious, 118–19
hyperobjects, 190
hyperreflexivity, 141

I, the, 234n25; diffusion of, 131; endless production *vs.*, 109; Not-I and, 110–12, 114–17, 128–29, 131, 139–40, 147; pure, 105–6; subjectivity linked to functioning of, 115; as surface, 110; as transitional object, 87, 165
"If Only I Were Not Obliged to Manifest" (Schwab, G.), 13
illness, of sister, 2–5, 64–66, 68
illusion of representability, 123–24
imaginary, 20–21; body, 107–8; cultural, 32, 157; language, 204–5; the real and, 121, 145–46; silence and end point, 125; subjectivity, self-reflexivity and, 147; transitional, 72. *See also* apocalyptic imaginaries
Imagination Dead Imagine (Beckett), 11, 187–88, 197
immaterial, 192, 204–5
immobility, 157–58

immortality, 107
indetermination, 198–200, 202
indifferentiation, 186, 201, 202
individuality, 123–24
infancy: differentiation and, 201; native indetermination, poetics and, 197–200, 204
infinite play of language, 53, 54
infinitude, despair of, 125–26
inhuman, 198, 203; child, adult and, 200, 202; politics resisting, 201–2; as radical antihumanism, 199
Inhuman, The (Lyotard), 174
inner space, 82, 195
insecurity. *See* epistemological insecurity; ontological insecurity
insomnia, 25–26
inspiration, 209, 216, 220
intelligence, artificial, 184–85
"Intermediate Area Between Life and Death, The" (Schwab, G.), 19
intimist exoticism, 193
inventing: inversion of, 120–21; *The Unnamable*, being invented and, 117–24
inversion: of creative act, 120–21; emotional, 159–60; moral, 158
Irigaray, Luce, 212
Iser, Wolfgang, 2, 7–8, 12

"Jacques Derrida and Waiting for Godot" (Schwab, Manu), 15
Joyce, James, 19
"Joyce—Beckett" (Hassan), 19

Kant, Immanuel, 173–74, 183, 202–3
katechon (waiting before apocalypse), 30
Kawin, Bruce, 137
Kenner, Hugh, 177
Kentridge, William, 65
Kermode, Frank, 31, 48
Kierkegaard, Søren, 125
Klee, Paul, 191
Klein, Melanie, 111, 166
Knowlson, James, 216

landscape, 193–94
language: beyond, 124; *biolingua*, 154, 170; catachresis of, 34, 47, 156, 157, 223; de-aestheticization of, 170; dissolution of, 136–37; emotions and, 128–32; experimental critique of, 104–5; foul, 135; imaginary, 204–5; infinite play of, 53–54; meaning separated from, 137; molar organization of, 191; primary process of, 180–82; speaking and, 116–17, 127–28
language games, 88, 230*n*1; apocalyptic imaginaries undermined by, 38; self-presentation and, 56–57
Lapoujade, David, 55
laughter, 15; *Endgame* inspiring, 62–63; guilty, 171; stifled, 172
life, death in, 76, 208
Lifton, Robert J., 158
light: in *Breath*, 216–18; into darkness, 218–19; paradoxical resilience of, 190

limbs, amputated, 107
limits, 55, 96
l'immonde, 194–96, 198
linking, attacks on, 168–69, 240n41
L'innomable (Beckett). See *The Unnamable* (Beckett)
literary subject, 97–106, 235n37; free of body, 106–7; the self in, 105–6
literature: body in, 107–9; internal ear and eye through, 191–92
Literature of Silence, The (Hassan), 19
Lost Ones, The (Beckett), 75, 173–205; aesthetic experience of, 203–4; all of nothing in, 187; artificial intelligence and, 184–85; beauty in, 183–84; climate conditions in, 178–79; cylindrical space of, 174–78, 182, 187, 204–5, 243n54; end times in, 176, 185–90, 194; epistemological doubt embraced in, 38–39; human and posthuman characters in, 176–77, 185, 190; human liminality in, 193–94; indetermination ambivalence and, 202; infancy, children and, 197–201; little people in, 177, 182, 195, 201, 204; narrative agency/voice in, 176–83; objectivity in, 182–83; the self in, 196–97; soul in, 173, 179–80, 183, 194–96, 204–5; transitional space in, 185; vanishing in, 182, 187–88, 192, 195–96; virtuality, 175–77
love, 185–86

lung, cyst on, 212
Lyotard, Jean-François, 85, 175, 188, 196–203; on aesthetics, 202–3; "Can Thought Go on Without a Body?" by, 180, 184; *Discours, Figure* by, 180–81, 191–92; on event, 192–93; on infancy, 197–200, 204; on inhuman, 199–203; on landscape, 193–94; on *l'immonde*, 194–96, 198; native indetermination of, 198–99; on poetics, 195–98; "Scapeland" by, 193–94; on soul, 204; on sublime, 203; *The Inhuman* by, 174; on totalization, 200; on unworlding, 195–96, 198; writing against culture by, 199

madness: moody, 165, 167; systematic, 38, 174, 183, 191–92
"Making of Beckett's '*End* Game,' The" (Joyce), 19
Malone (character), 88–89, 117, 166; breath of, 208–9, 219, 223; decomposition fascinating, 85; possessions inventoried by, 84, 86
Malone Dies (*Malone Meurt*) (Beckett), 72; "The Calmative" tangling with, 80; transitional space in, 36, 84–85
Mbembe, Achille, 226n23
McNulty, Charles, 29
meaning: audience depending on, 63–64; condensations mobilizing, 60–61; disbelief and

withholding, 235n37; double, 58–59; in end times, 54; Hamm stressed by, 57–58; language separated from, 137; representation beyond, 124; beyond speech, 59
meditation, 126, 137, 221
Memory and Desire (Woodward and Schwartz), 19
Merrell, Floyd, 131, 140, 237n70
Milton, John, 167
mime, 211
mind, empty, 137
minimalist text, 236n57
misery, comedian of, 159
mobility, downward, 158
Molloy (Beckett), 83–84, 166; *Endgame* echoing, 81–82; inner space invoked in, 82; transitional space in, 81
Molloy (character), 35, 117
moral inversion, 158
Moran (character), 84
Morton, Timothy, 190
mysticism, 124–27
Mythologies (Barthes), 185

native indetermination, 198–200
negation, 56–57, 126; consequences of, 129–30; discrediting, 130; forms of, 128–29; inverting, 128–29; philosophy of, 135–36; by the Unnamable, 99–100, 128–30, 133, 135
negative hallucination: in end times, 29–30; of Winnie, 164–65, 171–72

negentropy, 192, 243n54
Nell (character), 172
Nietzsche, Friedrich, 210, 212
nonbeing, limitless, 112
nonverbal self, 132–33
nothing, all of, 187
nothingness, God as pure, 126
Not-I, 79–80, 87; the I and, 110–12, 114–17, 128–29, 131, 139–40, 147; pronouns and, 115–16, 138; within transitional space, 89
Not-I (Beckett), 1, 26, 115, 210
nuclear apocalypse, 156–57

"Ode on a Distant Prospect of Eton College" (Gray), 166–67
old age: characters experiencing, 91; transitional objects of, 90–91; transitional space of, 88, 92–94
On Beckett (Badiou), 184, 211
"One daren't even laugh anymore," 15
"On the Dialectic of Closing and Opening in Fin de Partie" (Schwab, G.), 33
ontological abyss, 197, 202
ontological insecurity: container space for, 66–67; schizoid positionality produced through, 36–37; the self disintegrated by, 99, 196; systematic madness induced by, 38
Ophelia (character), 164
Oppenheimer, Robert, 157, 239n16
optimism: cruel, 159–60, 163–65; gene, 160

Order of Things, The (Foucault), 189
organless body, 107–9
organs: new, 148, 238*n*75; sexual, 107
Other, the, 132; gaze of, 120; Hamm unmasking, 56; pure form of, 117–18; self-identity feigned as, 121; self-images imposed by, 103; self-undermining genesis and, 117–19; voice of, 120
others, 93; anonymous, 117, 142–43; characters mirrored by, 78; hermeneutic mediation of, 143; unity of self and, 122
oxygen, 213–14

pain, 154–55
pandemic, 246*n*24; bookstores in, 221; fatigue, 220; waiting during, 29, 221. *See also* COVID-19 pandemic
pandemic surrealism, 25, 221–22
Paradise Lost (Milton), 167
paradox, 229*n*44, 235*n*39; contradiction and, 129; epistemological, 122; in happiness, 155; of light, 190; reformulated as, 121–22; self-presence and, 127; speech acts of, 124, 138; of subjectivity, 131–32, 142, 237*n*70; of theatrical reality, 161–62, 168–69
paranoia, creative, 93
Particular Matter(s) (Saraceno), 218
pause, silence contrasted with, 3–4, 220

phantasms of the body, 36–37
philosophy, 233*n*11; definition of, 96; Eastern, 126, 137; of negation, 135–36; psychology replacing, 54; *in The Unnamable*, 97–106, 126, 137, 143
Philosophical Investigations (Wittgenstein), 101
Pirella, Agostino, 5–6
plague, 25, 39–40; brain, lungs and, 207–8; theater and, 207
Plato, 104, 109–10
pneuma (breath and light), 218
poetics, 195; of end times, 26–40, 181–82; native indetermination, infancy and, 197–200, 204; of unknowable, 180; unworlding in, 196; from void, 197
poetry, 14–16; in "The Calmative," 77
politics, 201–2
Porush, David, 177, 205, 241*n*14, 243*n*54
possessions, 84, 86
posthuman characters, 188; *in The Lost Ones*, 176–77, 185, 190
Pothast, Ulrich, 123
Powers, Richard, 160, 172
projections: of audience, 52, 57–58; *Endgame* reflecting, 61–62; game of, 169; self, 98–100, 110–11, 113–14, 129, 237*n*70
pronouns: Not-I and, 115–16, 138; subjectivity in, 114–17
psychiatric hospital, in Arezzo (Italy), 5–6, 68

psychic life, 195
psychoanalytics, 12
psychology, 54
psychosis, 111
Purgatorio (Dante), 174, 185–86

Quad I and *Quad II* (Beckett), 221
queer, 79

Rabaté, Jean-Michel, 87, 89–90, 223
Rathjen, Friedhelm, 215
reader, 144
reality: imaginary and, 121, 145–46; reorganization of, 119–20; transitional space, fiction and, 145–46, 147. *See also* theatrical reality
reflexivity. *See* self-reflexivity
representability, illusion of, 123–24
Rosa (patient), 68–69
routines, 51–52
Royal Shakespeare Company, 17
The Rubaiyat of Omar Khayyam (Fitzgerald translation), 167
rubbish, 215–16

Sails of the Herring Fleet (Beckett), 18
"Samuel Beckett's dramatische Sprache" (Iser), 7–8
Samuel Becketts Endspiel mit der Subjektivität (Schwab, G.), 10
Saraceno, Tomás, 218
"Scapeland" (Lyotard), 193–94
scapelands, 190
Schillertheater, 24

schizoid positionality, 36–37
schizoid structure, of *The Unnamable*, 99–100, 103–4, 109
schizoid subject, 234nn21–22; disintegration threatening, 100–1
schizophrenia, cultural, 103–4
Schwab, Gabriele, 1–26; sister (Stefanie) of, 2–5, 64–66, 68; Winnie played by, 24, 153–54
Schwab, Leon, 17–18
Schwab, Manu, 13–15
Schwab, Martin, 13
Sein oder Nichts (Henrich), 23
self, the, 237n70; cultural objects reconstructing, 89; as depth, 110; figurations of, 110, 112; first-person narrator and, 118, 125, 140; implosion of, 196–97; literary subject reflecting in, 105–6; in *The Lost Ones*, 196–97; nonverbal core of, 132; ontological insecurity disintegrating, 99, 196; the Other and, 103, 117–19, 121; speech weaning, 90–91; storytelling and, 78, 85–86; unity of, 122; vanishing of, 195–96
self-alienation, 127
self-genesis, 118–19
self-identity, 122; absolute, 123; feigned as the Other, 121
self-manifestation, 136
self-observation, of body, 106–7, 111–12

self-presence, 127
self-presentation, language games and, 56–57
self-preservation, 170
self-projections: extreme, 129; on the Unnamable, 98–100, 110–11, 113–14, 129, 237n70
self-realization, 127
self-reflexivity: collapse of, 134, 136; as cutural reaction, 146–47; metalevel of, 141; spirals, 115–16, 120; textual, 118–19, 142, 147; of theatrical reality, 169
Senna, Danzy, 20–21
sensations, little, 194–95
"A Sense of Unending: Fictions for the End of Time" (Gontarski), 210
sexual organs, 107
Shakespeare, William, 162, 164
Sheehan, Paul, 208–9, 219
Shenker, Israel, 95
sickness, 125
silence, 16; breath and, 210, 220; in end times, 48–49, 220; as imaginary end point, 125; mystical, 124–27; pause contrasted with, 3–4, 220; unattainable, 124; in *The Unnamable*, 72, 124–28, 138
singularizer, 175
Smith, Patti, 21–22
Smuda, Manfred, 236n57
soul: climate influence on, 179–80; love/hope of, 185–86; making, 204–5; raw, 196; transference of, 173, 183, 194–96, 204–5; violent domestication process for, 194
soulscapes, 38, 190
space, 153; container, 66–67; inner, 82, 195; virtual, 177. *See also* transitional space
speaking, 204; against language, 127–28; language relationship to, 116–17; old style, 150–51, 153, 239n16
speech, 121; affective cathexis of, 133–34, 136–37, 180; ambivalence of, 131–32; characters obscured through, 55–56; death haunting, 91; disowning subject by, 130–31; glossolalia of, 134–35; meaning beyond, 59; organless, 107–8; of paradox, 124, 138; performance, 71, 88, 93, 152, 230n1; recursive loops in, 92; self-reference in, 115–16; the self weaned through, 90–91; validity of, denied, 98. *See also* language; voice
spirare (breath and inspiration), 209, 216, 220
storytelling: emotional turmoil mitigated through, 76; the self and, 78, 85–86; as transformational objects, 79–80
Studiobühne (theater), 23–24
subjectivity: the I functioning linked to, 115; nonverbal core and, 132–33; paradox of, 131–32, 142, 237n70; pronouns use in, 114–17; reader transformed and, 144; reorganization of, 119;

self-reflexivity, imaginary and, 147; textual, 142; in *The Unnamable*, 95–96, 98, 101–2, 109, 130, 139, 142
sublime, 203
suffering, 102–3, 154, 172, 179
symbols, 60
symptomatology, 99–100
systematic madness (*vesania*), 38, 173, 183, 191–92

Testot, Laurent, 219
Theater an der Grenze, in Kreuzlingen, 3, 14
Theater and Its Double, The (Artaud), 207, 214
"Theater and the Plague, The" (Artaud), 39–40
Theater of the Absurd (Esslin), 18
theatricality: abstraction shaping, 49–50; without actors, 211, 214; cruelty and, 152–53, 154, 214; exposing, 46; life as, 151; mime and, 211; plague and, 207; spacetime, de-aestheticization and, 170; transitional space of, 153
theatrical reality, 151; paradox of, 161–62, 168–69; quasi-referential techniques and, 170
Theodorakopoulos, Tessa, 23
theology, 126
Thiher, Allen, 103–4
thought: without body, 38, 180, 184; unthought known and, 67, 195–96, 203

thought images (*Denkbilder*), 49
timelessness, 161
Tophoven, Elmar, 9, 221
toxic air, 212
transcoding, 190, 198, 209, 211
transformational objects, 67, 79–80, 167
transitional character, 89–90, 144–48
transitional imaginaries, 72
transitional objects, 19, 36, 229*n*51; the I as, 87, 165; of old age, 90–91; transitional space creating, 86–87
transitional space, 4, 24, 59, 91; in *Malone Dies*, 36, 84–85; in *Molloy*, 81; Not-I within, 89; of old age, 88, 92–94; reality, fiction and, 145–47; of theatricality, 153; in "The Calmative," 72, 90; in *The Lost Ones*, 185; transitional objects created in, 86–87; Winnie occupying, 151, 162
"Transitional Spaces in Beckett's *Film*" (Schwab, G.), 13
Tranter, Rhys, 48
"Trying to Understand Endgame" (Adorno), 28, 44

unconscious, 62, 138–39, 141, 147
undifferentiation, 92, 196; differentiation and, 140–41, 202
University of California, at Irvine, 12
University of Constance, 2, 7, 19

unknowable, 180
Unnamable, the (character), 88–89; Basil and, 120; beyond boundaries of lifetime, 111–12; fantasies of, 122–23; the I, Not-I and, 110–12, 114–17, 128–29, 131, 139–40, 147; illusion of representability, individuality and, 123–24; infinite discourse of, 125–26; literary fictions mocked by, 97; mocking tone of, 102; naming, 121, 123; negation by, 99–100, 128–30, 133, 135; self-projections on, 98–100, 110–11, 113–14, 129, 237n70; silence and, 72, 124–28, 138; Worm and, 112–13, 116
Unnamable, The (*L'innomable*) (Beckett), 19, 24, 36, 95–148; aesthetic experience of, 138–44; buried before time, never born and, 106–13; differentiation in, 117–18; discourse, form and, 128–32; empirical worlds in, 97–106; end times in, 95–96; inventing, being invented and, 117–24; language, rhythms of emotions and, 128–32; literary subjects and, 97–106, 235n37; philosophies and, 97–106, 126, 137, 143; schizoid structure of, 99–100, 103–4, 109; silence and, 72, 124–28, 138; subjectivity in, 95–96, 98, 101–2, 109, 130, 139, 142; as transitional character, 144–48; unavoidable subject in, 113–17

unthought known, 67, 195–96, 203
unworlding, 195–96, 198

vesania. *See* systematic madness
Vidal, John, 246n24
violent domestication, 194
virtuality, 175–77
voice, 241n14; breath linked to, 209; of Other, 120; poetic, 180–82; recording/narrative, 85, 176–83

waiting: apocalyptic imaginaries linked to, 30; for the end, 42–43, 55; during pandemic, 29, 221
Waiting for Godot (*Warten auf Godot*) (Beckett), 15, 30, 33; Asmus directing, 17; Blau performing in, 18; cartoonist on, 221, *222*; on German TV, 1–2, 208
We do not all breathe the same air (Saraceno), 218
Wellmer, Albrecht, 11–12
"What Does Fiction Know?" (Powers), 160
What Is Philosophy? (Deleuze and Guattari), 96
Whitelaw, Billie, 210
Willie (character), 151, 155
Winnicott, Donald W., 22, 86, 89, 145, 165
Winnie (character), 17, 37–38; actresses playing, 23–24, 153–54; burial in sand, 149, 151, 156, 157, 208, 215; as burning, 161–62; as comedian of misery, 159; consoling objects of, 165–68;

environmental conditions addressed by, 152–53; future as now and never for, 163; hallucinatory suggestions by, 151, 167–68; immobility of, 157–58; moody madness of, 165, 167; negative hallucination of, 164–65, 171–72; old style speaking by, 150–51, 153, 239*n*16; optimism of, 159–60; pain/discomfort of, 154; paradise regained by, 167; playing role of, 153–56; psyche of, 161–62, 170; recoiling about life by, 158–59;

terror felt by, 155; transitional space occupied by, 151, 162; trilingual staging of, 153–54

Wittgenstein, Ludwig, 101, 110

Woodward, Kathleen, 18, 19, 86

word-forming experience, 202

World War II, 43–44

Worm (character), 112–13, 116

writing: breath connected to, 219; against culture, 199; as decomposition, 83–84

Zur Dialektik von Moderne und Postmoderne (Wellmer), 12

GPSR Authorized Representative: Easy Access System Europe, Mustamäe tee 50, 10621 Tallinn, Estonia, gpsr.requests@easproject.com

www.ingramcontent.com/pod-product-compliance
Lightning Source LLC
Chambersburg PA
CBHW031237290426
44109CB00012B/325